Books by Richard L. McElroy

The Best of Baseball Trivia

American Presidents

James A. Garfield: His Life and Times, A Pictorial History

American Presidents, Volume II

William McKinley and Our America, A Pictorial History

Christ Presbyterian Church of Canton, Ohio: A Sports Ministry

American Presidents and First Ladies, Volume III

The Stark County Wall of Fame: Our Greatest Sons and Daughters

Battlefield Presidents: Zachary Taylor and Benjamin Harrison and Their America

American Presidents and First Ladies, Volume IV

Battlefield Presidents: Zachary Taylor and Benjamin Harrison and Their America

Thank you for serving our country.
Enjoy my book & All Best Wishes.

By
Richard L. McElroy

Psalm 139

5/ 6/ 2011

Printed in the United States of America

ISBN-13: 978-0-692-00389-3 (Softbound Edition)

ISBN-13: 978-0-692-00388-6 (Hardbound Edition)

Library of Congress Control Number: 2009905158

Dedication

This book is dedicated to my many relatives, some of whom gave their lives in the service of their country as members of the Armed Forces of the United States. With my ancestors such as Roger Williams (founder of the Rhode Island Colony and a soldier during King Phillip's War in 1676), Joseph Manchester and Nathaniel Mitchell who served under General George Washington in the Revolutionary War, as well as subsequent veterans in other conflicts, more recent family members come to mind. These include my father Lee M. McElroy (1915–2002), brother Raymond, son Matthew and nephew Eric. In addition, my uncles Bill Faber, Jack and Dan Prosser, Burke Downer and Julian Yokum, and cousins Frank, Bob and Richard Moore (my namesake) are all part of my heritage. Indeed, I give a hearty salute to all the men and women who have worn the military uniform of our country. Lastly, I dedicate this work to my late mother, Virginia Cooper McElroy (1916–2008), who served as a nurse's aide during World War II and, among other things, introduced me to the world of literature and history. Her thirst for reading and travel inspired me to learn more about our nation and its people.

Acknowledgments

I wish to thank the following individuals for their assistance in this work: Librarians Janet Metzger of the Rodman Public Library in Alliance, Ohio; Karl Ash of the President William McKinley Museum and Library; Bette George of the Mount Union College Library and Mary Artzner Wolf of Walsh University in North Canton, Ohio. Also, Patty Rhodes of the National First Ladies Library; Professor Dr. Beverly Orkes Heiman of Ashland College who lives in North Canton; Helen Straus of Smithfield, Ohio; and Dr. Eric Matthews of Mount Union College; Jennifer Capps and Dave Pleiss of the Benjamin Harrison Home in Indianapolis as well as Tracy and Rachael Knisely, Reverend Douglas Patton, Cindy Sober, Rita Zwick, Tammy Pancher, James and Mary Imhoff, Joe Halter and Tom Hayes, all of Canton, provided information and input, as did historian Jerry Sandifer of Alliance. Jerry's expertise and knowledge of photography and photocopying added much to the manuscripts. Thanks too to the fine staff at the Bellaire Public Library in Bellaire, Michigan, as well as Roger and Terry Mason (also of Bellaire). Mary Hull, editor at Chestnut Productions in Russell, Massachusetts, was extremely helpful in her suggestions and criticism. A big thanks also goes to Harold "Skip" Hensel of Metairie, Louisiana; Ben Benson of Hartford, New York; historian/author Douglas Brinkley of New Orleans; Ryan and Amy Florek of Bellville, Illinois; and Karl Rove, FOX News analyst and former Chief Deputy of the White House. Additionally I am indebted to Curtis Cotton of Carrollton, Ohio; along with Andy Haren (Canton) and Marcia Mann of the Stark County District Library in Canton who both provided assistance in obtaining several pictures. A special thanks too goes to State Judge William Moody of El Paso, as well as his legal secretary Pam Foster. Bill, a historian and author in his own right, contributed information on Harrison's presidential tour in 1891. Furthermore, my wife Pamela offered many suggestions to improve this effort. Lastly, I want to offer my gratitude to colleague Dr. Bill Cunion of Mount Union College, without whose valuable advice and scrutiny, this book would not have been possible.

PART I

ZACHARY TAYLOR: Citizen Soldier

CHAPTER 1

Common Threads

AT FIRST GLANCE, IT WOULD APPEAR THAT ZACHARY TAYLOR AND BENJAMIN HARRISON had little in common. Despite having obvious differences, these two men of the 19th century shared many traits besides being military leaders whose exploits led them to the presidency.

Both Taylor and Harrison had a rich family heritage and each was related to a Virginia president (Taylor to Madison and Harrison to his grandfather William Henry Harrison). Their families were entrenched in military heritage and both Taylor and Harrison joined the army, becoming outstanding battlefield commanders. Taylor in fact served as a gallant young officer during the War of 1812 under the command of Benjamin's grandfather in the Northwest Territory. Both men were also descendants of England's King Edward I and each claimed ancestors who arrived on the *Mayflower*.

As children, Zachary Taylor and Benjamin Harrison grew up along the Ohio River (their boyhood homes are less than 90 miles apart). And though their concept of government differed slightly in the interpretation of the Constitution, Taylor and Harrison entertained very similar political views. In fact, Benjamin's father John was an avid member of the Whig Party which supported Taylor for president in 1848. John was elected to Congress just after Taylor's death in office.

Zachary Taylor and Benjamin Harrison were small in stature and both married exceptional women while leading exemplary lives. They both defeated Democrats to become Chief Executive, though their preparations for the presidency were scant. Taylor and Harrison each possessed a singleness of purpose along with a strong stubborn streak, and both men knew their country very well, having traveled more extensively than any other presidents of the 19th century. And what may be surprising to some historians and scholars, Taylor was a distant cousin of William Henry Harrison, and thus related to his grandson, the 23rd president. But here most of the similarities end, except for the fact that I find both men interesting and worthy of attention.

Zachary Taylor and Benjamin Harrison were not really contemporaries (when Taylor died at age 65 in 1850, Harrison was 16 years old), and Harrison's formal education contrasted sharply to that of Taylor's backwoods/schoolhouse learning. In terms of commanding troops on the battlefield, both men showed initiative, resourcefulness, self-discipline, and courage under contrasting but life-threatening circumstances. Each man differed in his style of leadership both in his military and elected life. Subsequently, both men believed firmly that people and nations are judged by their deeds.

Taylor and Harrison don't generally receive high praise in the ranking of presidents by historians, with Taylor getting slightly higher marks than Harrison. Neither is considered a great president, but both men made significant contributions during their term of office. During the last five decades, however, history has re-evaluated both Taylor and Harrison and looked more favorably upon their administrations.

Taylor and Harrison were ambitious men and strove to succeed, though it is doubtful that neither of them planned to be president, until the opportunity appeared in the immediate years preceding their election. When it was first suggested to Taylor that he be a presidential candidate, he told a friend, "Stop your nonsense and drink your whiskey."[1] In Harrison's case, he had no inclination to run until well after his term in the senate.

Zachary Taylor and Benjamin Harrison played an integral part of the American saga; they were not mere witnesses, but players who had a leading role upon the stage of history. Both were men of destiny, and when it called, they were ready to fulfill it. Their lives are forever intertwined and linked to the unfolding events of the nation. A closer examination of Taylor and Harrison and their times will give us a better understanding of our country's past and present. Let us have a look.

CHAPTER 2

Disobeying Orders

"OLD ROUGH AND READY" WAS REVERED BY HIS DEVOTED TROOPS, BUT THE GENERAL had been hesitant in recommending a strategy for victory in the Mexican War fought between the United States and Mexico from 1846–1848. Taylor's failure to provide President James Knox Polk with detailed reports and plans of the war had further eroded his reputation with Polk and his cabinet members. Polk wrote in his diary, "Gen'l Taylor, I fear, is not the man for command of the army. He is brave but does not seem to have resources or grasp of mind enough to conduct such a campaign."[1]

Under great pressure to end the controversial war, President Polk criticized Taylor for having allowed captured Mexican soldiers at Monterrey to go free with their sidearms, horses, and some of their cannons. But Taylor had a reason for this action. He had been unable to guard or feed his prisoners, so he released them, promising Mexican General Pedro de Ampudia a two-month head start south before pursuing them. The American Army was weary and sick and Taylor believed his gesture to Ampudia might even end the fighting and gain them the sympathy of the Mexican populace. There was also a problem with desertion within the American army. These defections mounted and on one occasion 30 men from a single company of

Irish Americans deserted en masse. They were captured and later executed, under Winfield Scott's command.

Concerned about Taylor's behavior, Polk instructed his Army Chief of Staff, General Winfield Scott, to go to Mexico and reduce Major General Taylor's forces. Polk wanted Taylor to "abandon Saltillo [his supply station] and make no detachments except for reconnaissance and immediate defense" around Monterrey.[2] Taylor, however, was an aggressive leader. He chose to interpret Polk's directive as a suggestion rather than an order. Instead, Taylor left six hundred men at Saltillo and marched the rest of his men seventeen miles south to engage the enemy.

Taylor's army of 14,000 was reduced to 4,700 when Scott reassigned them to his own command. The bulk of Taylor's forces were sent to the coastal city of Veracruz, Mexico, where they were to join up with Scott in large scale invasion. The remainder of Taylor's army was made up mostly of volunteers and inexperienced soldiers. In his written orders to Taylor, Scott added, "I know this to be the wish of the government, found on reason in which I concur."[3] Believing he had removed Taylor from the spotlight, Polk hoped a frustrated Taylor would give up his command and return home.

Disaster nearly struck in early January of 1847 when Scott's official written orders were intercepted. The American courier carrying the dispatches was captured and killed by Mexican guerillas. The papers not only contained Taylor's instructions, but also Scott's plans of invasion and the number of troops and cannons at various locations. These messages were quickly delivered to Mexican President Antonio de Santa Anna.

Santa Anna, who sported a wooden leg, had been deposed and exiled eight times as the Mexican leader. He returned to power in 1846 after the Mexican armies had suffered several defeats in his absence. He convinced his countrymen to try and take back California, Texas, and other regions Mexico had lost to the United States. Seeing an opportunity to destroy Taylor's depleted army, the Mexican leader left the city of San Luis Patosi. He was elegantly dressed and seated in a golden chariot pulled by eight white mules. Leading an army of more than twenty thousand, Santa Anna was escorted along the way by fighting cocks and scores of dancing women who strewed flowers in his path. But ahead lay the Mexican Desert and Zachary Taylor was three hundred miles beyond that.

Santa Anna hoped to cut Taylor's supply lines between Monterrey and the Rio Grande, destroy the American army, retake Saltillo, then head south to

Veracruz to crush General Scott. By mid-January a copy of Scott's intercepted orders finally reached Taylor. Much to President Polk's regret, Taylor refused to relinquish his command. He wrote in February, "In this I shall disappoint them, as I have determined to remain & do my duty."[4]

Saltillo, a Mexican city of more than fifteen thousand and the capital of the Mexican state of Coahuila, was also a key position to the passes through the range of the Sierra Madre. Taylor had already disregarded previous orders in November of 1846 when he occupied the city. Leaving Saltillo protected, he moved the rest of his small army to the hamlet of Agua Nueva, hoping to lure Santa Anna into a trap.

General Taylor figured Santa Anna would have to go through a narrow passage near the large ranch of Hacienda Buena Vista. Another American General, John Wool, feared an immediate attack, but Taylor seemed unconcerned. "Let the Mexicans come," he said, "and damned if they don't go back a good deal faster than they came."[5] Taylor realized the enemy would first have to cross the hot, dry stretch of rugged terrain. As he predicted, the enemy followed the route and nearly three thousand Mexican soldiers died or deserted during the march. Though hot and tired, Santa Anna's remaining large force was still anxious for a fight.

On Sunday, February 21, 1847, Texas Rangers spotted the Mexican army. By the next day the Americans had placed their five cannons on the flat plateau near the pass at Buena Vista. Commanding this artillery was Major John Washington, a distant relative of the nation's first president. Taylor had General Wool erect barricades of felled trees and thick brush in front of their big guns, which were placed above a series of deep, dry gullies known as arroyos.

After inspecting his lines atop his trusted horse "Whitey," Taylor waited patiently. On the morning of February 22, the Mexicans came within sight. Santa Anna held a numerical advantage, outnumbering the American forces four to one. He sent some cavalrymen to the American lines under a white flag of truce to deliver a written message to Taylor, urging him to surrender and avoid a catastrophe. Santa Anna personally wrote, "You are surrounded by twenty thousand men, and cannot in any human probability avoid suffering a rout, and being cut to pieces with your troops; but as you deserve consideration and particular esteem, I wish to save you from a catastrophe, and for that purpose give you this notice, in order that you may surrender at discretion, under the assurance that you will be treated with the consideration belonging to the Mexican character; to which end you will be granted an hour's time to make up your mind, to commence from the moment when my flag of truce arrives in your camp."[6] Taylor politely wrote Santa Anna a refusal, responding, "In reply to your note of this date summoning me to surrender my forces at discretion, I beg leave to say that I decline acceding to your request." He then handed his note to the Mexican officers and calmly announced before they departed, "General Taylor never surrenders. Santa Anna can go to hell!"[7]

General Taylor gathered his nervous officers and troops and announced, "Soldiers, I intend to stand here, not only as long as a man remains, but so long as *a piece* of a man is left."[8] That evening Taylor rode the seventeen-mile trip back to Saltillo to inspect his army there. During his absence, minor skirmishing broke out at Buena Vista.

The Battle of Buena Vista began in full force just after sunrise on the February 23. Mexican infantry and horse soldiers charged through the arroyos toward the plateau and the waiting American forces. Some Americans panicked. The Second Indiana Regiment, suffering heavy losses, withdrew its position. Taylor arrived around 9:00 a.m. with four companies of men from Saltillo. He was approached by General Wool, who suggested a retreat. Wool told Taylor, "General, we are whipped!" Taylor would not hear of it and responded, "That is for me to determine."[9] He then ordered Wool to round up stragglers and reform his lines. Taylor next sent the Mississippi Rifles forward to stem the retreat.

Santa Anna, sensing victory, tried to pierce the center of the American lines by sending in more cavalry. The Indiana and Mississippi regiments waited until the Mexicans were within fifty yards, then let loose a devastating volley of gunfire. Hundreds of men and horses fell. Colonel Jefferson Davis—Taylor's former son-in-law, who would one day be president of the Confederacy during the Civil War—led a gallant charge into the fray. Davis rushed his cavalry in a V-shape, which confused the Mexicans. Though seriously wounded with a bullet in his foot, Colonel Davis stayed in the saddle, assisting his infantry in using sabers and Bowie knives during the savage hand-to-hand combat. Now it was the Mexican Army's turn to panic. They retreated with Davis' troops in hot pursuit. Taylor, amazed as he watched Davis lead the attack, was nearly killed when two bullets ripped through his shirt, one grazing his arm and another tearing away a button.

Santa Anna's hope to break through and take Saltillo turned into defeat. As his army fled toward the nearby mountains, a sudden torrent of hail and rain drenched the area for fifteen minutes, producing a brilliant rainbow that spanned the battlefield. The trapped enemy, seeking cover in a ravine at the foot of the mountains, became the target of murderous cannon and rifle fire from the revitalized U.S. Army.

A pair of Mexican officers and their aides rode forward with a white flag. Taylor ordered a ceasefire and sent General Wool out to meet them. This lull in the conflict allowed Santa Anna's trapped men to retreat. Mexican officers quickly reorganized their forces and renewed the attack. Taylor, realizing he had been tricked, ordered the batteries to "Double shot your guns and give 'em hell!"[10]

The night of February 23 was a cold one; few soldiers slept. All through the dark hours the Americans listened to the flapping of vultures' wings, howling wolves, and the screams and groans of the wounded Mexicans. At dawn, the Americans witnessed a sad sight—hundreds of Mexican women and children knelt weeping beside their dead husbands and fathers. Santa Anna and the remnant of his army were gone. General Taylor's men, needing a rest, did not pursue. The general sent some aides, including his son-in-law Dr. Robert Wood, to locate Santa Anna and negotiate an exchange of prisoners. Some fighting in surrounding areas continued, however, when an Ohio battalion en route to Monterrey was attacked.

American losses at Buena Vista were heavy, with 670 men killed and wounded. Taylor personally saw to it that Davis' wounds were attended to. Among the dead were George Lincoln, a relative of Congressman-elect Abraham Lincoln; Major Edward Webster, son of Senator Daniel Webster; and Lieutenant Colonel Henry Clay, Jr., son of Kentucky Senator Henry Clay. Also killed were Whig Party leader Colonel John Hardin of Illinois, Congressman Archibald Yell of Arkansas, and Colonel William McKee. Enemy losses, however, were much greater. Santa Anna suffered nearly 1,900 men killed and wounded, and another 2,000 missing, taken prisoner, or deserted. Taylor's letters did not reflect much jubilation in his triumph. He wrote his brother Joseph, "The great loss on both sides . . . has deprived me of everything like pleasure."[11]

Buena Vista was one of the greatest victories in American military history, but there was little joy in the White House. When President Polk heard the news of the battle a month later, he shook his head in disbelief. He had difficulty understanding how a man who disobeyed orders had won a battle against impossible odds. Though newspapers proclaimed Zachary Taylor the greatest hero since George Washington, Polk refused to allow

Congress to give any special honors to "Old Rough and Ready." Taylor's popularity, however, could not be ignored. One young songwriter, living in Cincinnati at the time, wrote "Santa Anna's Retreat from Buena Vista," a piano quick-step which sold well. The composer was Stephen Collins Foster.

The twentieth century American General Douglas MacArthur once observed, "It's the orders you *disobey* which make you famous." MacArthur was very familiar with the role of high-ranking officers in warfare, and may have had Zachary Taylor in mind when he made this comment.

Zachary Taylor's prominence grew after his military victories in the Mexican War. All three major political parties in the United States—the Democrats, the Whigs, and the Know-Nothings—announced their intent to nominate him for President in 1848. Taylor, however, was not popular with Democratic President James K. Polk, who considered him a political rival. Polk's efforts to replace Taylor were met with opposition in Congress, as well among the newspapers and the public, and it was this hostility which helped propel Taylor to national prominence.

Taylor was well aware of his popularity and had entertained ideas for seeking the high office of the presidency. In August of 1847 he wrote a six-page letter to Jeff Davis, back home in Mississippi recovering from his wounds, predicting, "...if the election was to take place immediately or even next November, I would in all probability be elected to that important office."[12]

CHAPTER 3

Ancestry and Boyhood

ZACHARY TAYLOR'S PATERNAL AND MATERNAL ANCESTORS CAME FROM ENGLAND. One direct descendant on his mother's side was William Brewster who came to America on the *Mayflower*. He became a powerful and influential spiritual leader in the Plymouth Colony of Massachusetts and his daughter Fear Brewster married William Strother, resulting ultimately in making Taylor a fifth cousin six times removed. Brewster died in 1644. Taylor was also related to Issac and Sarah Allerton who came over on the *Mayflower*.

Zachary's great-great-grandfather James Taylor left Carlisle, England, and settled in what is today King and Queen County, Virginia, in 1635. He became a prosperous farmer and landowner. James' son, also James (1673–1729), accumulated more land and served in the House of Burgesses. This man, Zachary's great grandfather, was also the great grandfather of James Madison. Zachary Taylor was also fourth cousins to both Robert E. Lee and Franklin D. Roosevelt. Other Virginia families directly related to the Taylors included the Pendletons, Hunts, Gaineses and the Barbours. The Taylors were also related to the Benjamin Harrisons of Berkley County, Virginia, through the Saville and Pilkington families.

Zachary's father, Richard Taylor, was a graduate of William and Mary College in Virginia, and had an adventurous spirit. He served in the Revolutionary War, rising to the rank of Lieutenant Colonel after fighting against both the British in the East and the Indians in the Ohio Valley. He was not content, however, to stay in one place very long.

Taylor's mother was Sarah "Sally" Dabney Strother (1760–1822). Her family had also been longtime settlers in Virginia. She was raised in Culpepper County and in 1779, the eighteen-year-old Sally married thirty-five-year-old Richard Taylor. She was well educated for her time, having been taught by private tutors.

It was during the war that Sally had a terrible accident. It happened while she was making bullets. A niece bumped into Sally, who spilled hot molten lead on her hands. Most of her fingers were severely burned and disfigured. In spite of her disability, she continued to sew and take care of household chores as if nothing had happened.

As a bonus for his service in the war, Richard Taylor was given 8100 acres of land in northern Kentucky. This was an area of which Taylor was familiar. According to records, in 1769 Richard Taylor and his brother Hancock made the first trading voyage down the Ohio River, leaving Pittsburgh then following the Mississippi to New Orleans. After a short stay and selling their goods, they returned to Virginia by sea. Hancock Taylor was later killed by Indians on another expedition to the Ohio Valley.

Zachary Taylor was born on November 24, 1784, at Barboursville, a relative's home in Orange County, Virginia, located about 16 miles northeast of Charlottesville. His father Richard had moved there temporarily before heading West to claim his land in Kentucky. Named for his grandfather Zachariah who died in 1768, Zachary was the third of nine children. One of his brothers, George, died in infancy. His other siblings included Hancock (1781–1841), William (1788–1808), Joseph (1796–1864), Elizabeth (1792–1845), Sarah (1799–1851), and Emily (1801–1841).

After Zachary's birth, Richard left for Kentucky to build a two-story log cabin on the land he had been granted. He planned to move his growing family there. When he returned to Virginia, Richard loaded up his wife and children and made the arduous trip once again to Kentucky. The Taylors traveled by wagon, then took a flatboat down the Monongahela and Ohio Rivers, stopping near Louisville, Kentucky, at the falls of the Ohio. Their cabin was located about six miles northeast of the town of Beargrass Creek. Zachary was nine months old when his family moved into their new house. Many years later, he described this home as, "a small log cabin, about twelve feet square . . . this residence was on the edge of a dense canebrake. Here we were saluted at night by the howling of wolves."[1]

Richard Taylor held local office, having been appointed a port collector in Louisville, and later elected to the state legislature. His income as port collector, combined with the products he shipped from his farm, mostly hemp, tobacco, and whiskey, made him a wealthy man. Though Louisville with its population of about 600 in 1801 was a hub of activity, the area around it was under constant threat of attacks from British-supplied Indians. Despite these dangers, Richard purchased another 10,000 acres of land spread throughout seven counties in Kentucky. By 1810 he owned thirty-seven slaves, some of whom lived in the basement of the large three-story brick house the family had moved into. He called this home "Springfield." It became a popular gathering place for guests and relatives. One visitor recalled, "You can always get a good cigar and the finest goblet of wine at the Taylor place."[2]

Young Zachary helped out with chores at an early age. There was also plenty of time for play, but he was required to stay close to the cabin. As the boy grew older he learned to carry wood, chop trees, plow fields, and harvest crops. He helped build log cabins for neighbors and slept lightly in a second floor bedroom opposite his parents' room. He remained alert to any disturbance caused by wolf packs, hungry bears, or hostile Indians. Rifles were kept loaded and stacked at different locations throughout the house in case of trouble.

Zachary's family paid for tutors to educate him. One was Elisha Ayer, a Connecticut schoolteacher who taught him to love books and appreciate history. Ayer observed that his pupil was "quick in learning and still patient in study."[3] Another tutor was Kean O'Hara, an Irish Catholic immigrant and classical scholar. Though Taylor developed an appreciation for formal learning, he was always a poor speller. In addition, the boy showed a fondness for music and often enjoyed beating on the drum. But one habit noticed by those who knew the boy was a stuttering problem, which dissipated as he grew older.

Taylor's most unusual "instructor" was Lewis Wetzel. Nicknamed "Deathwind" and "The Avenger" by settlers, Wetzel was a legendary hunter and Indian fighter whose personal one-man crusade against the Indians reaped him more than a hundred scalps. He was fearless, bloodthirsty, and a great marksman. After some of Wetzel's family had been killed by Indians near Wheeling, Virginia, he had vowed to destroy all natives, even those friendly to the United States. Wetzel taught Taylor how to use a rifle and knife, track Indians, and hunt animals. After a short-lived stay with the Lewis and Clark Expedition, which he found too tame, Wetzel settled in Mississippi where he died in 1808. He had provided young Zachary with the type of learning he never received in a classroom, the kind which proved to be practical and lifesaving.

By the time he was nine, Zachary began attending a one-room schoolhouse. It was not uncommon for the Taylor boys to carry their rifles to and from school because of the threat of wild animals and unfriendly Indians. One day in 1793, Zachary and several classmates were on their way home from school when they came to a fork in the forest path. The three Taylor brothers waved goodbye to their friends and headed in another direction toward their log cabin. In an instant a piercing scream cut through the woods. A small war party of Indians had split up to chase both groups of youngsters. In the distance, the Taylors could hear their mother yelling for them to hurry. Arrows flew around them and the boys fired their rifles at the band of warriors. Another shower of arrows followed as the boys zigzagged down the path to their cabin. In a final burst of speed, they reached the cabin, where Sally Taylor slammed the door and placed a heavy wood bar across it. The Indians tried to get in but failed. After it was safe to come out, the Taylor boys discovered that their classmates had been killed and scalped.[4] Such were the dangers of obtaining a formal education.

Among Zachary's other boyhood friends were some future American heroes. One was George Croghan Jr., son of the famous Ohio explorer. Croghan would later defend Fort Stephenson in Ohio against overwhelming odds, repulsing several attacks by the British and Indians in 1813. Another one of Zack's friends was Robert Anderson, who later defended Fort Sumter when it was fired on by the Confederates in 1861. Zachary also had the chance to meet his boyhood idol, Daniel Boone, though the famous pioneer was old and had lost most of the land he had claimed. It was little wonder he soon came to admire the life of military leaders and frontier heroes like his father.

When Zachary mentioned his ambition to pursue a military career, his mother was less than thrilled. She did not share her husband's enthusiasm for the military. Sally Taylor told her son, "I shall be happy to know that your skill with a musket will be confined to shooting an occasional deer or grouse for dinner."[5] Young Zachary respected his mother, but he also envied daring pioneers and soldiers like his older brother William, who served as an artillery officer in the army. Zachary Taylor decided he wanted to shape his own military legacy.

CHAPTER 4

The Military and Matrimony

By 1802 Zachary Taylor was almost a man. At the age of seventeen, he performed an amazing feat of strength and endurance by swimming across the Ohio River and back. What made this stunt so extraordinary was that he did it in March in the near-freezing waters.

Taylor stood five feet eight inches tall. He had hazel eyes, light brown curly hair, a long nose, a wide mouth, and a large head. His broad shoulders rested upon a barrel chest and a long waist. Taylor's bowed legs were very short. Later, during his military career, he needed help mounting a horse when could not reach the stirrups. He would get a boost from a soldier or use a stool to climb into the saddle.

Some sources claim Taylor served as a volunteer in the Kentucky militia in 1803; others believe he first joined in 1806. Whatever the actual date of his entry, he saw little or no action. Though there had been peace after the Treaty of Paris ended the Revolutionary War in 1783, the frontier still bristled with outbreaks of violence. Great Britain was still bitter over having lost the Revolutionary War. The British throne refused to give up its claims in the Northwest Territory and it continued to provide Native Americans with weapons and supplies. The British covertly encouraged the Indians to attack American settlements. As a result, both the British and the Indians were still hated and feared by the pioneers.

England, as well as France, also interfered with American shipping on the high seas. They stopped vessels, searched them, and forcibly removed sailors who were thought to be deserters of the British Royal Navy. These abuses continued for several years as President Thomas Jefferson did his best to reach a diplomatic solution to avoid another war. In 1807, when the British sank the U.S. ship *Chesapeake*, Jefferson was outraged and took steps to increase the size of the army, tripling it from 2,700 men to 9,000.

Zachary Taylor was eager and ready to serve his country at this time. He requested assignment to the newly formed Seventh Infantry Regiment, where it became Taylor's responsibility to enlist more troops. With help from a few Kentucky Congressmen, Taylor was commissioned a first lieutenant. The fact that his cousin, James Madison, was the secretary of state may have helped the twenty-three-year-old Taylor obtain this position. In late June of 1808 Zachary learned his brother William had been killed by Indians at Fort Pickering, located on the bluffs above the Mississippi River near present-day Memphis, Tennessee.

As an army lieutenant, Taylor's pay was thirty dollars a month, plus twelve dollars for expenses. In September he was sent to Washington, Kentucky, to recruit more men. Not finding much success there, Taylor was transferred to Maysville, Kentucky, where there were more potential volunteers. After Taylor raised two companies of troops, he was assigned to General James Wilkinson in New Orleans, a city under the threat of attack by the British.

Life was very unpleasant in New Orleans. American soldiers, exposed to the travails of gambling, prostitution, and drinking, were also subjected to shortages of supplies. What began as an army of 2000 men was drastically reduced. The open sewers of New Orleans were piled with human filth and garbage, which were removed only when the city flooded. Hordes of flies and mosquitoes spawned diseases that decimated the military and civilian populations. Taylor and his men, many of them fellow Kentuckians, spent much of the time burying their dead. Shallow graves were dug and in a short while the legs and arms of the dead protruded through the dirt. Taylor never forgot this horrible sight.

General Wilkinson decided to move his army twelve miles to the south at Fort Pickering, but living conditions did not improve much. Nearly six hundred of his men were sick from dysentery and yellow fever, with only two doctors available. To add to the army's misery, their food, supplied by corrupt contractors, was spoiled and rotten. During a ten-month period in New Orleans, 700 soldiers died, 108 deserted, and 58 were discharged. Taylor also became very ill with yellow fever. His right eye was infected so badly, he wrote, "I have almost lost sight of it."[1] He was ordered to return home where he spent several weeks recovering.

In 1809 at a dinner party in Louisville, Kentucky, Taylor met Margaret "Peggy" Mackall Smith. Tall, shy, and attractive, Peggy was the dark-haired daughter of Walter Smith, a Maryland plantation owner from Calvert County. Her father had served as major and surgeon during the American Revolution.

Peggy had three brothers and three sisters. The twenty-two-year-old woman was devoutly religious and had been educated at a finishing school in New York City. She was visiting her sister's home in Louisville when she met the young, handsome Zachary Taylor. The two fell in love. During their courtship, Taylor had to return to duty in the Mississippi Territory.

Taylor soon received permission for a leave of absence. On June 21, 1810, he and Peggy were wed. Her parents only stubbornly approved of the marriage while Richard Taylor gave them 324 acres of land as a wedding present. Taylor built a log house on the land, which was located in what is today downtown Louisville, Kentucky. He bought a female slave to help his wife with the housework while he continued to recruit more men for the army. Taylor's pay was often late; during one stretch he was not paid for seven months. To supplement his income, the first lieutenant took on a job as a part-time surveyor and sold some land.

Taylor was soon promoted to captain and took command of Fort Pickering in Tennessee, where his older brother William had recently been slain by Indians. He moved to the fort with his wife, but Margaret became pregnant and returned to Springfield, the Taylor family home in Kentucky. On April 9, 1811, she gave birth to their first child, a daughter, Ann Mackall Taylor.

War clouds were gathering and Captain Taylor was assigned to Fort Knox, located on the Wabash River in Indiana, and named in honor of Revolutionary War hero and George Washington's Secretary of War Henry Knox. There had been problems at the fort, particularly with its commander, and U.S. General William Henry Harrison felt confident Taylor could restore order and properly train the men. Stealing and desertion were commonplace among the troops, so for weeks Taylor drilled and disciplined them. Harrison was so pleased with the results he wrote his superiors in Washington, praising Taylor for an outstanding job.

In November of 1811 Taylor was called back east to testify at the trial of James Wilkinson. This somewhat strange and nefarious officer had been a gallant soldier fighting against the British and Indians. He had become quite outspoken and was accused of lining his pockets with money made by unscrupulous means, including payments made to him by the Spanish for supplying information. Worse, he was charged with conspiring with Aaron Burr in treasonous acts against the government. Burr's plans supposedly were to raise an army, create his own empire by seizing parts of the Southwest, then attack Mexico. Friendship between Wilkinson and Burr ended when Wilkinson agreed to turn against Burr. The evidence against the two men seemed strong. Wilkinson and Burr were acquitted but both men's reputations were destroyed.

In June of 1812, the United States officially declared war on Great Britain. Some Native Americans tribes joined the War of 1812 and fought for the British. Tired of seeing every treaty broken, and failing to halt the constant flow of squatters on their lands, many of the tribes in the Northwest Territory felt compelled to stop the ever-advancing white settlers.

Led by the Shooting Star, Shawnee leader Tecumseh, the Indians and their British allies captured some key outposts. In Michigan Forts Mackinac and Dearborn fell, with all the inhabitants massacred. General William Hull then surrendered his army of two thousand to the British near Detroit without firing a shot. Morale was low and settlers were frightened. Captain Taylor was sent to Fort Harrison, a small garrison built of oak and honey locust above a sharp bend on the Wabash River, three miles from present-day Terre Haute, Indiana. The garrison held fifty-five men and nine women and children. Taylor had the men dig a four-foot trench on three sides. They also built blockhouses, which overlooked the river and trenches.

Friendly Indians informed the garrison that Tecumseh's brother, The Prophet, who had been defeated by General Harrison in November of 1811 at Tippecanoe, planned an attack. Although Taylor and thirty-five other soldiers were sick at the time, they readied the fort as best they could. On September 3, 1812, two farmers living about four hundred yards from the fort were shot and scalped. Taylor sent some soldiers out to recover the mutilated bodies, which were buried inside Fort Harrison. Several Indian men, with their wives and children, later approached the fort under a white flag, claiming to be starving. The flag bearer was Joseph Lemar, an Indian

Taylor knew all too well. Taylor did not trust the group and refused to let them enter the fort. Instead, he lowered some food over the walls. The Indians remained outside the gates for a while. Realizing this maneuver was an Indian ploy to study the fort, count its men, and determine any weak spots, Captain Taylor prepared for an attack. Though his men were incapacitated and their supplies low, Taylor noted, "Morale is high and there is little doubt that we are capable of overcoming any obstacles."[2]

The next evening, just after 11 p.m., Taylor was awakened as 450 Miamis, Kickapoos, and Winnebagos attacked the fort. Captain Taylor ordered every man, even those confined to their sickbeds, to arm themselves and report for duty. The handful of women inside helped load rifles. The Indians set fire to the fort's blockhouse. A couple of men climbed onto the roof to pull off burning shingles, while a woman named Julia Lambert lowered herself into a well to fill up buckets of water, which were passed to the blockhouse to dowse the flames. A terrific explosion shook the garrison when a barrel of whiskey exploded. Two soldiers, thinking the fort would fall, fled into the woods. The blast created a twenty-foot gap the enemy attempted to storm. Taylor met the Indians head on, driving them back and plugging up the hole with debris. The assault continued for hours into the next morning. As Taylor later reported to General Harrison, during the seven-hour attack "the Indians continued to pour heavy fire of ball and an innumerable quantity of arrows . . ."[3]

The livestock, assembled in a pen outside the fort, were all slaughtered—including horses, hogs, oxen, and sixty-five head of cattle. This dashed any hope the Americans had of transportation or food. The only thing left to eat was the green corn the Indians left standing in the fields.

When they realized the garrison could not be taken, the Indians laid siege to Fort Harrison for several days. They surrounded the area and guarded any escape routes. Fort Knox, near General Harrison's headquarters at Vincennes, was one hundred miles away. Taylor wanted to send for help. Two men volunteered to travel by canoe to Fort Knox, but they found the river blocked by Indians. Taylor then sent a sergeant and his companion on a trail through the forest, but Indians were waiting there as well. With all supplies cut off from the tiny fort, Taylor imposed a strict rationing of food until help arrived.

Despite the odds, both of Taylor's messengers eventually managed to thwart the Indians and go for help. They reached Fort Knox on September 15, where they learned that relief had already been sent. Knowing that enemy forces were in the region and that the fort would need supplies, Colonel William Russell had already sent his men on their way to Fort Harrison. Taylor's food was just about to run out when Russell arrived. After more than a week, the attacking tribes finally abandoned their blockade. Angry and frustrated, the Indians headed directly to a white settlement at Pigeon Roost on the branch of the White River, where they massacred twenty-one men, women, and children.

When President James Madison received the news of Taylor's victory at Fort Harrison, he was overjoyed. It was the first victory for the United States in the War of 1812 and it lifted the hopes and spirits of American soldiers everywhere. Afterward, most of the Indians left the region, heading north toward the western edge of Lake Erie and Canada where their British allies were. More recruits flocked to the U.S. Army as American confidence and morale increased. Newspapers proclaimed Taylor a hero, and Madison heartily approved of General Harrison's recommendation to promote Taylor to the rank of Brevet Major.

Major Taylor was assigned to General Samuel Hopkins, the commander of all the forces in the Illinois Territory. Among the new army volunteers were two thousand Kentucky riflemen, whom Taylor considered his kin. In November of 1812, Hopkins and Taylor marched their men on a mission to destroy two large Indian villages on the Illinois River. They were forced to turn back when their scouts got lost and supplies ran low.

In the summer of 1813, Taylor joined Colonel William Russell, and together they destroyed a few remaining abandoned Indian villages in Indiana. Now, with Fort Knox secure, Major Taylor invited his wife and daughter to join him. The rest of the year remained relatively calm for Taylor. He and his fifty-six men spent their time peacefully. Taylor was soon needed elsewhere and in early 1814 he was transferred to Fort Vincennes where on March 6, 1814, Peggy gave birth to a second daughter, Sarah Knox Taylor. Her middle name came from the fort where her father had served earlier.

CHAPTER 5

A Series of Ups and Downs

THE WAR OF 1812 BEGAN TO TURN IN FAVOR OF THE UNITED STATES. BY 1813, George Croghan Jr. had won a victory at Ohio's Fort Stephenson, Oliver Perry had destroyed the English fleet at Put-in-Bay on Lake Erie, and General Harrison had triumphed over Tecumseh's forces near the Thames River in Canada, where Tecumseh was killed. The British later burned federal buildings in Washington, D.C., and defeated the Americans at Bladensburg, Maryland, in 1814, but the young republic was fighting back.

In the spring of 1814, Taylor was reassigned to St. Louis, where he was put in command of four hundred fifty soldiers. General Benjamin Howard ordered Taylor to take his men to the upper Mississippi and Missouri River regions, where they were instructed to destroy Indian towns and build a fort. Departing in eight large boats, some equipped with small cannons, the army struggled upstream through rapids and shallow waters. They hoped to defeat Black Hawk, the young chief of the Sac and Fox Indians.

Years earlier, during the Revolutionary War, George Rogers Clark, an army commander in the Ohio Territory, had burned Black Hawk's village. Black Hawk, only a boy at the time, pledged he would never allow white settlements on the northern portions of the Mississippi, and that the red man would never be a slave to whites. He later allied himself with the British, who supplied them with weapons and goods. In turn, the Indians helped the British in the lucrative fur trade.

Black Hawk had recently enjoyed two victories over the U.S. Army. This boosted the confidence of the Indians as they prepared to fight Taylor. Taylor's advancing army was greeted by poor weather and an attack of the measles. Meanwhile, a large band of more than two thousand Indian warriors trekked along the shoreline, following the army's keelboats. Brevet Major Taylor kept a white flag beside him in his vessel in hopes of securing peace. Eventually, a severe storm forced his keelboats to stop. Rather than put ashore and be ambushed, or land on Credit Island, where the enemy was massed, Taylor decided to anchor in the middle of the Mississippi on a small islet just two hundred feet from Credit Island. He put his men under a strict night watch and had only two campfires built. The night was cold and there were gale force winds. Even though his men complained about the weather and the few campfires, Taylor held out. He expected the Indians to attack that very night.

Despite what some described as hurricane-like weather, the Indians, led by Black Hawk, opened fire on Taylor's forces before sunrise on September 14, 1814. In the dark, Taylor ordered his men to return fire only if they could see their opponents. Taylor's force managed to destroy some Indian canoes after sunrise when the weather improved. Then his soldiers were surprised when three British cannons fired on them from the shore. One of the shots went through the bow of Taylor's boat.

As Black Hawk's forces closed in, Taylor realized he was greatly outnumbered. For the first and only time in his military career, he ordered a retreat. Gathering his men and boats together in the choppy waters proved difficult. A valiant soldier, Paul Harpole, leaped into the high waves, exposing himself to enemy gunfire. While standing in chest-high water, Harpole threw a cable to another boat to keep it from drifting. Instead of seeking protection, he shot off fourteen rounds from muskets his comrades handed him. Harpole was shot in the forehead and, according to one witness, "tumbled forward into the river, where his body was obtained [by the Indians] and cut up into a hundred pieces."[1]

Taylor took his flotilla downstream, returning fire at the pursuing Indians for two miles. After a safe distance, he landed on shore to repair his keelboats and tend the wounded. Casualties were light—only three dead and fourteen wounded. Pressing on, Taylor reached the Des Moines River, where he erected a fort on the Illinois side. He called it Fort Johnson in honor of Colonel Richard M. Johnson, a fellow Kentuckian. Johnson was a hero at the Battle of the Thames and claimed to have killed Tecumseh. But Chief Black Hawk enjoyed a victory and he would prove to be a nemesis to Taylor nearly two decades later.

A dispatch soon arrived ordering Taylor to return to St. Louis. Taylor left Captain James Callaway to complete the building of Fort Johnson. He instructed Callaway to remain there and wait for reinforcements and supplies. Taylor's trip south was delayed a few weeks while he stopped to inspect other outposts. By the time he arrived in St. Louis he was astonished to find Captain Callaway there, too. The young officer, expecting help that had not arrived as quickly as anticipated, had evacuated and burned Fort Johnson. Taylor was furious, but the incident taught him a valuable lesson— the best way to accomplish an objective was to do it himself.

In January of 1815 Brevet Major Taylor was commissioned as a full major in the U.S. Army. Then Taylor learned that the War of 1812 was over. A peace treaty had been signed at Ghent, Belgium, in December of the previous year. Because General Andrew Jackson had not received word of the treaty, he had fought the British at New Orleans in January of 1815, winning a spectacular victory two weeks after the war was over.

Peace was followed by changes in the U.S. Army. The War Department reduced the army from 50,000 to 10,000. Of the 216 field officers, only 39 were retained. Taylor's recent rank of full major was reduced back to brevet major, which meant less pay. He went to Washington, D.C., to protest. Taylor was told that his demotion was an accident, but that since his promotion to full major had not been official until after the war's end, he was not considered a permanent major. As a result, he was not eligible for any benefits or pay increase.

To make matters worse, Taylor also learned that in 1814 two of his officers had sent letters to his superiors, complaining about his conduct. Following an investigation, however, Secretary of War James Monroe concluded that the complaints were not sufficient to tarnish Taylor's reputation. President James Madison sided with his cousin Taylor in this matter. Madison reminded the War Department of Taylor's heroics, writing "The defense of Fort Harrison has probably not been exceeded in brilliancy by any officer that has occurred."[2] Despite Madison's intervention, the decision to reduce Taylor's rank remained unchanged. Unable to hide his disgust and disappointment, Taylor resigned from the U.S. Army. The incident was a learning experience for Taylor, for he came to realize that petty jealousies, disappointment, and "backbiting" were a part of military life.

Zachary Taylor returned to Bluegrass Creek and settled in as a farmer. He planted corn, wheat, and tobacco, and worked long hours in the fields next to his slaves. He wrote a friend, "I have always welcomed a weary body that comes from a good day's labor."[3] He spent much of his time playing with his daughters and struck up a friendship with a neighbor, John Crittenden, the future senator and governor of Kentucky. Taylor was also reunited with his brothers, who had all fought in the war. Despite his setbacks in Washington, Taylor was nevertheless looked upon as a military hero.

Taylor's work on his plantation proved profitable. The port of Louisville was a hub of commercial activity. Farm products could be shipped more quickly to distant cities as a new mode of transportation—the steamboat—appeared. It revolutionized the trade industry and helped make a fortune for enterprising, industrious farmers like Taylor. In April of 1816, he wrote a relative, "I have commenced making corn and tobacco & am now in my cabbin [sic] where I will always be extreamly [sic] happy to take you by the hand . . . I can assure [you] I do not regret the change of calling or the course I have pursued . . ."[4] A few years later when a railroad was built nearby, farming became even more rewarding. Taylor's idyllic plantation life, however, would soon change. Farmer Taylor was destined to pursue yet another adventure.

CHAPTER 6

Summoned Again

Taylor's contributions as an army leader did not go unrecognized or unappreciated for long. Taylor discovered that, through the efforts of President Madison, he had been recommissioned as a major. By the summer of 1816, Major Taylor was back in uniform. His bitter feelings toward the military subsided, and he was assigned to Fort Howard at Green Bay.

Settled in 1764, Green Bay was Wisconsin's first permanent settlement. By 1816 about fifty families, living in crude log huts, inhabited the area. Most of the settlers were French trappers and laborers, living with their Indian wives and large numbers of racially mixed children. Very few of the people there spoke any English. Taylor sailed to Fort Howard in late November during a harrowing winter storm. He arrived to see the fort still under construction, its thirty-foot beams painted white. Behind the garrison lay a dense forest of pine, and beyond that, miles distant, were Indian villages. The U.S. Army considered Fort Howard the most important outpost in the Northwest. Located at the mouth of the Fox River, the fort was quite large. Major Taylor was warned that the Winnebagos might attack at any time, so he kept a watchful guard.

Taylor's assignment at Fort Howard was four-fold. He was to occupy the region, construct a road, protect the settlers, and pacify the natives. Another predicament Taylor had to address was the brisk illegal fur trade in the region. The British commonly smuggled furs from Canada into the United States without paying import duties. Taylor employed Indian spies to keep him informed of the illegal fur traffic. He rewarded them handsomely and gained their trust.

In 1817, after the area had been made safer, Major Taylor arranged for his wife and three daughters to visit him at Fort Howard (another girl, Octavia, had been born in August of 1816). According to the corporal who was assigned to drive a carriage for Mrs. Taylor, she carried a loaded pistol with her for protection. Conditions were still crude and certain supplies were scarce. There were food shortages, and in mid-January of 1818, Major Taylor wrote his superiors in Washington, "Unless considerable exertions are made to forward . . . provisions in the Spring, the troops here must suffer very much."[1] Taylor also wrote a brother: "Peggy says she is very lonesome and is in hopes you will be as good as your word in paying us the visit you promised. If you come over, Peggy says you must bring her some cotton for nitting [sic], which she wants mother to have spun for her."[2] Eventually, Peggy Taylor returned to Louisville with her daughters.

Discipline of the troops was a concern at Fort Howard. Taylor received his instructions from a captain at Fort Mackinac who had replaced the former commander there. Major Taylor outranked the captain, yet he took his orders from him. Taylor's officers were aware of this reversal in the chain of command, and some of them used the opportunity to refuse orders. Because of the shortages, food was rationed. When the whiskey ran out in February, Taylor announced that they would not be buying any more. Two lieutenants disobeyed him and purchased some whiskey anyway. Taylor had the men arrested, and even considered challenging one of them to a duel. Eventually the officers were court-martialed and allowed to resign.

During his time at Fort Howard, Major Taylor and three companies of infantry constructed a road from Green Bay, through Fort Winnebago, to Fort Crawford, a distance of one hundred fifteen miles. The road was completed at a cost of twelve hundred dollars. The route linked the forts and made the region easier to patrol. The Indians remained peaceful and the illegal fur trade was also slowed.

Inspector General John Wool paid a visit to Fort Howard and was much pleased with the progress Taylor had made. After nearly two years of enduring harsh winters and other hardships, Taylor was granted a furlough back to Louisville. In early September he reached home, happy to see his family.

For a year Taylor tended his plantation and supervised military recruitment in the Louisville area. In the spring of 1819 he received a promotion to lieutenant colonel and a pay increase to sixty dollars a month, plus expenses. Taylor was at home on July 27, 1819, for the birth of his fourth daughter, Margaret Smith Taylor. That summer Major Taylor traveled to Frankfort, Kentucky, where he was invited to join the governor of Kentucky, President James Monroe, and General Andrew Jackson for a dinner, followed the next morning with breakfast. It may have been at this point that Taylor took an interest in politics, though he kept any political views to himself.

A bitter conflict seemed imminent. By August, Indians were on the rampage in the lower Mississippi Valley—fighting against each other. The Choctaws and Cherokees were savagely attacked by several combined tribes. More than forty thousand warriors gathered along the Red River and American settlers felt at risk. In addition to the presence of Indians, the region was also threatened by white bandits, or land pirates. They preyed upon unsuspecting travelers, often robbing and killing traders who were taking their wares to New Orleans.

The army sent Taylor to Louisiana to establish a garrison known as Fort Selden. Fort Selden was upstream from the Red River, less than fifty miles from the Mexican border of Texas. After completing his mission, Taylor returned to Louisville but was soon ordered back to Louisiana. In February of 1820, he moved his family to Bayou Sara near St. Francisville, Louisiana, into the home of his wife's sister, Mrs. Samuel Chew.

One of Taylor's new assignments was to build a highway. Commanding 450 troops, he supervised construction of the 200-mile Jackson Military Road, which passed through Choctaw territory in Mississippi and went all the way to the Gulf of Mexico. When food and supplies for his men ran out, Taylor bought them on credit. During this time Taylor openly expressed his political views. Never shy about expressing these views to friends, Taylor said Americans were overextending themselves, and that it was impossible to maintain every outpost in the far reaches of the Northwest Territory and Louisiana Purchase. He also came to dislike many of the West Point soldiers assigned to him. He remarked in a letter, "Unless practice can be blended with theory, the latter will be of little service . . . Better to have a practical, than a theoretical soldier . . . the axe, pick, saw, and trowel, has become more the implement of the American soldier, than the cannon, musket or sword."[3]

Conditions in Louisiana were unhealthy. Typhoid, malaria, and yellow fever swept through the region. In July of 1820, Taylor's three-year-old daughter Octavia died. After her death Taylor returned to his regiment, only to receive word that his wife was deathly ill. Upon reaching Bayou Sara, Taylor himself came down with malaria. On October 22 his baby daughter Margaret died. Peggy recovered, but her health was permanently frail. Grief stricken and deep in despair, Taylor considered resigning from the army to stay with his family. After a slow recovery, however, he realized he needed to keep busy and eventually went back to his command. After many months of delay, the Jackson Military Road was finished. Taylor then set about constructing another outpost, Fort Jesup, which was completed in 1822.

By the spring of 1821, Taylor had made up his mind to leave the army *again*. Military pay was never very much and payment was often sporadic. He needed money and wrote General Thomas Jesup that he was retiring from the military without any regrets, saying, "I have no fears of succeeding tolerably well in civil life."[4] Taylor had also apparently made unsuccessful efforts to secure help from his cousin, ex-President James Madison. In disgust, he described Madison as "perfectly callous and unacquainted with the noble feelings of a soldier."[5]

Death continued to visit the Taylors. In 1822 Taylor received news that his mother, at age 62, had died. He worried about his father, Richard, now in his eighties. Taylor wrote his sister Elizabeth in Lexington, Kentucky, "I am truly sorry that it is not in my power to visit him frequently."[6] Richard Taylor was well cared for, however, and lived in his brick homestead Springfield with a host of relatives.

Without explanation, Zachary Taylor changed his mind and decided to remain in the army. When Fort Selden was ordered abandoned, Taylor was authorized to proceed to Kentucky. Taylor's command was then divided among duties at Fort Jesup, Fort Smith, and Baton Rouge. In January of 1823, he bought 380 acres of prime land 45 miles north of Baton Rouge. Taylor and his family moved into their new home and had their slaves transferred from Kentucky to this plantation. But Taylor's stay in Louisiana was brief, and duty soon called him back to Louisville.

The Taylors sailed up the Mississippi in February of 1824. Lieutenant Colonel Taylor found a cousin to supervise his Louisiana plantation and its two dozen slaves. Dividing his duties between headquarters in Louisville, Kentucky, and Cincinnati, Ohio, Taylor traveled frequently. Good news came on April 20 when his fifth daughter Mary Elizabeth or "Betty," was born.

For the next two and a half years, Taylor supervised the training of recruits and their transportation to numerous locations. He kept track of military costs and submitted detailed monthly reports to Washington, D.C. He got to know some powerful elected officials and enjoyed talking with them about the issues of the day. Though fascinated by political events, Taylor never voted in an election because he rarely stayed in one place long enough to establish a residency.

The 1824 presidential race generated great controversy and Taylor followed it with interest. Democrat Andrew Jackson received the most popular and electoral votes, but he failed to win a majority in either. The other presidential candidates included John Quincy Adams, Henry Clay of Kentucky, and William Crawford of Georgia. Because there was no clear winner, the U.S. House of Representatives was to decide the outcome of the election. Realizing he was unlikely to win, Henry Clay gave his support to Adams, and the House chose John Quincy Adams as the sixth President. Adams then appointed Henry Clay as his secretary of state. Jackson supporters claimed a "corrupt bargain" had been made and they vowed to put "Old Hickory" in the White House in the next election.

On January 27, 1826, Taylor's only son Richard was born. Shortly thereafter, the Lieutenant Colonel was ordered to Washington to sit on a military board of officers, whose goal was to suggest changes in the Army. After arriving in the nation's capital on October 13, 1826, Taylor was exposed to the pleasantries of Washington society, but he took little part in the cultural and political activities there. With Congress in recess and President Adams home in Massachusetts, Taylor saw a few friends and relatives. He met with Secretary of War John Barbour, a cousin, and was introduced to Postmaster General John McLean. McLean's daughter later married Taylor's brother Joseph. The military panel, on which Taylor served, managed to make a few minor changes to improve the army. In January of 1827 Taylor headed home. His arduous return trip included travel by coach to Wheeling, Virginia, where he boarded a boat that spent the next week plodding through the ice-choked Ohio River.

As soon as he arrived in Louisville, Taylor received new orders sending him to New Orleans, where he remained from February until June of 1827. He transferred his regimental headquarters to Baton Rouge to be closer to his plantation. Returning to New Orleans in November, Taylor remained there until May 1, 1828, when he left for a new location at Fort Snelling. Located at the junction of the St. Peter and Mississippi Rivers (near present-day St. Paul, Minnesota) this garrison was the northwestern most outpost in the

U.S. Army. Sauks, Winnebagoes, and Potawatomis had killed some soldiers and intrusive settlers there, including a few lead miners. After the Sioux announced their intent to join their Indian allies in opposing the Americans, General Henry Atkinson took 500 troops to Prairie du Chien, 165 miles south of Fort Snelling, to quell the outbreak.

Arriving in mid-May of 1828 to assume command of Fort Snelling, Taylor was pleased to find spacious living conditions in the eight-room stone house. He noted that the landscape consisted of vast prairie, dotted with many large lakes. Though the buffalo had vanished and deer and bear were scarce, there was still an abundance of beaver, elk, grouse, and wolves. The pure waters held fish of all kinds, and the soil yielded wild rice and potatoes. Local Indians bartered their furs for guns, ammunition, and clothing.

Despite the threat of an Indian uprising, Taylor felt the area was secure enough to invite his family to live with him. Protected by a stone wall, Fort Snelling was an imposing structure, and accommodations for the officers were excellent. Peggy Taylor created a school at the fort for white and Indian children, as well as a library for the adults. The Taylors had their mahogany furniture and delicate china shipped to the fort. Their daughter Ann, now seventeen, fell in love with the fort's surgeon, Dr. Robert C. Wood, and married him. In January of 1829, Taylor received news of his father's death. His estate at Springfield was sold to pay off his debts, and the rest of his property was divided among his children. Zachary Taylor made a handsome profit by selling his share of this Kentucky land.

In June 1829 the Taylors departed for yet another home. They sailed down the Mississippi by steamer to Fort Crawford at Prairie du Chien, where the Wisconsin River flows into the Mississippi. Taylor was ordered to build a new garrison to replace the old inadequate outpost. Commanding 210 men, Taylor completed the task, but not without difficulty. Drunkenness and disorder were prevalent. After a short time, Taylor had so many men jailed inside the stockade, he used them to build a road down to the river. Taylor also organized a temperance, or anti-alcohol society, and an officers' reading club. Among Fort Crawford's inhabitants were thirteen women, twenty-three children, and seventeen slaves.

Fort Crawford became a center of activity. The Taylors entertained guests and friends. They served liquor in small doses, but Taylor usually preferred iced milk. The soldiers put on plays, which were attended not only by whites, but also by the Indians and slaves. In early June of 1830, Taylor was again reassigned, leaving behind his oldest daughter and her husband Dr. Wood. Taylor's mission in the Northwest had been a success; Indian attacks had ceased and new settlements had been started.

Taylor spent the next several months back in Louisville where he inspected military facilities, recruited more men, and purchased 137 acres of land in Mississippi, not far from his Louisiana plantation. During the summer of 1831, Taylor commanded the New Orleans post, then returned to Louisville where he became sick and spent January and February of 1832 recovering.

In April of 1832, forty-eight-year-old Zachary Taylor was promoted to full colonel of the First Regiment. It had been a long wait, and he joined his men in a festive celebration held for him.

The day after the party, the soldiers witnessed a strange event. During a dress parade in which the troops demonstrated their marching skills and handling of weapons, Colonel Taylor noticed one new recruit out of step. As he fumbled with his musket, the young man was approached by Taylor. Unbeknownst to the Colonel, the soldier was a German who barely understood the English language. When the German stood improperly in line during inspection, Taylor grabbed him by the ears and shook him, a tactic he had used before in correcting fellow privates. The recruit swatted away Taylor's hands and landed a punch squarely on the colonel's jaw, knocking him down to the ground. Such an act was punishable by death. Fellow soldiers fixed their muskets on the mutinous recruit. Taylor scrambled to his feet, rubbed his chin, dusted himself off, and told his men, "Let the man alone! He will make a good soldier."[7] It was incidents such as this that won Taylor the admiration and respect of his men.

CHAPTER 7

Fighting, Farming, and Family

DESPITE THE ESTABLISHMENT OF MILITARY FORTS, THE LAND-HUNGRY SETTLERS OF northwestern Illinois and parts of the Wisconsin Territory feared a major Indian uprising in the early 1830s. After being driven into Iowa and Wisconsin, several tribes had moved back into their old lands, which had been guaranteed to them by treaties with the government.

Black Hawk, leader of the Sac Indians, was still an imposing figure despite his old age and five foot, four inch frame. The chief commanded respect, even among the tribes who were opposed to him. In 1832 Black Hawk and a large Indian force crossed over to the eastern side of the Mississippi. When white settlers challenged this move, there were outbreaks of violence.

Black Hawk announced that the Native Americans would be pushed no further off their lands. He also condemned other tribes for selling their lands, claiming those Indians were drunk at the time of the sale, the result of free liquor supplied to them by the U.S. government. General Henry Atkinson tried to avoid a conflict. He met with Black Hawk's emissaries, who told him, "His [Black Hawk's] heart is bad and if you send your officers to him, he will fight them."[1] Further negotiations resulted in bloodshed. American troops were called in as white settlers demanded more protection from their government. The resulting fighting was known as the Black Hawk War.

Missouri raised a thousand men and Illinois raised two thousand. Michigan and Indiana called for troops as well, many of them thirty-day volunteers. The steamship *Warrior* transported hundreds of men and guns up the Mississippi. Other officers and men, including Colonel Taylor, arrived by flatboats. Governor John Reynolds of Illinois accompanied the army into the north central part of the state, arriving at Dixon's Ferry on the Rock River. Among the recruits for the Black Hawk War was a young captain of the volunteers named Abraham Lincoln, who within a decade would become a Whig and work for Taylor's election as president. Lincoln saw no military action during the conflict, doing most of his fighting against mosquitoes.

It was at Dixon's Ferry that Lincoln met Jefferson Davis for the first time. Thirty years later these two men would oppose each other in a life-and-death struggle during the Civil War. But at Dixon's Ferry in 1832, Davis, Lincoln, and Taylor all dined together while discussing battle plans. Other dinner guests included brothers Albert Sidney and Joseph Johnston, officers who later commanded the Confederates against President Lincoln's Union Army. Colonel William S. Hamilton, son of Alexander Hamilton, and Nathaniel Boone, son of Daniel Boone, also attended the meal.

By July of 1832 Taylor and four hundred men had set out to defeat the Indians and capture Black Hawk. About forty miles north of Fort Crawford, the enemies clashed where Bad Axe Creek joins the Mississippi. Some units of the Illinois militia had refused to cross the Illinois state line. Taylor, keeping his temper, met with the militia, reasoned with them, and convinced them to march on. At the Battle of Bad Axe, Taylor leaped from his horse, waded to an island, and positioned himself where he could better direct his forces.

Black Hawk had successfully battled Taylor years before, but this time conditions were different. Though many Indians were on the verge of starvation, they put up a fierce resistance. Still, they were no match for the larger American army and its cannons. Black Hawk and his warriors retreated as other Indians deserted. More than a hundred of them drowned in trying to avoid capture. Taylor pursued Black Hawk, sending messengers to convince him to surrender and avoid further battle. In August, several chiefs, including Black Hawk and his two sons, were delivered into Taylor's camp. Sadly, the defeated Sac leader was later taken to eastern cities where he was put on exhibition. Black Hawk was eventually escorted to an Indian reservation, and he died near Eldon, Iowa, in October 1838 at the age of 71.

Zachary Taylor remained at Fort Crawford, where he took on the extra duty of Indian agent, maintaining peace and promoting trade between the tribes. He believed one of the major causes of the Black Hawk War was the American Fur Company, which employed Indians to trap animals for their furs. When Taylor had schools built for Indian children at several forts, the fur company protested because the schools kept the children from trapping. Because it had supported some congressmen in their elections, the fur company had great influence in Congress. Taylor believed Washington officials and army policy were being unduly influenced by the fur company. He complained that the American Fur Company people were ". . . the greatest scoundrels in the world."[2]

The Black Hawk War had cost the United States more than $3 million, a hefty amount for the struggling republic. In terms of human life, more than 1000 American soldiers and sailors had died, and at least twice that amount wounded. As in all conflicts, there were numerous mistakes made in the Black Hawk War, leading Taylor to write, "The entire affair was bungled."[3]

Taylor's family settled in with him at Fort Crawford, located at the mouth of the Fox River. His daughter Sarah Knox (called Knox by her family) fell in love with Lieutenant Jefferson Davis. Tall, proud, dignified, and a West Point graduate, Davis also studied law in his spare time. Such qualities and habits drew suspicion from Taylor. The two had disagreed over some regulations and minor infractions relating to a court martial in which they served as judges. Davis and Taylor had also argued over other matters and a rift developed between them. Tempers flared so badly that rumors persisted they would fight a duel against each other. Colonel Taylor banned Davis from his house at the fort, but Davis continued to meet secretly with Knox. The couple asked Taylor's permission to get married. Colonel Taylor, mindful of the sacrifices his wife Peggy had made for his army career, discouraged the union, saying, "I'll be damned if another daughter of mine shall marry into the army! I know enough of the family life of soldiers."[4]

In order to separate Davis and his daughter, Taylor sent Davis on several extended assignments to Kentucky and Louisiana. Though separated for two years, Davis and Knox continued to write each other. Ultimately, Jefferson Davis resigned from the Army and married Knox Taylor in Louisville on June 17, 1835. Taylor was outraged, but he did send the couple some money for a wedding gift. Knox Davis and her husband settled at the Davis plantation near Vicksburg, Mississippi. Knox Davis wrote her mother, "Do not make yourself uneasy about me; the country is quite healthy."[5] Disaster struck, however, when Jefferson Davis and his bride both contracted malaria. Twenty-one-year-old Knox Davis died on September 15, 1835.

Except for this tragic interlude, Taylor enjoyed life at Fort Crawford. The outpost contained a theater, library, and school, thanks in large part to Peggy Taylor, who worked to have the facilities built. She always sought to improve conditions wherever they lived. In the fall of 1834, Taylor took a leave of absence and, with his family, visited Kentucky and Louisiana for a few months. Back at Fort Crawford, he continued to train his men and settle disputes between Indian tribes. In the summer of 1835, Taylor and his men built a road and constructed bridges from Fort Crawford to Fort Winnebago—a distance of one hundred and ten miles. Also during this time, Colonel Taylor was instructed by the government to purchase more land from the Indians, whose numbers had been depleted by outbreaks of smallpox.

The Taylors entertained many friends and important visitors at the fort. One special guest who stayed for a while was General Winfield Scott, nicknamed "Old Fuss and Feathers." Though Scott and Taylor became friends, the two officers differed greatly in their style of command. Scott was a West Point graduate who put much importance in appearance and neatness. Taylor, who had a mistrust of West Point graduates, was more of a practical "soldier's soldier." His independent, sometimes carefree manner, contrasted sharply with most other officers of similar rank.

Zachary Taylor was forty-nine years old when he adopted a change in politics, becoming very anti-Jackson in his sentiments. Two decisions by President Andrew Jackson caused Taylor to turn against him. During the 1830s President Jackson refused to grant a second charter for the Bank of the United States, located in Philadelphia. He considered the bank a tool of the rich and he disliked the bank president, Nicholas Biddle. Jackson ordered all federal deposits withdrawn from the bank. Eventually, the Bank of the United States went bankrupt and the nation suffered a financial crisis as a result.

Taylor also opposed President Jackson's harsh treatment of the southern Indians. When gold was discovered by whites on Indian lands in Georgia, greedy prospectors killed many peaceful Indian natives there. The whites were never arrested and Indian appeals to local officials were ignored. The Cherokees appealed to the U.S. Supreme Court, which ruled that they could keep their lands. Nevertheless, Jackson ordered the Indians removed. Over the course of several years, thousands of them were forcibly relocated from

Georgia, Tennessee, and Florida. They were made to march along the "Trail of Tears" toward the Oklahoma Territory. Along the way, hundreds died from starvation, cold weather, and disease. It was one of the most shameful episodes in U.S. history. Taylor, who had always treated the Indians fairly, was appalled by Jackson's action. He began to identify more closely with Jackson's opposition: a new political party known as the Whig Party.

Colonel Taylor remained at Fort Crawford until 1837, when another major Indian uprising, known as the Seminole War, demanded his attention. For three centuries before it became a state in 1845, Florida had been claimed at various times by Spain and England. During the early 1800s, Spain regained control of the Florida peninsula from the British, despite the fact that American settlers had also claimed the territory. The Seminole and Creek Indians who lived there frequently attacked American settlements, often at the encouragement of the British. Some runaway slaves found refuge among the Seminoles, which angered slave owners.

In 1818 during the First Seminole War, American forces, led by General Andrew Jackson, had invaded Florida and defeated the Seminoles. They drove out the last vestiges of British and Spanish influence. The U.S. government forced the Indians to sign a treaty, and several tribes were relocated to distant western reservations. A few thousand remained, however. When another treaty was signed in 1832, many of these remaining Seminoles were forced to move.

During the 1830s, thousands of Americans pioneers poured into Florida. The Seminoles who continued to live there after 1832 were determined to stay. They and their Negro followers fled into the swamps, occasionally attacking American outposts. In 1835, the Second Seminole War broke out, lasting seven years. The young Seminole leader Osceola organized his men into an army. Osceola, however, was tricked into discussing peace talks under a white flag of truce with General Thomas Jesup. The Seminole chief was seized and put in prison, where he died in 1838. More than a thousand Indians, now led by other chiefs such as Alligator, Wild Cat, and Abraham, directed the resistance begun by Osceola.

During the Second Seminole War, Colonel Zachary Taylor was given command of all American forts south of Tampa. While stationed at Tampa Bay, Taylor supervised the organization and training of his army. Rather than push inland ahead of his supply lines, Colonel Taylor ordered his provisions sent ahead to existing forts. During the time Osceola was in prison, Taylor met with Seminole Chiefs Jumper and Oulatoochee to negotiate a ceasefire. The Indians decided to continue to fight.

Taylor faced other dangers beside Seminoles. His army also had to deal with snakes, alligators, quicksand, mosquitoes, and the dense growth of cypress trees in the murky swamps. In addition, there was a shortage of medical supplies and doctors. Taylor's army had no vegetables and their flour was infested with insects. Though fish were plentiful, the army's meat was spoiled. All of these conditions took a toll on Taylor's forces. Nevertheless, Taylor moved his forces further inland to locate and defeat the Seminoles, building bridges and supply stations as they advanced. Though small bands of Indians were captured, Taylor relentlessly pursued the main body of Seminoles. Those who were captured were sent to prisons in New Orleans, Louisiana, and Charleston, South Carolina.

Using friendly Indians as guides, Colonel Taylor discovered a force of Seminoles on Christmas Day, 1837. After leading his army over 150 miles through rivers, swamps, bayous, and tangled brush, Taylor found more than seven hundred Indians camped on the north shore of Lake Okeechobee in south central Florida. In front of them lay a foot-deep swamp which Taylor's men would have to cross in a frontal attack. The bulk of the Indian force was led by Chief Sam Jones, who patiently waited for the enemy.

Dressed in a straw hat and coveralls, Taylor looked more like a farmer than a soldier. This casual outfit served a purpose—he would be more difficult to spot in battle by Indians who made an effort to kill officers.

Taylor's men loved him because he was truly one of them. He camped with his men and slept with them around their campfires instead of separating himself and staying in his own command tent or sleeping on a cot. He didn't dress in fancy uniforms and never bragged of his exploits. It was during this time that Taylor's men gave him the nickname—"Old Rough and Ready."

Come morning, Taylor mounted his trusted horse Claybank and ordered a charge against the Seminoles. At first the battle went poorly for the soldiers. Taylor withheld his trained infantry and sent his inexperienced Missouri volunteers to test the enemy's power. The Missouri men sank in the mud, and heavy enemy gunfire forced them to retreat. Taylor then used his trained regiments, but their casualties quickly mounted as well.

During the next three hours, all but one of Taylor's officers were killed or wounded. With help from his brother Joseph, a career army officer who served with him, and his son-in-law Dr. Wood, Taylor evacuated the dead and wounded across two small bridges he had constructed, then pressed the attack. Just when the situation looked bleak, Taylor's troops, with one final volley of gunfire, drove the Seminoles from Lake Okeechobee.

Because the Indians were led by three different chiefs who were also rivals, they lacked a coordinated command and refused to take orders from one another. This proved to be a weakness in their strategy. After the battle, Taylor counted 30 dead soldiers and 112 wounded. Using animal hides stretched between poles, he sent his wounded back to Forts Basinger and Fraser, two small supply stations he had constructed along the way. He did manage to capture a couple dozen hostiles. He wrote in a report, "I experienced one of the most trying scenes of my life . . . The victory was dearly purchased . . ."[6]

Taylor pursued the fleeing Indians. Though he failed to locate them, the next day he did manage to capture 300 cattle and 100 ponies belonging to the Seminoles. Taylor continued moving deeper into the swamps of the Florida Everglades. Convinced Taylor could not be beaten, many Seminoles gave up their fight. In April of 1838, Chiefs Alligator, Oulatooche, and Tustanuggee and 360 of their warriors surrendered and were marched back to Tampa Bay. They were confined to a prison camp before being sent to Arkansas and Oklahoma. Small bands of determined renegade Indians, however, continued to fight in Florida until 1842.

Back in Washington, and throughout the nation, Zachary Taylor was hailed as a hero. In 1838, Colonel Taylor became Brevet Brigadier General Taylor. During the next two years he erected more than seventy forts and supply stations, constructed 3,600 feet of bridges and causeways, and built nearly 900 miles of wagon roads in Florida. This was an astonishing achievement, despite encountering scattered groups of Seminoles, who were living on wild roots and any food they could steal.

One band of three hundred Seminoles who surrendered to Taylor included fifty escaped slaves. Taylor, opposed to the spread of slavery into territories (Florida was not yet a state), informed the War Department he would not seize the Negroes, nor would he return them to their white masters. Besides, it was not his job to impound runaway slaves and escort them back to their owners. His decision angered slave owners, but Taylor remained firm in his decision. Eventually as many as four hundred blacks accompanied their adopted Seminole families to reservations in Oklahoma.

Taylor stayed an extra year in Florida and served as an Indian agent, supervising the movement of Cherokees westward and settling disputes among the few remaining tribes. He believed the policy of forcing Indians to move was unjust and voiced this opinion to his superiors in Washington, writing, "We have committed the error of attempting to remove them when their lands were not required for agricultural purposes; when they were not in the way of white inhabitants."[6] Despite his opposition, Taylor was a soldier taught to follow orders.

Zachary Taylor's service in Florida took its toll on his health. He had been seriously ill there twice, and he became weak and haggard. Military leaders encouraged him to seek rest. In 1840 Taylor, after regaining his health, was ordered to Washington, D.C., to file an official report on the war. President Martin Van Buren, who replaced Jackson in 1837, also wanted to personally thank him for his service. On their trip east, Taylor and his wife stopped in Philadelphia to pick up their youngest daughter Betty, who took time off from boarding school to travel with her parents. They visited Washington D.C., New York City, Niagara Falls, and Boston.

Richard Taylor, their thirteen-year-old son, was left with a tutor in Lancaster, Massachusetts, so he could prepare for college. Richard, who had worked on his father's sugar plantation, was later sent to Scotland and France to learn Latin and literature. In 1843 he was admitted to Harvard as a junior and later switched to Yale. During the Mexican War he became his father's aide-de-camp until he was stricken with malaria and sent home. In 1856 he was elected to the state senate in Louisiana and in 1860 decided to cast his lot with the Confederacy. Becoming a general, Dick Taylor proved a gallant leader. In May of 1865 he surrendered, becoming the last Confederate general to lay down his arms. After his property was confiscated or destroyed by Union forces during the Civil War, Taylor built up his career as a successful businessman and later wrote a book entitled *Destruction and Reconstruction*.

In early 1841 Zachary Taylor was given command of the Second Military District, an area that included the present-day states of Oklahoma, Arkansas, Louisiana, and southern Missouri. He set up a temporary headquarters in Baton Rouge. Taylor felt privileged when his former commander General William Henry Harrison, who had been elected president in 1840, sought his advice for a cabinet recommendation. Taylor suggested John Bell of Tennessee as Secretary of War, and Bell was chosen. But Taylor's letter of support and congratulations did not receive a response from Harrison. A Whig who shared Taylor's views, Harrison died in early April of 1841, just one month after he took office. His vice-president, John Tyler of Virginia, became president. Tyler, however, had little in common with Whig Party leaders. As a slave owner with independent views, Tyler met strong opposition in Congress from Northerners and other Whigs who opposed slavery. Bell joined most of the other cabinet members and resigned after Tyler took office. Bell shared sentiments with Zachary Taylor in that he supported slavery but opposed its extension. Not only was John Tyler's administration unsuccessful, there was even a move in Congress to impeach him.

Taylor was soon sent to Fort Jesup near the Texas border, then assigned to Fort Gibson, deep in the Oklahoma Indian Territory. Conditions there were deplorable. The hospital was dirty and overcrowded, and the blockhouses were rotting and on the verge of collapse. Taylor's living quarters were also poor. Several officers' wives died at Fort Gibson, due mainly to disease and lack of medical attention. When informed there were no government funds to make improvements, Taylor, upon the advice of his superiors, moved his family to Fort Smith, Arkansas.

Life at Fort Smith was more pleasant. Taylor hunted and fished with his men. One day two newly arrived young officers approached Taylor, who was casually dressed in civilian clothes. Fresh out of West Point, the men greeted Taylor by saying, "Good morning, old fellow!" Engaging in small talk, they then invited Taylor to have a drink. The elderly man joined them but did not drink anything. When Taylor got up to leave, one of the West Pointers told him, "Give our love to the old woman and the gals." Later that day the two men called on General Taylor when he was dressed in full uniform. To their shock, they discovered he was the "old man" they had been joking with earlier. Taylor returned their salute, then introduced the men to his wife and daughter Betty, telling them, "Here are the old man and the gals." He left the young officers with one piece of advice: "Never judge a stranger by his clothes."[8]

During his tenure at Fort Smith, Taylor surveyed an area for the building of Fort Washita in Oklahoma Territory. The new fort was built after another outpost was abandoned because it had been located within Cherokee lands. Despite protests from settlers, Taylor had vacated the old fort. He also constructed Fort Scott in southeast Kansas.

In 1842 and 1843, Taylor hosted two Indian conferences to settle disputes among the tribes. When the Chickasaws and Cherokees complained about raids from the neighboring Kickapoos and Shawnees, Taylor investigated the problem. As many as a dozen tribes attended Taylor's conferences. John

Ross, the leader of the Cherokees, worked with Taylor to resolve problems, but Indian violence persisted for some time.

Zachary Taylor was fifty-nine years old in 1843. He looked forward to becoming a full-time farmer, husband and father. The Mississippi plantation he had purchased in 1823 had proven to be a disappointment. Profits on his crops, especially cotton, were unstable. Floods, droughts, hurricanes, and insects made farming a constant struggle. In 1841 Taylor sold three properties in Mississippi and Louisiana to buy another plantation. In early 1842 he purchased a 1923-acre plot near Rodney, Mississippi, along with eighty-one slaves, paying $61,000 in cash and $35,000 in notes. Taylor called the place Cypress Grove.

The Taylors soon remodeled their new home. A veranda was built around the large four-room house so there was always shade somewhere. Peggy, with the help of slaves and soldiers recruited from the sick list at the barracks, had an Episcopal chapel built on the property. She and several officers' wives conducted Bible classes. Peggy's husband took only a passive interest in the affairs of the Episcopal Church, but he was devoted to reading the *Scriptures*, remaining in his large library. Taylor's daughter Betty observed of him: "He was a constant reader of the *Bible* and practiced all its precepts, acknowledging his responsibility to God."[9]

With his military career, Taylor was seldom home, so the job of running the plantation fell upon Peggy and the family overseer. Her husband gave her strict instructions by mail about managing the place. He ordered that the slaves be well fed and cared for, and given money for Christmas. Growing cotton was a main priority, but when cotton prices fell after 1840, Taylor's plantation still made a profit by raising sheep, chickens, hogs, cattle, peas, tobacco, and hay.

When it came to farming Taylor seemed well ahead of his time. He was an advocate of crop rotation, soil conservation and diversification. Not relying simply on a single crop, Taylor diversified and planted corn, oats, sugar cane and other vegetables in addition to his cotton.

Among the horses grazing at the plantation was Taylor's longtime companion Claybank, who had accompanied him on many military ventures. Taylor once described Claybank as "smarter than most ordinary folk and all politicians."[10] But Claybank was getting "long in the tooth" and Taylor needed another horse. He chose a beautiful white stallion called "Whitey" to carry him in his next mission.

CHAPTER 8

The Mexican War

In 1836 Texas gained its independence from Mexico when Sam Houston's army defeated Mexican General Santa Anna at the Battle of San Jacinto. Texas declared itself a republic and Houston became its President. By 1843, most Texans favored statehood. This status would provide their rapidly growing population with better protection from a foreign invader, be it France, England, or Mexico. President John Tyler announced that he favored Texas joining the Union. In 1843 officials from Texas and the American government met to discuss annexation.

But there was trouble brewing in Texas again. Mexican officials claimed the Nueces River, not the Rio Grande, was the southern boundary of Texas. The difference between the two rivers involved millions of acres of land. There was also the issue of slavery. Most Northerners opposed Texas' admission to the Union because many Texans were slave owners. In fact, Northerners did not want to see slavery expand *anywhere* in the United States. Mexican officials also opposed the existence of slavery in Texas. And the Indians living in Texas objected to the influx of more white settlers, but they lacked any political power to prevent it.

Democrat James Knox Polk, a Tennessee slaveholder and a former Speaker of the U.S. House of Representatives, was elected president in 1844.

Polk campaigned on the idea of promoting what later was termed "Manifest Destiny"—the belief that America was destined to expand its borders. Polk claimed that the Oregon Territory and the vast Southwest were part of America. He said he would annex these regions even if it meant going to war. Polk sent special envoys James Mason and John Slidell on a secret mission to negotiate a settlement with the Mexicans on the Texas issue. Mexico, however, was torn by revolution, with a new leader seemingly every several months. The Mexicans refused to see Mason and Slidell. This made President Polk furious with the Mexican government.

There was also a dispute at this time with England over the northern boundary of the Oregon Territory. The situation reached a critical stage, and Polk feared Great Britain would join forces with Mexico in a war. War with the British, however, was avoided through diplomatic negotiations. The United States accepted the forty-ninth parallel, instead of the fifty-fourth, as Oregon's boundary. This solution left Polk free to concentrate on the dispute with Mexico.

During the negotiations over the boundary of Texas, General Taylor was ordered to Fort Jesup, Louisiana, to await further instructions. While he was on leave on February 25, 1845, Taylor had a chance encounter in Baton Rouge with soon-to-be Congressman Jefferson Davis. It was their first meeting since Davis' marriage to Knox Taylor and her death ten years earlier. The bitter feelings which once existed between the two evaporated, and Taylor even wished Davis and his future bride, Varina Howell, good luck.

General Taylor was hoping to see his son Richard graduate from Yale where he had been attending college, but in 1845 he was ordered to occupy Texas. His job was to protect settlers and keep a close watch on the Mexicans. Spending three weeks on board the *Alabama* with the bulk of his troops, Taylor and his army of four thousand reached Aransas Bay and disembarked in the shoals of the Nueces River delta. The army then moved by land and positioned itself at the village of Corpus Christi, not far from the mouth of the Nueces.

Taylor's army of observation could now be called an army of occupation. For four months the restless soldiers endured storms and unsanitary conditions in their city of tents. While Taylor slept, many of his men visited the nearby town to experience the nightlife of drinking, gambling, and prostitution, which flourished in the makeshift brothels outside the camp. Many officers disregarded the rules that forbade them to indulge in such activities. Officers broke other rules by not bothering to shave or going hunting when they were supposed to be on duty. Taylor demanded the resignation of those who were caught disobeying him. Order was at last maintained as the army waited for possible action against Mexico.

On December 29, 1845, Texas was admitted to the Union as the twenty-eighth state. Secretary of War William Marcy ordered Taylor to advance to the Rio Grande, where several American warships would meet him. In March of 1846, Taylor's long wagon train left Corpus Christi. It was a grueling journey through the beating sun, and Taylor's men, with cracked lips, peeled noses, and sunburned faces, had to have their water rationed since good drinking water was hard to find. The Americans encountered Mexican patrols along the way, but there was no exchange of gunfire. With David Twiggs leading the cavalry and Braxton Bragg in charge of the artillery, the Army finally reached the banks of the Rio Grande where it encamped. The small garrison built there was initially called Fort Taylor.

Taylor's presence was seen as an act of aggression by the Mexicans. Across the river lay Matamoros, where Mexican soldiers built a fort and aimed their cannons at the Americans. Taylor responded likewise, setting up artillery pieces pointed to the public square in Matamoros. He also blockaded Brazos Santiago and Matamoros, driving off two Mexican supply ships. Since Matamoros was about thirty miles from Point Isabel, Taylor had to make certain each vacated position was strong enough to defend itself. His major concern was an attack on his supply base. Two weeks passed without incident, except for an amusing encounter Taylor had with the Navy.

The general often drew criticism from other high-ranking officers for his informal habit of wearing a white ruffled shirt, straw hat, and baggy pants. His relaxed attitude irked a few important officers, particularly those educated at West Point who, despite weather conditions or circumstances, took great pride in their appearance. Taylor also proved he could be self-deprecating and he poked good-natured fun at military decorum, though he knew where to draw the line.

Taylor was scheduled to meet with naval officers from a squadron near the mouth of the Rio Grande. Naval Commodore David Conner, knowing of Taylor's casual style, had dressed himself in civilian clothes. The general meanwhile had cleaned his uniform, put on his sword and polished his boots to properly receive the Navy. The meeting proved initially to be some what strained and embarrassing, but the military enjoyed a good laugh over the event.

Another incident also attracted attention. According to Mexican War veteran Samuel Chamberlain, a young lieutenant came to see Taylor. The officer instead found an apparent elderly servant sitting outside a tent, cleaning a saber. Not seeing Taylor anywhere, he offered the old man a dollar to clean his sword as well. The lieutenant returned the next day only to discover that "Old Fatty," as he had called him, was General Taylor himself. Taylor handed the officer his sword and announced, "I'll take that dollar."[1]

In early 1846 Taylor received eight thousand volunteers, but many of the raw recruits were untrained and undisciplined. They were more inclined to drink whiskey than follow orders. Large numbers of these soldiers had signed up for only three months of service, and they complained bitterly about the scorpions, rattlesnakes, tarantulas, land crabs, and insects. Hot, dry days, cold nights, leaky tents, and brackish drinking water made life miserable in the camp. Texas farmers complained about stolen livestock, and their wooden fences were pilfered to satisfy the army's shortage of firewood. Nearly all other supplies were scarce.

The discord grew as small bands of U.S. cavalry and Mexican forces exchanged gunfire. When three Americans scouts were killed by Mexican soldiers north of the Rio Grande, General Pedro de Ampudia demanded that Taylor retreat to the Nueces River. Taylor refused, and in April of 1846, another scouting party was surrounded and slaughtered by Mexican forces. After learning of the incident, Polk claimed that American blood had been shed on American soil. This assertion was certainly subject to interpretation. President Polk asked Congress for a declaration of war against Mexico. On May 13, 1846, Congress adopted the measure, though the fighting had actually begun days earlier.

Polk's opponents claimed he was looking for an excuse to declare war and had forced the Mexicans into firing the first shots. The young Whig congressman from Illinois, Abe Lincoln, introduced several "spot resolutions" in the House demanding to know the exact spot where American soldiers had died. In addition, Lincoln used strong language in denouncing President Polk. Many newspapers considered his remarks unpatriotic and politically motivated. One town back in Illinois passed its own resolution calling Lincoln the "Benedict Arnold of our district."[2] Even his own party felt some of his comments against Polk were too inflammatory and he failed to get reelected. Lincoln's career in 1848 seemed to come to an end.

The majority of Mexican troops were poverty-ridden conscripts, forced into service by press gangs and commanded by generals who bought their commissions. Civilian-led militia groups roamed the countryside as well, posing a constant threat. Indeed, the Mexicans would prove to put up great resistance.

Some New England states were reluctant to send troops or supplies. They suggested that Polk had forced the war in order to extend the power of slavery by annexing Texas and the Southwest. Henry David Thoreau, a freelance Massachusetts writer and philosopher, spent a day in jail because he refused to pay taxes to support the war effort. In his work *Civil Disobedience* he bettered Jefferson and Thomas Paine when he wrote, "That government is best which governs not at all."[3]

General John E. Wool, under Taylor's command, marched toward the Mexican border. Along the way the Americans improved roads, built bridges and sent back detailed scouting reports. Supervising these activities was a daring forty-year-old Virginian and West Point engineer named Robert E. Lee. Taylor and Lee were cousins and it was Lee's skill and valor which allowed Wool to succeed. Lee was promoted, eventually to lieutenant colonel, and then given orders to transfer. No doubt Taylor was disappointed several months later when Lee was reassigned to General Winfield Scott's army as it made its way to Vera Cruz and Mexico City. Lee, of course, would later oppose Scott and many other officers when the Civil War erupted. And though Wool and Taylor had some fundamental disagreements over strategy, after a while they got along quite well.

Taylor and his army had left Point Isabel on the evening of May 7. His line extended several miles as 300 wagons and cavalry made its way toward the Mexican border. Ten teams of oxen, which was also the army's meat supply, pulled cannons (among them two large eighteen-pounders) because of a shortage of horses. Taylor's earlier request for more supplies had been delayed. At dawn on May 8 the columns moved out of camp then, after marching a few miles, rested near a swamp surrounded by clumps of chaparral, a dense thicket of shrubs. The spring of 1846 in southern Texas had been unusual in that heavy rains and small tracts of resaca (depressions) of prairie were filled with water. This is where the enemy placed its cavalry.

The Mexican army, led by General Mariano Arista, readied to attack General Taylor. Even some American civilians rushed to join Taylor's army in the first major battle of the Mexican American War. Near a watering hole at Palo Alto, Taylor's 2,500 men were attacked by more than 6,000 Mexicans. The struggle continued all day and into the night as American artillery inflicted heavy casualties. Taylor, mounted on Whitey, chewed tobacco while taking notes and giving orders. American cannons started a brush fire, which swept through the underbrush and high grass. Among those under Taylor's command who struggled forward was Lieutenant Ulysses S. Grant, later commander of the Union Army in the Civil War and serve as the eighteenth President of the United States. Enemy losses in killed and wounded were 500, while the Americans lost 50. Among those Americans killed was one of Taylor's most valuable officers, Major Sam Ringgold, who had a bullet tear through his thigh. Ringgold refused to leave the battlefield and died three days later at Point Isabel.

The evening following the battle, Taylor called a council of war to meet with ten fellow officers to decide the army's next move. Seven of them voted to stay and wait for reinforcement from Point Isabel. Taylor, after listening to all of his officers, overruled them and ordered an attack, remarking, "Gentlemen, you will prepare your commands to move forward."[4] By the next day, May 9, 1846, the Mexican army was still north of the Rio Grande, positioned in a large clump of dwarf oaks near an old riverbed eight miles north of Fort Taylor. It was called Resaca de la Palma.

To prevent being cut off from his supplies and reserves at Fort Brown and Point Isabel, Taylor decided to drop back eastward. He knew Arista would regard this move as a retreat. Taylor felt he could then turn upon Arista's rear should he divide his forces. This is exactly what happened when the Mexican general split his forces, one to attack Fort Brown and the other to assault Taylor's main army.

Near the area where the Battle of Resaca de la Palma was to take place, a friendly camp peddler told Taylor that he was too close to the enemy. With sword in hand, "Old Rough and Ready" replied, "Let us ride a little nearer."[5] Taylor ordered his men forward into the tangled web of brush and thickets where enemy soldiers hid.

In his report Taylor provides some insight, describing the enemy's artillery positioned between its cavalry and infantry: "These batteries were opened upon us, when I ordered the columns halted and deployed into line, and the fire to be returned by all our artillery...The first fires of the enemy did but little execution, while our eighteen-pounders and Major Ringgold's artillery soon dispersed the cavalry which formed his [Arista's] left....the Fifth Infantry repelling a charge of lancers by promptly forming, like Wellington's regiments at Waterloo, the moving square, and not only firing, but using the bayonet along the threatened fronts, and the artillery doing great execution in their ranks."[6] These actions were enhanced by the use of Ringgold's mobile howitzers which were fired with quickness and precision, a tactic some military experts described a "flying artillery." After Ringgold was mortally wounded his artillery battery had been put under the command of Randolph Ridgeley.

After nearly three hours of hand-to-hand combat, the Mexicans fled. The Americans had performed magnificently, capturing enemy supplies and even a Mexican general. American losses were 150 in killed and wounded while the enemy's casualties were well over a thousand. Though General Santa Anna had gained a foothold during the battle, he failed to take any terrain considered critical.

Euphoric over their victory, Americans cried "On to the halls of Montezuma." Taylor's son Richard, who had fought at Palo Alto, also took part in the action at Resaca de la Palma. Congress passed a formal resolution congratulating Taylor and ordered a gold medal struck in his honor. President Polk, however, was not altogether pleased.

On May 18 Taylor's army crossed the Rio Grande, but it needed supplies and men. Point Isabel and Fort Brown were vulnerable and needed protection as well. General Taylor was not about to stop; he was looking to move further south.

In 1846 there was already talk of Taylor becoming president. Influential newspaperman Thurlow Weed of Albany, New York, met his old friend Colonel Joseph Taylor on a Hudson River steamboat. Weed remarked to Taylor, ". . . your brother is to be our next President." Joseph Taylor replied, "That is preposterous . . . He knows nothing of civil affairs. When I tell you that he is no more fit to be President than I am, you will see how absurd your proposition is."[7]

One of Taylor's officers, Lieutenant George Meade, who later gained fame in the Civil War at Gettysburg, had written his wife, "Gen. Taylor is a gallant brave old man, who knows not what fear is . . . I consider him the best General I have yet served under . . ."[8] The Duke of Wellington, living in London, had followed the battle and also announced his praise for Taylor.

One incident during the Mexican War demonstrated both Taylor's humility and respect for his soldiers. Major Jacob Brown had earlier built an outpost near Matamoros, Texas (located across the Rio Grande from the Mexican town of the same name), and named it in honor of his commander, General Taylor. Not long after its construction, Fort Taylor was attacked by Mexican forces and Brown was killed. Taylor's men arrived after the battle.

Upon discovering Brown had been mortally wounded, Taylor renamed the garrison Fort Brown. It later became known as Brownsville, Texas.

Taylor encountered problems which constantly challenged his army. Unrest among his men and a shortage of supplies called for immediate action. In a report he wrote with frustration, "Desertion had already commenced to a shameful extent...Having no supplies, I, to obtain them, compromitted my private fortune and the credit of myself and friends. All this procured me the sum of $180,000."[9] Taylor's funds, along with the money he borrowed from a handful of wealthy friends, purchased enough supplies to last the army two weeks. Finally, after waiting three months, reinforcements and supplies arrived, including 1600 mules to carry all the baggage. He was of course reimbursed later by the federal government.

James K. Polk was a shrewd, hard-working, and strong-willed president. He was also partisan and narrow-minded. Because of Taylor's popularity, he may have feared him as a possible political rival in the next election. President Polk asked General Winfield Scott to take command of the war. Scott, living in Washington, was in no hurry to get to Mexico and waited several months before accepting Polk's offer. The war, however, was far from over.

The Mexican Army was low on ammunition, food, and supplies. It was also low on morale. Hundreds of enemy soldiers deserted, but those who remained still had some fight left in them. Retreating toward the city of Monterrey, the Mexicans reorganized their forces and made a stand there. Meanwhile Taylor made a trip back to Point Isabel to coordinate his land operation with naval strategy. On his way there, Taylor saw a drunken teamster run a baggage wagon into the back of a carriage, tearing off its rear wheels. True to form, Taylor rode Whitey up to the driver, yelled at the man, then grabbed him by the ears and shook him.

Taylor fell ill at this time, but by June 1846 he felt much better, especially after hearing that he had been promoted to full Major General—the highest rank that could be given. Thousands of more volunteers arrived for the war, including Jefferson Davis, who had resigned his seat in Congress to join the fight. Taylor's old friend, General Edmund Gaines, had recruited 8000 men from four southern states and sent them to Texas. Gaines had wanted to send 4000 extra troops but was ordered by the War Department not to. In July, Taylor moved his forces by steamboat, mule train, and foot toward Monterrey, leaving some of his men at various stations and forts along the way.

President Polk could not have possibly been pleased when Congress passed a formal resolution thanking Taylor for his actions, ordering a medal struck in his honor. The president did not try to prevent the recognition, for in doing so would have been politically unwise. Perhaps he took some solace when he learned the medallion would not be made of gold. It was issued in July of 1846.

Monterrey was a key city—its capture would allow the Americans to control the open passes in the eastern Sierra Madre leading toward the Mexican capital of Mexico City. But getting to Monterrey was a problem. Hard, sharp stones in the arid terrain made marching difficult. Temperatures reached 112 degrees. Diseases such as typhus, dysentery, and malaria accounted for hundreds of casualties, and the dead had to be removed from tents to make room for the dying. Taylor, anxious to see the war end, wrote his son-in-law Dr. Wood, "I am perfectly disgusted with the way things are going on …"[10]

As he neared Monterrey, Taylor sent his Texas Rangers unit ahead. The horse-mounted Rangers dressed in red shirts and wore sombreros or buckskin hats. They carried muskets and powder horns, along with Colt revolvers and Bowie knives, which they tucked in their belts. They looked fearsome and the Mexicans referred to them as "devils from hell." On September 19, 1846, Taylor rode down the slope of the San Juan River Valley. As he stopped to get a better look at Monterrey through his spyglass, a twelve-pound cannonball tore up dirt at his horse's hooves. The battle had begun.

Monterrey was a city of 11,000 civilians and more than 9,000 Mexican soldiers. Mexican General Pedro Ampudia considered his army invincible, particularly in the well-fortified city. Before Taylor could take Monterrey, he first had to capture or destroy the four outposts surrounding the city. On Monday, September 21, General William Worth and Colonel David Twiggs led a night attack against Bishop's Palace, a large stone building atop Independence Hill, which guarded the entrance to the city. This took the Mexican army by surprise. The Americans then captured three other forts, with Jefferson Davis, Ulysses S. Grant, and Joseph Hooker leading the way. After enemy soldiers fled into the city, the Americans turned their cannon on Monterrey and shelled it for hours.

The fighting at Monterrey was different from any Taylor had experienced. The general was deep in enemy territory with limited supplies. Mexican soldiers within the city hid in adobe and stone houses, waiting to fire on their aggressors. Upon entering Monterrey, General Taylor dismounted Whitey to direct the battle. Oblivious to danger, he led the First Ohio Regiment into the maze of streets. Each man fought for himself. Taylor's six thousand troops battled block by block and house by house, encountering soldiers and armed civilians. When ammunition ran low, Ulysses S. Grant made a daring ride through the streets to find General Twiggs, who delivered the ammunition just as the Americans were firing their last rounds. Eventually the Mexicans were driven toward the city's center, where General Ampudia made a stand. American cannons again rained deadly fire on the trapped soldiers. Finally, after five days of brutal conflict, Ampudia surrendered. While the Mexicans marched out of the city, the Americans marched in to the tune of "Yankee Doodle."

General Taylor promised Ampudia he would not pursue his army for eight weeks. It would take the Americans that long to recover their losses and get supplies. The defeated Mexicans were allowed to keep their muskets, ammunition, and horses, and they began marching south. Unfortunately, while Taylor's army occupied Monterrey, a few of his soldiers stole from Mexican civilians and raped Mexican women. When Taylor learned of the thefts and rapes, he quickly punished the offenders with demotions, discharges and time in the stockade.

President Polk felt Taylor's terms of surrender were too generous. Nor was he pleased with Taylor's losses of five hundred men killed and wounded at Monterrey. Earlier Polk had ordered the only officer with more seniority than Taylor, General Winfield Scott, to take command of the fighting in central Mexico. Just two days after the Battle of Monterrey, Scott wrote out orders to Taylor, reassigning most of Taylor's troops to his own command.

President Polk explained to his advisors he was displeased and suspicious of "Old Rough and Ready." In his diary, Polk wrote that Taylor was "evidently a weak man and has been made giddy with the idea of the Presidency. He is most ungrateful, for I have provided him, as I now think, beyond his deserts and without reference to his politics, I am now satisfied that he is a narrow-minded, bigoted partisan, without resource and wholly unqualified for the command he holds."[11]

After the Battle of Monterrey, Mexican President Mariano Paredes, who succeeded Herrera, resigned. Santa Anna, exiled in Cuba, convinced American officials he would negotiate a peaceful settlement to end the war. Having promised President Polk he would sign a treaty and accept the Rio Grande as Mexico's northern boundary, Santa Anna was permitted to pass through American lines. But the crafty Mexican general hated the Americans, referring to them as thieving "Gringos." Santa Anna was determined to defeat Taylor. After arriving in San Luis Potosi, Santa Anna declared himself president again and rallied the broken Mexican army.

Following Taylor's spectacular victory over Santa Anna at Buena Vista in February 1847, the general made his headquarters at Walnut Springs near Monterrey. Back in Washington, President Polk refused to sign an order for troops to fire a salute in Taylor's victory. He noted in his diary, "Had General Taylor obeyed his orders, and occupied Monterrey and the passes beyond it, the severe loss of our army, including many valuable officers, would have been avoided. It was great rashness to take the positions he did in advance of Saltillo. Having done so, he is indebted not to his own good generalship, but to the indomitable and intrepid bravery of the officers and men under his command for his success...from the beginning of the existing war with Mexico he has been constantly blundering into difficulties, but he has fought his way out of them but with very severe loss."[12] Additionally, Polk had some concerns about Scott who had declared himself a Whig.

Not all of the losses by Taylor, and later those of Scott, were directly related to the battlefield. More than half the deaths were due to disease and at the army field hospital in Perote on the road to Mexico City more than 500 men were laid up. Another constant problem Taylor dealt with was the behavior of his men at Walnut Grove, particularly the volunteers whose terms of enlistment would soon expire. When Taylor again received reports of stealing and the raping of Mexican women, he issued an order reminding his soldiers of "the great importance of respecting the rights of all Mexican citizens."[13] This directive was ignored by some Americans who held contempt for the Mexicans.

Many atrocities by the Americans, and there were hundreds, went unreported and unrecorded. Consequently, American stragglers or those soldiers separated from the main army, often paid a terrible price if captured. Such events intensified the deep resentment which already existed between Mexicans and Americans.

Meanwhile, beginning in April of 1847, General Scott, with a naval fleet and thirteen thousand troops, won battles at Vera Cruz, Cerro Gordo, Churubusco, Moleno del Ray, Chapultapec, and Mexico City. On September 14 the Americans, led by Scott, entered the Mexican capital among a cheering crowd that was happy the war would finally be over. Santa Anna resigned as president. While Taylor's victories had done little to shorten the war, Scott's military actions had helped bring the war to an end.

However, General Scott's losses in the Mexican War were also high and, like Taylor, he was criticized by Polk and some members of Congress. American losses during the Mexican War totaled nearly 2,000 battle deaths, 11,000 dead from disease, and more than 5000 more injured or disabled. The cost of the war was about $100 million. Many Americans, however, felt that the resulting immense territorial gain justified the expenditure.

One duty Taylor did not mind was answering his mail. His correspondence increased as military officials, admiring politicians, concerned mothers and adoring fans sent him letters. Though besieged with hundreds of messages, he tried to answer them all. While camped at Rhode Island, Texas, one of the letters he received was from a young boy, Charles Reynolds of Maumee, Ohio.

Reynolds asked Taylor to send him a sword and uniform so he could join the army and fight in the war. Taylor replied, "…gladly as I should wish to do you a favor you will perceive that having no means except by mail, it will be quite impossible to do as you wish. Let me advise you to wait until you shall arrive as mature age, then it will be ample time for you to put on sword and epaulette and do your duty to your country. I admire the patriotism of yourself and friends…"[14]

President Polk sent Nicholas Trist to negotiate a peace settlement with the new Mexican government. Trist, however, negotiated terms that differed from Polk's instructions. He also felt sympathy towards the shattered Mexicans. The emissary was placed under arrest, returned to the United States, and dismissed without pay.

By 1847 Taylor was ready to depart from Mexico and requested a six-month leave. On November 8, 1847, General Zachary Taylor bid farewell to his troops. On Friday November 26, he sailed down the Rio Grande onboard the steamer *Monmouth*, bound for home. Hundreds of sick and wounded American soldiers were on the boat and Taylor saw that the men were made comfortable. He even gave up his compartment for the wounded and slept on a mattress outside the boiler room. Upon nearing New Orleans, Taylor was met by a fleet of fourteen ships which guided his steamer into the city. Bells tolled from every church and one hundred cannons offered a salute as forty thousand people came out to greet their war hero. Parades, dances, fireworks, and ceremonies of all kinds were held in the general's honor. Upon reaching Baton Rouge, Taylor was so overcome with the huge welcome that he wept.

Zachary Taylor had performed admirably even if he was a bit unorthodox. One officer serving under him, Ulysses S. Grant, wrote years later, "No soldier could face either danger or responsibility more calmly than he. These are qualities more rarely found than genius or physical courage…General Taylor never wore a uniform, but dressed himself entirely for comfort. He moved about the fields which he was operating to see through his own eye the situation…He was very much given to sit [on] his horse side-ways, with both feet on one side, particularly on the battlefield."[15]

The war was not just controversial; it proved costly as well. Many of its participants, including Grant, saw it as an unnecessary conflict. The nation was nearly split in two over the war's aims. Negro abolitionist Frederick Douglass expressed the feelings of many Americans in his newspaper *The North Star*. Issued in an editorial on March 17, 1848, he praised the war's conclusion, writing that the "end is put to the wholesale murder in Mexico and is truly just cause for rejoicing." Furthermore, he advised his fellow Americans to seek the Almighty's pardon "for crimes at the hands of God whose mercy endureth forever."[16] The Whig Party led the charge in denouncing the Mexican War and in a twist of logic, chose two of the war's biggest heroes, Scott and Taylor, as its standard bearers.

Hundreds of soldiers and officers gained valuable experience which they would use later in the Civil War. The sacrifice was high but some parts of the country gave more than other sections. More than 49,000 volunteers came from the states bordering the Mississippi, while 13,000 came from the Northeast. The areas known collectively today as the Midwest gave its fair share as well. But the old quarrel over slavery was revived.

The Treaty of Guadalupe-Hidalgo, which officially ended the war, was not signed until February 2, 1848. The pact was so named because its negotiations were conducted in a small village of the same name near Mexico City. The United States paid Mexico $15 million for the vast territory it had acquired—an area including present-day California, Nevada, Utah, Arizona, New Mexico, and parts of Wyoming and Colorado. This region of nearly 524,000 square miles equaled a domain greater than the combined areas of Great Britain, France, Germany and Switzerland. The Rio Grande became the undisputed boundary between Texas and Mexico and the United States also agreed to pay all past claims filed by American citizens; these totaled more than $3 million. Taylor took no part in the discussions and had no wish to. He was a soldier, not a politician or diplomat. But politics was on his mind.

CHAPTER 9

Politician and Candidate

TAYLOR INTENDED TO SPEND THE REST OF HIS DAYS ON HIS LOUISIANA PLANTATION, devoting time to his family and giving his property some much needed attention. His plan to confine himself close to Baton Rouge began by accident. He soon discovered that the months of exposure to the elements, hard riding, and worry over his army had all taken its toll. On January 20, 1848, Taylor suffered a severe attack of rheumatism and was bed ridden for a month.

He ventured into New Orleans on several occasions, attending operas, plays, and banquets. One evening Taylor encountered a young New England poet, Walt Whitman, at the St. Charles Hotel. Both were in the city to see a play. After Whitman congratulated Taylor on his battlefield victories, he wrote, "The house was crowded with uniforms and shoulder straps. General Taylor was almost the only officer in civilian clothes; he was [a] jovial, old, rather stout, plain man, with a wrinkled and dark-yellow face, and, in ways and manners, show'd the least of conventional ceremony or etiquette I ever saw."[1]

The hero was in so much demand that he had to refuse many requests. One invitation Taylor did accept was from the civic leaders of Pass Christian, Mississippi, located just west of Gulfport. A large reception was held in his honor, and he humbly explained to a crowd, "It was not due to me that the enemy with which I contended was vanquished, but to the brave soldiers that stood by and sustained me in times of peril. To them belong the glory and to them I frankly yield all claims to the laurels that adorn their brows."[2] Comments such as these came from the heart and endeared Taylor to nearly all listeners.

Zachary Taylor's reputation was becoming legendary. Hundreds of songs were written about him and his portrait adorned thousands of homes and businesses throughout the nation. His likeness graced ice carts, wagons, and cigar boxes. New villages and streets were named Buena Vista, Monterrey, and Taylor. Over the next year many artists visited Taylor's plantation to paint his portrait. In January of 1848 the Tennessee legislature, in a joint resolution, recommended his selection as candidate for president. Not even Old Whitey escaped stardom. Following the war, souvenir hunters began plucking hairs from his tail.

Taylor knew he would soon have to make a decision about seeking the presidency. His letter to Captain John S. Allison, an influential Kentucky businessman and politician, announced he would accept a nomination if the Whig Party offered it. Taylor had stated, "I have consented to the use of my name as a candidate for the Presidency...I am a Whig. If elected I would not be the mere President of a party...I would endeavor to act independent of party domination...."[3] This written response was sent by Allison to newspapers throughout the country. Allison knew the general quite well; he was married to Taylor's sister Emily.

There was no shortage of presidential candidates in 1848. Among the Whigs seeking the White House were three Senators: Henry Clay of Kentucky, Thomas Corwin of Ohio, and Daniel Webster of Massachusetts. Supreme Court Associate Justice John McLean and General Winfield Scott also sought the nomination. Taylor initially favored Clay, who had lost three previous presidential races to John Quincy Adams, Andrew Jackson, and James Polk. Taylor again announced he had no desire to be a candidate, but said he would not refuse a duty if called upon by his fellow citizens.

Clay was hoping General Taylor would endorse him, and he was disappointed when Taylor refused to withdraw his name from contention. When asked what his politics were, Taylor announced, "I am a Whig, but not an *ultra* Whig."[4] A second letter to Allison in September was made public and reassured voters he was not an extremist. Meanwhile, Clay reminded the Whigs of Taylor's inexperience as a politician. Clay and other southern Whigs were alarmed when "Old Rough and Ready" spoke about limiting the spread of slavery. On the other hand, northerners and abolitionists (those who opposed slavery) could not ignore the fact that Taylor owned three hundred slaves. They were at least satisfied that he treated them well.

Ironically, in early September of 1847 Taylor had earlier been nominated for president in Philadelphia by a minor anti-immigrant third party, the Native American Party. Taylor appreciated their support but he was not running on *that* ticket. National support for Taylor took a firm hold in December of 1847 when Whig Congressman Abraham Lincoln organized a "Taylor Club" among House members. The group included several southern Representatives who referred to themselves as the "Young Indians." Taylor's old friend John Crittenden of Kentucky worked to organize a campaign there. Another friend, Alexander Stephens, established a Taylor Club down in Georgia as well.

Meanwhile, Taylor kept busy, making public appearances, tending to his properties and responding to his ever-increasing volume of mail. Typical was a request by A. D. Haslett who wrote Taylor asking for a lock of his hair. In late March of 1848, Taylor sent Haslett a letter, writing, "Your request as stated to have a lock of my hair as a keepsake is with much pleasure complied with…much of the larger portion of the same has turned from black to white or gray…as it has been bleached while I have been in the service of our common country."[5]

Several Whig leaders in the state of New York also admired Taylor. Former Governor William Seward and Thurlow Weed agreed to "educate" the public and "sell" Taylor to the voters. Weed was the state party boss and editor of the influential *Albany Evening Journal*. Another Whig leader in that state was the powerful and influential Millard Fillmore who had recently lost the governor's race to the Democrats. He was no friend of Seward and Weed, but expressed no opposition to Taylor.

President Polk was not among the Democratic frontrunners for the nomination. Though his administration had been successful, Polk had proven too independent in dealing with party leaders. He was also totally exhausted. Earlier in his term he said he would not seek reelection, and Democrats took him at his word. When the Democratic delegates convened in Baltimore on May 22, 1848, they had several candidates to consider. The most notable contenders were General Lewis Cass of Michigan, former Congressman and Secretary of State James Buchanan of Pennsylvania,

Senator John C. Calhoun of South Carolina, Polk's Vice President George Dallas, and former President Martin Van Buren.

The 1848 Democratic convention in Baltimore was the scene of much controversy, especially over the pivotal issue of slavery. Northern and southern delegates also disagreed on the issues of tariffs (taxes on imports) and states' rights. The convention delegates ultimately selected Lewis Cass as their presidential nominee. His qualifications were admirable. He had been a war hero, governor of the Michigan Territory, Secretary of War under Andrew Jackson, and Minister to France. General William Butler of Kentucky, a hero of the War of 1812, former Congressman and an aide to Taylor in the Mexican War, was chosen as the Democrat's vice presidential candidate.

When the Whigs met in Philadelphia on June 7 to choose their candidates for the election of 1848, Zachary Taylor already had much support. One of those in attendance was Horace Greeley, editor of the influential *New York Tribune* (twenty years later he would be defeated by Grant in the race for the White House). Greeley announced his support for Henry Clay, then John McLean of Ohio, then Daniel Webster; anyone was better than Taylor. Greeley fought hard against Taylor's nomination. He wrote friend Schuyler Colfax (later Grant's vice president), "We cannot with any decency support General Taylor….his unqualified devotion to slavery; his destitution of qualifications and principles, place him at an immeasureable [sic] distance from the Presidency…we may elect him, but we destroy the Whig Party…I wash my hands of the business."[6]

Taylor led in the voting from the start. But another anti-Taylor delegate, Charles Allen of Massachusetts, choked with rage as it appeared Taylor would win the nomination. Jumping up on a table he yelled, "The free states will not submit!" The party, Allen believed "is dissolved."[7] By the fourth ballot, Taylor had enough votes to win the nomination, easily defeating Clay, Scott, and Webster. Immediately following the nomination, many Northern Whigs and Clay supporters created chaos. For fifteen minutes a steady gavel rapped for order. It was only a motion to select a vice presidential nominee which ended the chaos.

New York politician Millard Fillmore, a former congressman, state comptroller and a "tariff man," was selected as Taylor's running mate, beating out fourteen other men for the honor, including Thurlow Weed, Ohioan Thomas Ewing and New York's Abbot Lawrence, a millionaire and generous Whig contributor. Fillmore's views on slavery were not as extreme as other Northern Whigs. Though opposed to slavery, Fillmore believed (correctly) that the federal government had no power to outlaw it where it existed. Amazingly, no party platform was adopted, as in doing so might offend or alienate different sections of the country.

Following Taylor's nomination, Greeley returned to New York City in disgust, branding the convention and Taylor's victory as a "slaughterhouse" of Whig principles. Over the course of the next few months, Greeley's views about Taylor would soften, but he was correct in predicting the end of the Whig Party.

Taylor was unaware of the convention's proceedings and waited at his plantation for news. He first learned of his nomination when a telegraph message was sent to Memphis, then delivered to New Orleans by steamboat. Until he received official notice from the convention, Taylor did not consider himself the Whig nominee. When the official letter of notification arrived from Philadelphia, Taylor had it sent back unopened because it had no postage. Zachary Taylor was not going to pay the ten cents. As a national hero, Taylor received a tremendous amount of mail, much of it with insufficient postage. Rather than pay the postage, he routinely returned the mail unopened. Luckily, a Whig leader in Philadelphia noticed the returned letter and paid the postage to send it on the long voyage again.

In the days before the Civil War, presidential candidates campaigned very little themselves—that was done by their political party's legion of loyal lieutenants—governors, congressmen, and local officials who tried to rally support for their candidate. Taylor kept to tradition and stayed home. There was plenty to do which demanded his attention. With more and more mail arriving, he was inundated with letters from office seekers, newspapers, friends and supporters, not to mention autograph hounds. Just one of hundreds of examples for those asking for his signature was a letter from Henry Wiley of Saxtons River, Vermont. Taylor wrote him, "…your esteemed letter…asking my autograph was this moment received which request is with much pleasure complied with…accept my best wishes for your continued health & prosperity throughout a long life."[8]

Taylor's views were known to some because he had voiced his opinions prior to the convention. He favored the Whig philosophy of higher tariffs, selling public land to generate more revenue for the government, and building internal improvements such as canals and roads.

The 1848 campaign had its share of mudslinging. Clay, bitter at his defeat, refused to support Taylor, saying the general "exhibited such instability and vacillation; he will inevitably fall into the hands of others who will control his administration."[9] Clay, whose son had been killed at the Battle of Buena Vista where Taylor was commander, further described Taylor as "that swearing, whiskey-drinking fighting frontier colonel."[10]

Thomas Ewing cautioned Taylor to stay home and not speak out on the issue of slavery, lest he offend voters everywhere. Other Whigs asked that he stop writing letters to newspapers, explaining that his views might cost him votes. The Democratic Party lay in waiting for the best moment to attack Taylor's character.

The Whigs rejoiced when Martin Van Buren, having failed to win his party's nomination, decided to leave the Democratic Party. Van Buren met with abolitionists and Northern Democrats, nicknamed "Barnburners", and decided to run on a third party ticket. Van Buren was nominated in Buffalo, New York, by a strong anti-slavery group known as the Free Soil Party. Whigs hoped Van Buren would help split the Democratic vote, taking enough votes away from Lewis Cass to ensure Taylor's victory.

Meanwhile, the Whigs worked feverishly to discredit Democratic candidate Lewis Cass. He was criticized for getting rich at the expense of the Indians when he served as an Indian agent years before. Abraham Lincoln attacked Cass in speech after speech, telling voters that Cass's military record during the War of 1812 was greatly exaggerated. He also reminded them of the candidate's obese frame and joked that the word "Cass" rhymed with "gas." With his double chin, large bags under his eyes and a poorly-fitted red hairpiece, Cass became a target of ridicule and the darling of critical Whig cartoonists.

Cass had been born and educated in New Hampshire and rose to prominence in Michigan politics. As a Senator from Michigan he promoted the idea of popular sovereignty whereby the people of a territory could decide for themselves if they would permit slaveholding. Like his colleague, Stephen Douglas of Illinois, Cass felt his views on the slave issue could satisfy the demands of both the North and South.

The presidential race of 1848 was characterized as a candidate-centered contest and had some exciting moments. A Cincinnati wagon, festooned in Whig symbols and having Taylor's image painted on it, carried women in bloomers urging men to vote for Taylor. In appealing to some European immigrants, books about Taylor were printed in German by the Whigs and widely distributed. In New Orleans a fight broke out between Whigs and Democrats resulting in the Whig headquarters being completely destroyed.

Perhaps the oddest incident took place in Philadelphia, where a drunken prostitute was stopped by police. When she gave her name as "Rough and Ready" she was thrown into jail.

One of the issues that dominated the campaign of 1848 was the Wilmot Proviso, a bill which dealt directly with the controversy over slavery. The Founding Fathers had legalized slavery in the Constitution, but most northern states had since taken it upon themselves to ban it. David Wilmot, a member of the House of Representatives, introduced a piece of anti-slavery legislation, only to see it defeated. His measure proposed to ban slavery from any territory acquired as a result of the Mexican War. Cass opposed the bill and said he favored "popular sovereignty," whereby the settlers in the territories could decide for themselves whether slavery would be allowed. Cass further stated that the federal government should not interfere with slavery.

The Democrats did their best to tarnish Taylor. He was depicted as a semi-illiterate, greedy individual who treated his slaves cruelly. Sketches of him in opposition newspapers showed him in wrinkled, dirty clothes. Taylor was called a "military autocrat" and compared to Caesar, Cromwell and Napoleon. Citizens were warned that he wanted to become president to gratify his lust for glory. Taylor was sensitive to these attacks, remarking that the 1848 campaign was characterized by "the vile slanders of the most unprincipled demagogues this or any other nation was ever cursed with, who have pursued me like bloodhounds."[11]

The campaign in the South took some interesting twists and turns. Voting overwhelmingly for Polk in 1844, Southerners would have to be convinced by Taylor supporters that their man was the best choice. In Alabama most of the political battles were waged between Democratic factions. When Governor Reuben Chapman, however, announced that Cass could not be trusted, Taylor became the beneficiary of his remarks.

In South Carolina, Calhoun made public his displeasure with Cass. Being the only state still voting through its legislature in presidential elections, South Carolina was heavily influenced by their fiery spokesman. Calhoun expressed his concern and "the impossibility of finding a candidate at the North, and the hazards of looking to that quarter."[12]

Louisiana, where plantation owners favored a high tariff on sugar, had supported Clay in 1844. To make certain the state stayed in Whig hands, Taylor's powerful friends there took no chances. Samuel Peters and Maunsel White worked feverishly to promote their candidate. Peters was president of the New Orleans Chamber of Commerce and White, who would later appraise Taylor's estate in late 1850, was a Democrat in the state legislature.

Georgia was a Taylor stronghold with Alexander Stephens, Robert Toombs and T. B. King well organized. In Virginia, the situation was less stable. The western counties were controlled by the Whigs but the rest of the state lay in Democratic control, due mainly to the power and influence of former President John Tyler and South Carolina's Calhoun.

In Kentucky the Whigs were firmly entrenched, even though there was fighting among themselves. Senator Henry Clay, Taylor's main rival, held much sway, as did John J. Crittenden who was leaving the Senate to run for governor. Crittenden appealed to the masses and before leaving his Senate seat, had been honored at a rousing Whig banquet in Washington. On his way back home, he stopped in cities like Pittsburgh to tell crowds that he wholeheartedly endorsed Taylor.

In New England, the Whigs fared well, winning four of the six states there, losing New Hampshire and Maine. The efforts of several stump speakers including William Seward and Abraham Lincoln reaped dividends for Taylor. Years later this campaigning paid off for Lincoln as well, for he met his future secretary of state Seward for the first time.

In 1845 a law had established the first Tuesday after the first Monday in November as Election Day. As a result, the national election on November 7, 1848, was the first in which the whole country voted on the same day (with the exception of Massachusetts). Nearly 3 million men cast their ballots. Though Cass won Ohio and Indiana, he captured Alabama, Virginia and Mississippi by razor-thin margins. South Carolina as expected went for Cass as did Illinois in a fairly close election.

Zachary Taylor did not learn of the election results right away. News traveled slowly to the South; telegraph wires still stopped at Memphis and messages from there were sent by horseback and paddle-wheel steamers. Ironically, the vessel carrying the news downstream was the *General Taylor*. Upon receiving the news of his victory, Taylor showed no emotion whatsoever.

Taylor's victories in Georgia, Tennessee, North Carolina and Kentucky were complemented by the electoral votes won in New York, Pennsylvania and Massachusetts. Taylor defeated Cass in a close race, winning the popular vote by 140,000. When the Electoral College met in December, Taylor garnered 163 votes to Cass' 127. Of the 30 states (15 in the North and 15 in the South), Taylor won eight Northern and seven Southern states. It was certainly not a landslide victory, but enough of a comfortable win to give Taylor a small mandate for action.

Peggy Taylor had pleaded with her husband not to run for president. She even prayed he would not be elected and if he was, she vowed she would not accompany him to Washington. After years of moving from place to place, Peggy was looking forward to a quiet and stable home life with her husband. She felt if he became president it would deprive him of a happy home and "shorten his life by unnecessary care and responsibility."[13]

Peggy disliked Washington, D.C., with its social elegance and snobbery. When rumors circulated in Washington that she was unsociable and smoked a corncob pipe, the first lady remarked, "I don't care what they think about that. I disapprove of them for lots of reasons."[14] In reality, Peggy Taylor did not smoke—tobacco smoke made her so nauseous that guests never smoked in her presence. Her husband, however, regularly chewed tobacco.

Zachary Taylor had a deep, abiding love for his wife. He had once written, "I am confident the feminine virtues never did concentrate in a higher degree in the bosom of any woman than in hers."[15] And he told Jefferson Davis, "My wife was a much better soldier than I was."[16] Taylor's goodbye or good evening to his wife always ended with the expression reminding her to always be prepared: "Keep your powder dry."

Nor was Peggy enthusiastic about living in what she called "that big white barn in Washington."[17] Vowing not to partake in public functions or entertain politicians and diplomats, Peggy was grateful when her daughter Betty, recently married to Colonel William Bliss on December 5, agreed to act as official hostess at the White House. Bliss was a noted linguist and had served as Taylor's adjutant general. He would prove a valuable asset to Taylor at the White House.

Mrs. Taylor did not make the lengthy voyage to Washington with her husband because of "the discomforts of travel at the season."[18] She planned to take a different route and stop in Baltimore to visit her sister. Later, she would join her husband in Washington, D.C.

Though Taylor won the election for president, he refused to meet with Whig leaders who wanted to offer him advice and make political demands. In December Colonel Bliss ordered two new suits made for the president-elect from a New Orleans tailor. When some Whig office seekers learned about this, they bribed the tailor to put their letters in the pockets of the suits. Taylor spent much of his time readying for his new destination, even taking care to transport Old Whitey to the White House.

After arriving in the nation's capital the horse was allowed to retire and put out to pasture, the pasture being the Executive Mansion. While he grazed on the White House lawn, visitors in Washington pulled out hairs from his tail to take home as souvenirs. By 1850 not a single hair remained in Old Whitey's tail.

During the last week of January, 1849, Taylor started on his month-long sojourn to the nation's capital. The president-elect's trip from Baton Rouge to Washington was both exciting and exhausting. Taylor traveled on eight different steamboats up the Mississippi and Ohio Rivers, making more than a dozen stops at cities such as Vicksburg, Nashville, Louisville, and Cincinnati. A chance encounter with Henry Clay on board a paddlewheel led to a reconciliation, at least for a while. The president-elect consumed so much food at the lavish dinners held for him that he developed indigestion several times. Everywhere the ladies lined up to kiss or embrace him. This was hard work—but a lot easier than dodging bullets and cannonballs on the battlefield.

During his first trip by steamer Taylor met a passenger aboard ship when the man, unaware of who he was, began a conversation about politics. He asked him if he was a "Taylor man." The president-elect replied, " Not much of a one—that is, I did not vote for him, partly because of family reasons and partly because his wife was opposed to sending 'Old Zach' to Washington, where she would be obliged to go with him."[19]

Near Memphis, the steamboat Taylor was on broke its rudder, putting him behind schedule. By the time the steamboat arrived in Cairo, Illinois, it was 3:00 a.m. and he was in bed. The local officials there had been waiting hours and were angry when Taylor did not appear. As the packet left the landing, the town leaders had a three-cannon salute fired "to make sure and waken him up."[20]

In Taylor's hometown of Louisville, Kentucky, the sidewalks, doorways, and roofs were lined with hundreds of spectators who wanted to get a glimpse of their hero. He attended a formal banquet there then traveled the next day on another steamer, the *Sea Gull*, to Frankfort. Toward evening Taylor tripped over some luggage in a poorly-lit passageway. He fell and bruised his ribs and back. In Frankfort he appeared at another dinner and met with an old friend—Governor Crittenden. Taylor asked the former senator to be his secretary of state, but Crittenden refused and suggested Senator John M.

Clayton instead. At a stop in Madison, Indiana, Taylor was struck by a trunk being loaded on board. The collision injured his side, which was already inflamed from the previous day.

In Cincinnati, Ohio, Taylor was welcomed at a great reception. Hundreds of women pressed forward for kisses. Taylor shook so many hands he developed blisters. He also experienced severe stomach cramps and caught a cold. Taylor needed rest, but that was almost impossible. Boarding the fast steamboat *Telegraph No. 2*, Taylor went up the Ohio River. The ship had to stop below Wheeling at Moundsville because of the ice floes. Taylor then rode a sleigh into Wheeling where ten thousand people greeted him.

The next day, February 21, the president-elect departed by sleigh and stagecoach for Cumberland, Maryland. From there he boarded a train to Baltimore where he was reunited with his brother Joseph, his wife Peggy, and his daughter Betty and her husband. That evening, he boarded another train and headed toward Washington, D.C. The entire route was marked by bonfires lit alongside the tracks. Upon arriving in Washington, the hero was whisked away just as the large excited crowd began to get unruly, but many in the throng followed Taylor to his hotel.

One of Taylor's most ardent supporters, Congressman Lincoln, had hopes that Taylor would exercise his authority as chief executive and make strong decisions. Lincoln told John Clayton that Taylor "must not appear a mere man of straw."[21]

The Family Crest of Zachary Taylor

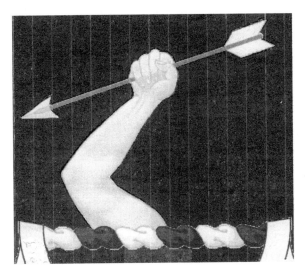

The Motto under the crest is, "He attains whatever he attempts."

Legendary woodsman, scout and Indian fighter Lewis Wetzel. Called "The Avenger" and "Gun-Always-Loaded," Wetzel hunted down Indians in the Ohio Valley after they killed some of his family. John Madison, Zachary Taylor's cousin and brother of the fourth president, hired Wetzel while surveying the Kanawka River region in western Virginia. Madison and Wetzel were attacked and Madison was killed.

One of Wetzels' personal "students" was teenager Zachary Taylor, who learned valuable skills of hunting, shooting and scouting. Wetzel briefly worked with Lewis and Clark on their historic trip, but left because the expedition was too slow and not exciting enough for him. Wetzel died in 1808 at the age of 44.

A sketch of Lewis Wetzel at age 26, based on a detailed description.

By artist Doug Martindale
(Author's Collection)

Taylor first gained national attention in his defense of Fort Harrison in Indiana during the War of 1812 on September 4, 1812.

Stark County (Ohio) Historical Society

Fort Crawford in the Wisconsin Territory where Taylor served over a span of several years. From a painting by Henry Lewis published in *Das Illustrite Mississippihal Leipzig* in 1854.

Stark County (Ohio) Historical Society

Chief Black Hawk of the Sac and Fox tribe. Black Hawk fought against the advancing white man and Taylor's armies from 1814 until his capture in 1832.

Library of Congress

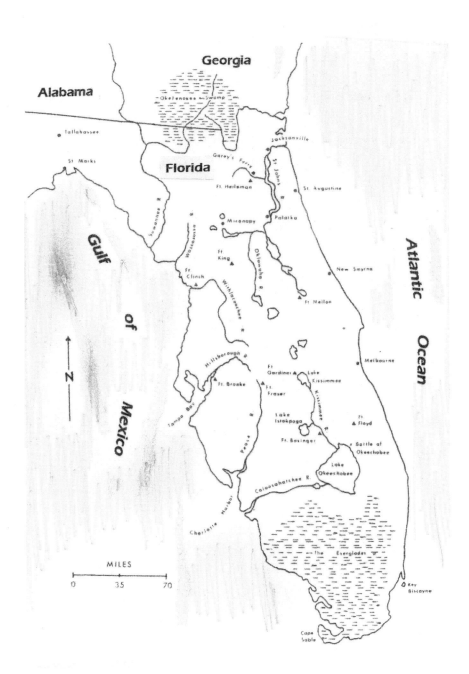

The Florida peninsula where Taylor commanded troops for nearly five years, during the Second Seminole War.

A close-up of Taylor at his Spanish Cottage home at Cypress Grove. Taylor retired to his plantation after the Mexican War then was sent to the White House as the twelfth president.

Library of Congress

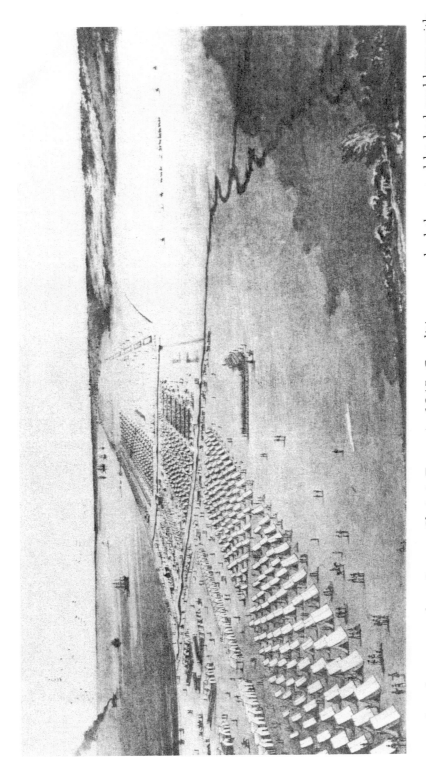

General Taylor reported to Corpus Christi, Texas, in 1845. Conditions were bad there and he had problems with his troops, particularly the short-term volunteers. This camp scene is from a lithograph by Captain D. P. Whiting in Taylor's army.

Library of Congress

A lithograph depicting another view of Cypress Grove Plantation where Taylor lived for a few years. Located near Baton Rouge, Louisiana, the home no longer stands.

Stark County (Ohio) Historical Society

The Mexican War
1846–1848

The fighting at Resaca de la Palma was savage. This is a drawing by
H. A. Ogden.

National Teachers' Union

Taylor atop Old Whitey on a hill overlooking Monterrey.

Library of Congress

The battle for Monterrey went from house to house. This is a sketch drawn by H. A. Ogden.

National Teachers' Union

The Mexican army could not stop the advancing Americans at Monterrey. Taylor forced the Mexicans into the city's main plaza where they surrendered on September 24, 1847.

Library of Congress

"General Taylor never Surrenders"

→ BUENA VISTA ←

GRAND TRIUMPHAL MARCH

Composed in Honor of

('MAJOR GENERAL TAYLOR'S')

VICTORY IN MEXICO

Many songs were written about Taylor after his victories in the Mexican War. This is a songsheet cover of music composed after the Battle of Buena Vista.

Stark County Historical Society

General Antonio López de Santa Anna; president of Mexico eleven times and overthrown each time. Beginning in 1836 at the Alamo and Golead in Texas, General Santa Anna fought against the Americans until he was defeated by Taylor at Buena Vista in 1847. Santa Anna returned to Mexico City in 1874 and died in poverty there two years later.

Library of Congress

This anti-Taylor lithograph was published by Peter Smith of New York. Taylor is depicted as a military figure who built his career on the death of others.

Stark County Historical Society

THE JUGGLER IN TROUBLE

General Taylor, in the role of a Chinese juggler, says: "I berry much 'fraid dat some of dese d------n knives tumble down an' cut my finger. I can't keep um up much longer." From *The John-Donkey*, a humorous magazine of 1848. This political cartoon was originally reproduced by The Ohio State University.

Stark County Historical Society

This is the best known photograph of President Taylor, taken by Mathew Brady in 1849.

Library of Congress

John C. Calhoun, the firebrand Senator from South Carolina. Calhoun urged the southern states to withdraw from the Union and opposed Taylor on a number of issues. A strong proponent of slavery, Calhoun died in 1850 shortly before Taylor's death.

National Archives

John Clayton, Taylor's Secretary of State. An outspoken and blunt man, Clayton negotiated the controversial Clayton-Bulwer Treaty with England in 1850.

Library of Congress

Colonel William Bliss with his father-in-law Zachary Taylor. Bliss served with Taylor in the Mexican War, then as a private secretary to President Taylor. This photograph is from a daguerreotype probably taken in 1849.

Library of Congress

Richard Taylor (1826–1879), only son of President Taylor. A Yale graduate, Richard served briefly in the Mexican War with his father, then as a secretary at the Taylor White House. Dick Taylor was a Confederate officer later in the Civil War, and was the last general to surrender to Union forces in 1865.

Library of Congress

Ann Mackall Taylor Wood (1811–1875), oldest daughter of the President. Ann was the wife of Dr. Robert C. Wood. This daguerreotype was discovered in the photograph collection of Ann's grandson, Trist Wood.

Library of Congress

Betty Taylor Bliss (1824–1909), served as official White House hostess because her mother was chronically ill.

National First Ladies Library

Margaret "Peggy" Taylor refused to sit and have her portrait painted, but she did pose for this Mathew Brady daguerreotype, only recently discovered. Peggy made very few public appearances while her husband was president, except for attending Sunday church services.

Stark County Historical Society

Jefferson and Varina Davis. A Senator from Mississippi, Davis had been Taylor's son-in-law, but after the death of Davis' wife, Knox Taylor Davis, the two men did not speak for years. Davis and Taylor established their friendship during the Mexican War when Davis was wounded while serving as a gallant officer. The Davises were frequent guests at the Taylor White House and Varina was perhaps the closest friend of Margaret Taylor, helping to organize White House social activities. Jefferson Davis later served as president of the Confederacy. This Brady photograph was taken during Taylor's administration.

National Archives

Mathew B. Brady opened a photography studio in New York City and Washington. At age 24 he began photographing the leading celebrities and politicians in the nation's capital, including President Taylor and his family.

Library of Congress

Frederick Douglass. After escaping slavery in Maryland disguised as a U.S. sailor, he settled in Massachusetts where he became a celebrated anti-slavery speaker. After a trip to England, where friends raised $700 to buy his freedom, he returned to America and in 1847 founded *The North Star*, an abolitionist newspaper. President Taylor, deeply concerned over the slave issue, felt northern abolitionists were too extreme and troublesome. Forty years after Taylor's death, the aging Douglass was appointed minister to Haiti by President Benjamin Harrison.

National Archives

A few women began wearing pantaloons—or bloomers—during Taylor's rise to office. The outfit was named for Amelia Bloomer (depicted here) who first popularized them. As an advocate of women's rights, Bloomer attracted much attention during her lectures. After 1860, women stopped wearing long pants in public until the 1930s.

Stark County Historical Society

This 1847 daguerreotype of Abraham Lincoln was taken during his single term as a Whig Congressman. Lincoln was an avid Taylor supporter and campaigned for his election.

National Archives

Dolley Madison at age 80. This Brady photograph was taken a year before her death. A friend to a dozen presidents, Dolley's eulogy was given by President Taylor.

Library of Congress

Stephen Foster — "The American Troubadour"

The nation's most prolific songwriter of the mid-nineteenth century was Stephen Collins Foster. One of his earliest tunes was an 1848 piano quick-step, accompanied with flute and violin, to honor Taylor's victory in the Mexican War. The piece was titled "Santa Anna's Retreat from Buena Vista" and enjoyed mild success.

This portrait of Foster was done by Thomas Hicks.

Library of Congress

Audiences loved the fiery dramatic style of actor Edwin Forrest, pictured here playing Spartacus. Forrest was the most popular American-born stage star. During a British tour in 1845 he exchanged insults with England's Shakespearean actor Charles Macready. Their rivalry resulted in a bloody riot four years later in New York City when common citizens, resenting Macready's aristocratic attitude, attacked the theater where he was performing.

National Archives

The Washington Monument, as it appeared after President Taylor's visit and his subsequent collapse on July 4, 1850.

Library of Congress

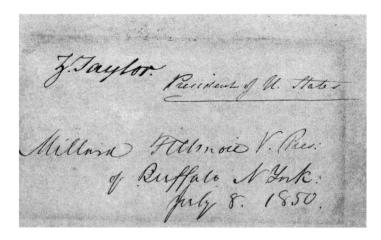

These two signatures, signed at different times, are from a page of an autograph book, now in the possession of Harold "Skip" Hensel of Metiarie, Louisiana. Note the date of Fillmore's signature, penned his last full day as vice president.

Harold Hensel

Vice President Millard Fillmore did not play a major role in the Taylor administration. Though he and Taylor disagreed on the Compromise of 1850, Fillmore remained a loyal ally of Taylor. After Taylor's death he replaced the entire cabinet with his own appointees. Denied renomination in 1852, Fillmore ran for president again in 1856 on the American, or Know-Nothing Party, a national organization opposed to Catholicism.

Bowman Publishing Corporation

The White House as it appeared during Taylor's administration.

Library of Congress

The twelfth president's tomb, located at the Zachary Taylor National Cemetery in Louisville, Kentucky.

Author's Collection

CHAPTER 10

Chief Executive

ACCORDING TO CUSTOM, PRESIDENT-ELECT TAYLOR SHOULD HAVE PAID A PERSONAL visit to President Polk, but Taylor refused, feeling Polk had not given him proper respect during the war. Polk was equally displeased with Taylor and ordered his cabinet to stay away from him. Senator Jefferson Davis, however, intervened and persuaded both men to set aside their differences for the good of the country. On March 1, 1849, Taylor had dinner with Polk at the White House, though Peggy remained at the Willard Hotel.

Since Inauguration Day fell on a Sunday, the swearing-in was postponed until the next day out of respect for the Sabbath. Thus, for 23 hours the country was without a legal chief executive. David R. Atchinson of Missouri, president pro-tem of the Senate, claimed he was the sitting president for one day, but this was not true since his term had expired on Saturday at noon. However, on Monday, Atchinson, who was voted to serve a second term as pro-tem, was sworn in and *for several minutes* prior to Fillmore's oath, served as head of the government.

Monday March 5, 1849, dawned cold and gray with falling snow. At 11:05 Taylor left the Willard Hotel with Mayor Seaton and ex-Speaker of the House Robert Winthrop. His carriage stopped at the Irving Hotel where President Polk came out, extended a handshake, then entered the carriage to sit with Taylor and his party. Cannons boomed in celebration as the entourage rode to the Capitol with the inaugural parade in tow.

The Senate gallery was reserved for wives of Congressmen to witness the swearing in of Vice President-elect Millard Fillmore. Other folks had waited since 9:00 that morning to get in and when the Senate doors opened, amidst the rush three women had fainted. Fillmore was sworn in and made a few brief remarks. He thus became the official head of the government since Taylor had yet to take his oath. Just after noon, Polk and Taylor appeared on the steps of the East Portico of the Capitol, greeted with great applause. A special stage had been erected over the steps where Taylor and Fillmore sat on a sofa placed at the front of the platform.

Nearly thirty thousand people waited for Taylor to be sworn in as president. First, Taylor gave a brief address—the shortest one since Washington's inaugural speech. Though he usually spoke with a slight stutter, on this day his talk was flawless. Pulling down the glasses, which rested atop his head, Taylor read his remarks in a clear, loud voice, though Polk noted in his diary that Taylor read his speech "in a very low voice and very badly as to his pronounciation [*sic*] and manner."[1]

Prior to his arrival in Washington, Taylor had surprised some officials by voicing his opinion that Oregon and California were too distant to become states and that they should be granted status as independent nations. Whig leaders advised him not to mention the two territories or anything about slavery. Taylor half-heartedly concurred.

The new president promised to rely upon his cabinet for advice and told the people, "In the discharge of these duties my guide will be the Constitution . . ."[2] Taylor had said he would not be the president of a party, but of the entire country. He also pledged to keep the country impartial on foreign matters and promote "peaceful and friendly relations with all other powers."[3] He set the tone clearly by stating further, "In all disputes between conflicting governments, it is our interest not less than our duty, to remain strictly neutral..."[4] But it was what Taylor *did not* say that pleased many Whig leaders. He said nothing about his feelings regarding California and Oregon being too distant to become states. Whig leaders feared that if Taylor made his feelings known it would upset those who believed the country was destined to expand its borders. Nor did Taylor state his views on slavery, though many in the crowd were anxious to hear them.

Following his speech, Zachary Taylor placed his hand on the *Bible* for his oath of office. The *Bible* used in the ceremony had been brought from New

York City, the same one used in George Washington's first inaugural. Chief Justice of the Supreme Court Roger B. Taney administered the oath and Taylor kissed the *Bible*. Cannons roared and the Marine Band played "Hail Columbia." Polk was the first to step forward and shake Taylor's hand, remarking, "I hope, sir, the country may be prosperous under your administration."[5]

The short inaugural parade consisted mostly of military bands, a few political clubs, college students, and clergymen. President Taylor was touched when a band of Chippewas, an Indian tribe he had once defeated, performed a dance. That evening President Zachary Taylor and Vice President Millard Fillmore attended three inaugural balls held in their honor. Traveling in separate carriages without their wives, at 9:00 p.m. Fillmore and Taylor first stopped at Carusi's, where a military ball was conducted.

Their second stop was at Jackson Hall where many attendees were Democrats who tried to forget their political defeat amid dance and champagne. As 11:00 neared, the two men drove off to the third ball. At this last one, held at Washington City Hall, a midnight buffet was served. The men and women were separated in different dining rooms. While Fillmore ate with the gentlemen, Taylor dined with the ladies. Good manners were abandoned by the cold and hungry guests as a near riot broke out in getting to the food. Men tore the meat off of turkey skeletons and women dug their jeweled hands into cakes; champagne drenched gowns and suits. An Englishman observed it was "as though these people had not eaten in days."[6] Many in the large crowd there had clothing ruined as the chandeliers rained perpetual showers of melted candle wax. Another visitor described the scene "about as chaotic as Tammany [Hall] with the women thrown into the confusion."[7]

Both men and women fainted and were carried out into the heavy snow to be revived. Such behavior, however, was not uncommon at inaugural balls. Pandemonium had also occurred at Andrew Jackson's inaugural ceremonies where damage to the White House was in the thousands of dollars.

After Taylor arrived, he personally greeted more than four thousand people. His hand was already blistered from too much handshaking, so he bowed and spoke to each guest. After the meal, the servants fled, anxious to get home in the snowstorm. Thousands of coats and hats were left in a huge pile in the middle of the lobby. Taylor left around 1:00 a.m., and the revelry continued for another three hours. One of the many guests who had their clothing stolen was Abraham Lincoln. He walked back to his boardinghouse in a blizzard without his hat.

The new president inherited an unsettled Congress. Neither the Whigs nor the Democrats held a clear majority. Added to the mix were ten Free Soilers who had also been elected to the House. Choosing a Speaker of the House proved difficult in 1849. Finally, after three weeks and 63 ballots, Howell Cobb of Georgia was selected. But the Northern and Southern Whigs, along with the Democrats and Free Soilers, could not pass much legislation.

Taylor settled into the White House and worked hard at his job. The new chief executive genuinely liked meeting the people—he even rose at 6:00 a.m. at times to interview the jobseekers who were lined up outside his office to procure positions. One visitor, George Francis Train, recorded his visit with Taylor: "On arriving there I was at once ushered into the presence of General Taylor, who sat at his desk. The presidential feet rested on another chair . . . He wore a shirt that was formerly white, but which then looked like the map of Mexico after the battle of Buena Vista. It was spotted and spattered with tobacco juice. Directly behind me, as I was soon made aware, was a cuspidor, toward which the President turned the flow of tobacco juice. I was in mortal terror, but I soon saw there was no danger. With an unerring aim as the famous spitter in Dickens's *American Notes*, he never missed the cuspidor once, or put my person in jeopardy."[8]

The Department of the Interior was created on March 3, 1849. The bill's passage, however, was delayed by Congress until May because Democrats were reluctant to create more patronage appointments for Taylor and the Whigs. Under Taylor's authority the newly created cabinet post took over scattered and duplicated duties which had been performed by other departments and agencies. Under the Interior Department's umbrella now were the Bureau of Indian Affairs, the General Land Office, the Census Bureau, Patent Office and Pension Office. Additionally the department assumed control over the Commissioner of Public Buildings, the Board of Inspectors, the warden of the penitentiary in Washington and receiving accounts and records of federal marshals and officers of U.S. Courts.

Taylor's cabinet selections represented various sections of the country. After giving the matter a great deal of thought, he declared his choices to be "harmonious, honorable, patriotic, talented, hard-working and of irreproachable private character."[9] Within a year, however, Taylor would question his assessment of those he appointed.

The president's secretary of state was John Clayton of Delaware. Though Clayton graduated first in his class at Yale, his brilliance was offset by his lack of experience. He also lacked tact when dealing with foreign diplomats, but he was an honest and loyal man. William Meredith of Pennsylvania, who favored high tariffs, was Taylor's secretary of the treasury. George Crawford of Georgia was selected as secretary of war. As a chief spokesman for the South, he resigned his post after Taylor's death (as did the other cabinet members). Reverdy Johnson of Maryland, a lawyer who favored states' rights, was named attorney-general. Johnson was an expert on constitutional law and worked endlessly in the Taylor administration until he was replaced by President Fillmore in 1850. William Preston of Virginia, who opposed slavery, became secretary of the Navy. Originally chosen to be attorney-general, he was moved to naval secretary due to his lack of legal experience. Jacob Collamer of Vermont was chosen as postmaster general, and he initiated reforms in the Postal Department. The newly established Interior Department was headed by Ohio's Thomas Ewing, who came into the cabinet with experience and a reputation for integrity.

One decision made by Taylor early on in his administration concerned the presence of newly elected Senator William H. Seward at cabinet meetings. An anti-slavery Whig and former governor of New York, Seward served as an advisor to Taylor, which tended to draw criticism from both the newspapers and the Southerners in the cabinet.

Taylor put much of the responsibility of patronage—the practice of awarding government jobs to loyal campaign workers—on his cabinet and his close advisors. To appoint a Whig to a position meant firing a Democrat, and the Taylor administration was not shy in using the "spoils system" to hand out jobs. Taylor had explained to Meredith, "There are plenty of Whigs, just as capable and honest, and quite deserving of office, as the Democrats who have held them through two or three presidential terms."[10] In the Postal Department alone there were 3,406 removals during Taylor's first year in office. In addition, hundreds of other clerks and employees were replaced. Taylor did not interfere when his subordinates removed Democratic office-holders. One of the Democrats displaced was Nathaniel Hawthorne who worked in the Salem Customs House. Out of work, Hawthorne began working on a novel he titled *The Scarlet Letter*.

Taylor brought other changes to the administration. The White House's previous occupants, the Polks, had not allowed dancing or drinking at any White House functions. This drab atmosphere changed when Taylor became president. His daughter Betty Bliss, who served as the official White House hostess, was immensely popular. She appealed to the social crowd of

Washington and at age 22, the dark-haired, dark-eyed beauty entertained in place of her mother. Festivities at the mansion took on a less solemn tone and alcoholic beverages were served on occasion at formal dinners.

After attending finishing school in Philadelphia, Betty had married Colonel William Wallace Bliss, whom Taylor nicknamed "Perfect Bliss." Betty's mother shied away from large receptions, even refusing to sit for an oil portrait, sending daughter Betty as a stand-in. Peggy preferred to visit with relatives and family friends who were invited to her upstairs parlor at the White House. The first lady also attended Sunday morning services at St. John's Episcopal Church, where only a few people recognized her as she arrived quietly and left without fanfare.

Taylor was saddened when he learned of the death of 81-year-old Dolley Madison. One of the nation's most beloved citizens, she died on July 12, 1849, at her home. Dolley Madison had known every president from George Washington to Zachary Taylor, serving as a hostess in the Executive Mansion under Jefferson and her husband. Her receptions were spectacular non-partisan social events where all public officials enjoyed her kindness and elegance. Dolley often said she hated politics but loved people.

After James Madison's death in 1836 she had moved back to Washington where she continued to welcome guests. Her son from her first marriage, John Todd, twice squandered her estate and she lived in poverty. During her last few years Dolley was so destitute she had to rely upon the generosity of others, including Daniel Webster, just to eat. It was her informality and down-to-earth approach which endeared her to others. After President Polk was sworn in as president in 1845 he made a stop at Dolley's house on LaFayette Square. When he arrived there he found the 77-year-old matron running barefoot outside, racing with two teen-aged daughters of a friend.

Her funeral at St. John's Church was attended by hundreds in Washington, including most members of Congress, the Diplomatic Corps and Taylor's cabinet. Thousands more waited outside to get a glimpse of the coffin. President Taylor delivered the eulogy, remarking, "What an extraordinary great lady she was! America will never know another like her…She will never be forgotten because she was truly our First Lady for a half century."[11]

During the time he was in office, Taylor took only four trips away from Washington. Taylor, along with his family and Vice President Fillmore, left Washington beginning on the second week of August in 1849, touring Pennsylvania and New York. His vacation was well timed, for a cholera epidemic surfaced in Washington and spread with deadly results in Cincinnati, Philadelphia, St. Louis and Milwaukee.

Epidemics were commonplace every decade or two and thousands of Americans perished. The outbreak in 1849 was so bad that in early July Taylor proclaimed a national day of fasting and prayer against the epidemic. Being removed from Washington, Taylor avoided the deadly clutches of the disease, but he was not totally immune from its effects.

Taylor visited several Pennsylvania cities including Philadelphia and Harrisburg. During the excursion the president toured some of the iron and coal mines of western Pennsylvania. While Taylor was vacationing in the mountains there, he had dinner at a tavern. A man shook the president's hand and announced he had not voted for him. "You said you would be president of all the people and not a party, but you've turned out the Democrats and nobody else," the man complained. Taylor replied, "Who else could I turn out? All the office-holders were of your party, and they held the offices for nearly twenty years."[12] Almost without exception, the First Family was well received everywhere and large crowds turned out to greet them.

On August 13 Taylor suffered from vomiting and diarrhea in Carlisle. He believed he got sick from drinking the brackish water there. The party left for Pittsburgh, arriving there on the 18th. He gave a speech to a large crowd, promising to protect their coal and iron industry by supporting tariffs. He then headed north to Waterford and Erie and met with a delegation of Whigs from nearby Warren, Ohio. While in Erie Taylor became ill again, developing the "shakes" and spent two days in bed. Dr. Wood, his son-in-law, expressed deep concern but Taylor recovered quickly. The next morning, on the 28th, he and his entourage boarded a side-wheeler, the *Bay State*, and headed for Oswego, New York, and Niagara Falls.

On September 3, the president took a carriage ride across the new suspension bridge to visit Canada. This was the first time an incumbent president had ever set foot on foreign soil. After his sightseeing at the falls, Taylor stopped in Albany on September 6. By then he was so weak he could hardly walk to his carriage. Gathering up his strength, Taylor spoke before a large crowd but his voice was so weak he could hardly be heard. He then headed off to New York City, then returned to the White House where he finally got some much need rest.

This lengthy tour yielded two major results. The trip demonstrated the president's susceptibility to illness, as he was nearly exhausted upon its completion. Another problem was when news of his visits reached the southern newspapers, many supporters in the South felt uneasy.

On October 10 the President felt much better and resumed his travels, going to Baltimore to see his brother Joseph. He also made three appearances at the state fair, attending a cattle show held there. Once again, a huge gathering met him, and women crowded forward for kisses. When a young, handsome Maryland military officer volunteered to take Taylor's place in kissing the ladies, he was told, "You forget, Sir, that duty belongs alone to the Commander-in-Chief!"[13] A tired president returned to Washington on the evening of the 12th.

Taylor's pale and haggard looks, his constant indigestion, fever, lack of energy, and a history of near-fatal maladies had slowly but steadily weakened him over the years. A few of those close to him were deeply concerned, but both Taylor and most of his family dismissed his condition as normal exhaustion from meeting so many people and eating so much food at countless banquets. Yet the president's health was not good. In the spring of 1850 Thurlow Weed noticed a change in Taylor's demeanor and was so alarmed he made a special trip to Baltimore to alert former army surgeon Dr. Robert C. Wood.

Certainly the political pressures took their toll. By December of 1849, the numbers in the House were thus: there were 112 Democrats, 105 Whigs and 12 Free Soilers. The one burning issue which refused to go away was slavery, as well as a renewed controversy, the Wilmot Proviso. In December of 1849 Taylor informed Senator Robert Toombs of Georgia that he would *not* veto the Wilmot Proviso if Congress saw fit to pass it. Toombs, a "Cotton" Whig, wanted the bill killed as did most other pro-slavery members in Congress.

The Wilmot Proviso (previously mentioned in Chapter 8) first surfaced on Saturday, August 8, 1846 when President Polk submitted an appropriations bill to Congress, requesting $2 million to facilitate expenses for negotiations with Mexico over the settlement of the war. With Congress scheduled to adjourn the following Monday, most Democrats arranged for the bill to be immediately passed during a night session. Polk was confident that fellow legislators, eager to get back home, would pass the appropriation without opposition or debate. However, David Wilmot, a Pennsylvania Democrat who had supported Polk in 1844, introduced his bill attached to the monetary measure. To hasten its adoption, debate was severely limited. The House passed the bill in a close vote, 85 to 80. The Senate, however, rejected the Wilmot Proviso but accepted the appropriation part of the bill.

Wilmot and his anti-slavery friends weren't done. In 1847 he attached his amendment to a $3 million appropriation bill which requested additional negotiation money to acquire more land and pay Santa Anna an agreed-upon stipend. Once again it passed the House but failed in the Senate. In 1848, Wilmot tried again to affix it to another piece of legislation, this time the Treaty of Guadalupe-Hidalgo. And once again, his bill to limit slavery failed in the Senate. Taylor's old friend Senator Sam Houston of Texas, though opposed to seeing slavery expand into the new Oregon Territory, had joined Calhoun in defeating the measure while clashing with congressional abolitionists.

Toombs and other "Cotton" Whigs were extremely disturbed. Speaking for many of his Southern colleagues, Toombs told a group of Senators in session, "We have the right to call on you to give your blood to maintain the slaves of the South in bondage. Deceive not yourselves, you cannot deceive others. This is a pro-slavery government; slavery is stamped on its heart!"[14]

With Taylor's assurance he would sign the Wilmot Proviso into law, he also promised not to actively seek its adoption. And while the bill was an unsuccessful congressional amendment, the Wilmot Proviso proved to be a battle cry for opponents of slavery. Many discontented Whig and Democratic Congressmen in the North, along with the Free Soilers, contrived to form the new Republican Party in 1854.

Even though Taylor could not resolve the growing crisis over slavery, he was able to achieve a victory of sorts for his former son-in-law. When Senator Jefferson Davis and Congressman William Bissell exchanged insults, accusing each other of cowardice during the Mexican War, the men agreed to settle the issue by a duel. Taylor intervened and prevented bloodshed when he announced that both men had performed heroically.

In February of 1850 Taylor made a short sojourn to Richmond, Virginia, where he attended the laying of the cornerstone for a Washington Monument there. He also made a speech to the Virginia legislature, proclaiming his devotion to the Union. The president's last stop was in Fredericksburg, Maryland, where he feasted at another dinner and warned southern firebrands about disunion and secession. Some southerners, opposed to the tariffs and anti-slavery measures advocated by northerners and the federal government, felt their only recourse was to break away from the Union and exist as independent states. Taylor was a strong supporter of the Union and warned the southern states against trying to break away from the country.

More disturbing news reached President Taylor when he learned of attempts by American citizens to seize more land. Private armies of American mercenaries had been organized in two different parts of the nation to forcibly take parts of Canada, which belonged to Great Britain, and Cuba, which belonged to Spain. Weapons, provisions, and recruits had been gathered to supply insurgents. Taylor quickly sent word that any action taken against Canada or Cuba was an act of treason. He announced that the perpetrators would be arrested and imprisoned. As a result, both armies disbanded. Taylor did not share the view of those who believed the country was destined to expand its borders, particularly if it meant grabbing land from weaker or foreign nations under the guise of spreading slavery.

Relations with Spain had never been healthy, going back to the early 1800s. In trying to hold on to her shrinking empire, the Spanish-held colonies in the Americas were ruled with harshness on native populations. Expansionists in Congress, especially those dedicated to the concept of Manifest Destiny, saw Spain as a cruel taskmaster exacting blood from its subjects. Fomenting a rebellion against Madrid would, in their opinion, be advantageous to the U.S.

American nationalists favoring Cuban independence procured money and arms and established a base in New Orleans. General Narciso Lopez, in seeking to circumvent the 1818 neutrality law which Taylor had invoked, led the crusade. Lopez, a misplaced Venezuelan adventurer, was a man of wealth who had strong connections to rich planters who were also interested in seeing slavery and cotton growing expanded into Cuba. Most of Lopez's 400 men were American mercenaries, including many Mexican War veterans, ready to take over the Spanish government in Havana.

Lopez once lived in Cuba but had lost his large estate there. He met personally with several American officials to aid his cause. Wanting to free Cuba of Spanish rule and retake his property, Lopez approached both Robert E. Lee and Jefferson Davis to lead his expedition. He offered each man $100,000, plus an extra $100,000 once the invasion force succeeded. This was a tremendous sum of money but both men declined the offer. The Spanish ambassador in Washington, however, learned of Lopez's plans and protested to Taylor. President Taylor could not allow such a scheme to occur and ordered the navy to take action.

Procuring a steamer and two sailing ships, Lopez and his well-stocked force left New Orleans and landed at Cordevas, about 80 miles east of Havana. Despite the fact that his two sailing vessels had been captured by the U.S. Navy, Lopez established a beachhead with his invasion force. He was soon attacked by Spanish soldiers. In heavy fighting, the rear guard of Kentuckians killed 30 Spaniards and held their position. But the victory was short-lived. More Spanish troops arrived and overtook Lopez, whose losses totaled more than 70 in killed and wounded, in addition to some prisoners taken by the Spaniards. The expedition thus failed and Lopez and his remaining men barely made it back to their steamer *The Creole*, which had been grounded offshore. Lopez ordered all weapons and ammunition thrown overboard so the loaded vessel could escape. The Spanish *Pizarro* pursued the Americans. Reaching Key West safely, the beaten and battered army found themselves as part of a diplomatic upheaval.

Southern newspapers, particularly Democratic ones, charged Taylor with inciting Spanish tyranny. Great Britain also voiced its disapproval. The captured American prisoners in Cuba were put in chains and taken to Contoy, while Taylor pressed for the prosecution of those who made it back. In the end, Taylor and Secretary of State John Clayton gained a victory of sorts. A Louisiana court acquitted the returning nationalists, and a Spanish court found the 49 prisoners not guilty and within a year were released. Lopez, incidentally, attempted another assault, was captured by Spanish authorities and publicly strangled in Havana on August 24, 1850.

On other foreign policy issues Taylor ignored pleas from revolutionaries in Hungary who were struggling against the Austrians. Though he could not provide any kind of aid, his sympathies were clearly with the Hungarians. There were also existing claims against the Portuguese, which had interfered with American commerce, but these problems remained unsolved because of Taylor's death.

On March 11, William Seward gave a speech in the Senate. In his address he voiced he was appealing to a "higher" power than the Constitution when he gave his anti-slavery views. Seward's remarks came as a surprise to Taylor. Since Seward was a trusted advisor, his speech met with disapproval from Taylor, who was by no means an abolitionist. Their relationship became a bit strained. But that was politics and Taylor's forgiving nature did not let Seward's address stand in the way of their friendship.

To avoid spending money on extra hired help, President Taylor brought fifteen of his slaves to work at the White House. They slept in the eight rooms located in the attic. One of them had been Taylor's personal servant and had accompanied him to Mexico during the war. Most of the slaves at the White House remained out of the public eye, for the country was sensitive to the issue of slavery at the time. The president cut costs in other ways as well. He employed his son-in-law Colonel Bliss as his personal financial manager. Bliss oversaw expenditures, managed White House functions, and worked with the cooks, caterers, and servants. Richard Taylor, the president's son, served as his personal secretary. It was also during this time that Taylor purchased another Louisiana plantation for $115,000 (the price included the cost of 90 extra slaves). His business had been doing very well and he felt he could expand. Taylor called his new property in St. Charles Parish Fashion Plantation and he raised mostly sugar cane. His son Richard, though living at the White House throughout most of the year, remained as manager of the cotton plantation in Jefferson County, Mississippi.

Zachary Taylor's main family concern, however, was the well-being of Peggy. He once told Jefferson Davis, "You know, my wife is as much a soldier as I was."[15] During their marriage the couple lived in no fewer than two dozen locations. By the time she was first lady, Peggy Taylor was exhausted and her frail health provided an excuse for fewer dinner parties. On rare occasions when she appeared at afternoon events, no food or liquor was served.

Peggy Taylor was not a total recluse. She attended church regularly, sometimes several times each week. She disliked protocol and shunned most formal activities at the White House. Her daughter Betty, Rebecca Taylor (the President's niece) and others, including Varina Davis, served as hostess. On one occasion she welcomed her Sunday school group to the mansion and accepted a lifetime membership in the American Sunday School Union. Her passion for gardening, however, was left to the discretion of the servants at the Executive Mansion.

As previously mentioned, contrary to rumors, Peggy Taylor did not spend most of her time shut up in a White House room smoking a pipe. In 1848 several Democrat newspaper cartoons had depicted her as such and circulated derogatory comments during her time in Washington. Hearing this gossip only reinforced her belief that Washington was no place for her.

Peggy's grandson John Bliss described her as "a strict disciplinarian… intolerant of the slightest breach of good manners."[16] He went on to say she was also a kind, thoroughbred Southern lady. One young woman from

Natchez visited Peggy at the White House and characterized her as gentle and refined. Varina Davis may have provided a more in-depth view when she wrote, "Mrs. Taylor's bright and pretty room where the invalid, full of interest in the passing show in which she had not the strength to take her part, talked most agreeably and kindly to many friends who were admitted to her presence."[17]

The Taylor grandchildren frequented the White House, some of them staying for extended visits. Four of Taylor's grandchildren lived in Baltimore. The two oldest boys, John and Bob Wood, were in military school, John at Annapolis and Bob at West Point. The two younger girls, Blandina (or Nina) and Sarah (known as Dumple) brought great joy and kept company with grandpa and grandma, as did their teenage niece Rebecca Taylor. Another frequent guest was her close friend Fanny Calderon de la Bera, wife of the Spanish ambassador.

The Taylors did purchase some new furniture for the Executive Mansion, along with some inexpensive items such as washstands, candlesticks, pitchers, towels, and tables. The President also had Commissioner Ignatius Mudd enlarge the gas system inside the White House to improve the lighting. This saved money, minimized the need for candles, and reduced the risk of fire. Gas pipes were installed and overhead burners were placed in the basement as a safety precaution.

There weren't many pets at the Taylor White House. Besides his horse Old Whitey, the president and first lady owned a pet canary named Johnny Ty. The bird died just a few months after the Taylors moved in. They had tried to pair Johnny Ty with a mate, only to discover that the other bird was also a male!

There was a more pressing need, however, in matters of the household. Upset by the high rates the gas company was charging, Taylor sent Commissioner Mudd to argue with the organization's owners. It was soon discovered why the White House gas bill was so high. Some of the hotel owners along Pennsylvania Avenue had secretly tapped into the gas lines, splicing pipes of their own in order to enjoy free gaslight. Mudd had the hotel pipes capped. To encourage competitive prices for consumers, he also convinced Congress to charter more gas companies.

As president, Taylor was very accessible to the people. He would meet with anyone, and when the Marine Band performed outdoors, he mingled freely with the guests, wearing his black silk hat tilted back on his head. Visitors, no matter what their politics, were welcomed. Taylor's friend James Buchanan, a former secretary of state, once brought a group of young ladies to meet the president at the White House. Taylor was impressed with Buchanan's selections and remarked, "You always pick out the prettiest ladies." Buchanan responded, "Why, Mr. President, I know your taste and mine agree in that respect." Taylor made the ladies blush when he loudly proclaimed, "Yes, but I have been so long among Indians and Mexicans I hardly know how to behave myself, surrounded by so many beautiful women!"[18]

Taylor never tired of meeting the people and showing up at social functions. During the Christmas season of 1849 he opened the White House to meet the public. Folks of all stations mixed freely, but in the large crowd pickpockets did their business. In May of 1850 he attended the wedding of Secretary of the Interior Thomas Ewing's daughter Ellen. She was marrying a young Mexican War veteran, William Tecumseh Sherman.

Zachary Taylor's popularity with the people and public officials couldn't isolate him from controversy. He faced numerous challenges as president and one embarrassing incident turned into a full-blown scandal, and it was not without complications.

The George Galphin family of Georgia, partly made up of Creek and Cherokee tribe members, had a longstanding claim against the United States dating back to the time when Georgia was an English colony. The British government, upon receiving lands in South Carolina and Georgia ceded by the two tribes, agreed to pay the Galphin claim for its sale. The amount totaled $43,500 and in 1775 some Creek and Cherokee Indians agreed to receive $50,000 from the government in exchange for their land. A small partial payment was apparently made but when the Revolutionary War erupted the rest of the installment was discontinued. After the war George Galphin became an Indian commissioner and the U.S. Congress officially thanked him for securing his land and keeping it out of British and Indian hands.

The Galphins claimed that the deal was illegal and mismanaged, and that their Indian ancestors had never received any of the payment. As the years passed, the Galphins demanded the full amount, in addition to the interest that had accumulated over the past decades. Georgia officials ignored the demand for repayment, even though the family had been told it would receive the money. The Galphin heirs kept submitting their formal complaint and in 1848, Congress authorized payment of a remaining principal of $9,700 to the Galphin family. President Polk's Secretary of the Treasury, Robert J. Walker, paid the amount, but he refused to pay the $191,353 in interest that had accumulated over the 75-year period.

The Galphins, through their lawyers, continued demanding total compensation. During Taylor's term, Attorney General Johnson ordered Treasury Secretary Meredith to disburse the funds. Both officials had been advised to do so by the Secretary of War George Crawford, himself a Georgian. They also agreed the claim should be paid with full interest. It was not disclosed, however, that Johnson had been the Galphin family attorney and that Crawford was the legal representative of the Galphin estate (he had been the family lawyer since the mid-1830s). And in place of receiving half of the original claim of $43,750 for his fee, Crawford felt he was entitled to half of the $191,353. Instead of getting nearly $22,000 in legal fees, Crawford got more than $90,000. Johnson and Meredith paid the claim with government funds but they later denied any knowledge that Crawford was involved in the matter.

When the money was paid Johnson and Meredith were rumored to have received some compensation for their efforts, but there was never any proof they personally profited from the transaction. Congress and the newspapers learned of Crawford's actions and the apparent conflict of interest. After an investigation, the House of Representatives condemned the actions of all three cabinet members, charging Crawford with plundering the Treasury. The Democrats, who controlled both the House and Senate, threatened to impeach Taylor but he denied any knowledge of Crawford's role. Seward felt that Crawford should resign, and so should anyone else who was involved.

Taylor was distraught over the affair. In comments made to advisor Thurlow Weed, Taylor said, "I'd like to throw out the lot of them. I have nothing but complaints about this department or that secretary. Now this! Would it not be the best course to dismiss the whole damn bunch?"[19] On July 3, Taylor met with Weed and told him he would announce replacing Crawford, Johnson and Meredith. Before the controversy could be resolved, however, Taylor died. Fillmore asked Taylor's cabinet members to resign and the Compromise of 1850 took precedence over all other political matters.

Another issue, having to do with transportation, was raised during Taylor's administration. At the time, land travel from America's eastern seaboard to the West Coast was long, dangerous, and difficult. So was the passage by sea, as ships had to sail around the tip of South America. Many travelers chose an alternate route—taking a ship to Central America then traveling by mule through the tropical forest to the Pacific Coast. This was also dangerous, due to disease and other perils. Businessmen had long dreamed of a water route across Central America to remedy this problem.

When the United States acquired territory on the Pacific Coast during President Polk's term, the dream of a water route across Central America had been revived. Wealthy investors, a few members of Congress and shipping magnates like Cornelius Vanderbilt proposed the building of a canal to link the Atlantic and Pacific Oceans. Great Britain agreed there was a need for a waterway shortcut. From their colonies in Latin America, the British made plans to finance the construction of a canal, with some of the money coming from men like Vanderbilt.

Yet there was a problem. In the United States, the Monroe Doctrine of 1823 had forbidden further colonization in the Americas by foreign powers. England, and later France, hoped to build a canal and retain complete control of it. Americans saw this as a violation of the Monroe Doctrine. Great Britain, however, did not view its plans as an attempt to establish a permanent settlement. President Taylor took offense at the British plan and remarked, "No European nation shall operate such a waterway in the western hemisphere . . . A canal of this nature should be independently operated for the benefit of all nations."[20] However, the United States lacked the funds to sponsor such an ambitious project itself. It could only take part in the building of a canal if the costs were shared with someone else. While the British proceeded with their plans, Secretary of State John Clayton met with Sir Henry Bulwer, the British Minister in Washington, to reach a settlement.

The result was the Clayton-Bulwer Treaty of 1850, whereby both England and America agreed to share equally in the construction, maintenance, and control of a canal to be built across Nicaragua (the decision to build it across the isthmus of Panama would be made later). Democrats in Congress, many of whom still promoted the expansionist idea of Manifest Destiny, felt betrayed. They denounced the treaty because they felt the United States was denied dominant influence in the region. On the other hand, the treaty guaranteed both nations as partners in a joint effort. No single nation would control the canal—it would be jointly shared. Though Great Britain eventually abandoned the canal project, diplomatic relations between Britain and the United States improved as a result of their collaboration. In one of his last official acts, President Taylor signed the Clayton-Bulwer Treaty on July 5, 1850.

Three other problems, minor ones compared to dealing with the English over foreign policy, were resolved. A petty dispute with the French foreign minister over a shipping matter off the coast near Veracruz, Mexico, was settled through diplomatic channels. In another matter, when Taylor learned that Comanches had raided ranches and killed settlers in Texas, he dispatched the U.S. Cavalry there to subdue them. Then, turning his attention towards the Plains Indians, in late June of 1850 Taylor asked for the resignation of Orlando Brown who was the commissioner of Indian affairs. Taylor felt Brown had been both incompetent and unfair to numerous tribes.

During Taylor's sixteen months in office (486 days to be exact), the nation teetered on the brink of civil war. Slavery and states' rights dominated business on the floor of Congress as members from the North and South engaged in stormy debate over whether slavery would be allowed in the new territories gained from Mexico. Even Virginia, the state of Taylor's birth, gave the president headaches. The state legislature passed a resolution declaring it would oppose any federal interference with Southern institutions, and would take action if necessary. Vermont, on the other hand, debated a law which it soon passed, declaring that fugitive slaves who escaped to that state would not be turned over to federal authorities. Needless to say, the South was outraged by such blatant disregard for the law.

Tearing at the heart of the Taylor administration were Henry Clay's proposals before Congress, which later became known as the Compromise of 1850. The crucial issue was whether the federal government had the power to prohibit slavery in the western territories. To avoid a civil war and try to please both the North and South over the slavery issue, the seventy-three-year-old Clay introduced a series of bills in the Senate. No one was more aware of the explosive issues of slavery and disunion more than Taylor.

Three years before he had expressed his concerns to Davis about the possibility of an armed conflict between the North and South. And if that happened, according to Taylor, "The Union in that case will be blown to atoms, or will be no longer worth preserving. But I pray to God this state of things will not occur in my day or in yours, or that of my children…"[21]

Henry Clay was a patriotic American and a master politician. Three decades before he had introduced the Missouri Compromise of 1820, which kept the number of slave and free states equal, thus avoiding a clash between the North and South. By 1850 California desired statehood, but having California enter the Union as a free state would upset the sectional balance of power in the Senate. Clay used all his charm, patience, and eloquence to guide his proposals through the Senate. He put forward the following provisions: 1) admit California as a free state; 2) organize New Mexico and Utah into territories and let the people there decide on the issue of slavery; 3) pay Texas for giving up her claims on lands in New Mexico; 4) end the slave trade, but not slavery, in Washington, D.C.; 5) enforce a strict fugitive slave law to help slave owners retrieve their escaped slaves.

Debate over Clay's bills dragged on for nearly a year. Senators Robert Toombs of Georgia and John C. Calhoun of South Carolina talked of secession if the measures were passed. The Southern states would depart peacefully, they announced. In a speech, Senator Daniel Webster responded, "Peaceful secession is an utter impossibility. I see that disruption must produce such a war as I will not describe...."[22] Webster initially opposed Clay's compromises, but later surprised his fellow legislators when he announced support for the bills. Webster reasoned that compromise was better than seeing the country split in two.

President Taylor announced that he favored the admission of California as a free state. He also urged settlers in New Mexico to apply for statehood, bypassing the territorial stage. Taylor and everyone else realized that if 100,000 new treasure-hunting adventurers drafted a state constitution, slavery would never be approved.

Taylor disagreed with other parts of Clay's proposals, and this angered Southerners. Many Texans wanted to expand the borders of their state, and they demanded land from New Mexico Territory. Taylor was determined to see this boundary question with Texas settled by legal procedure. In 1849 he sent a vanguard of military officers to New Mexico to protect its borders. But Texas was insistent on taking the land, so Taylor decided to send federal forces to New Mexico to help defend it. Secretary of War Crawford, however, refused to sign the order for more troops, so Taylor told him, "Then I will sign the order myself."[23]

The New Mexico dispute was a sticking point, and alienated Taylor with some members of Congress. Senators Stephens and Toombs, though on good terms with Taylor, warned that if he sent troops into New Mexico, the South would stand by Texas. And if there was an armed conflict with federal authorities there, not only would the Dixie states defend slave-holding Texas, but articles of impeachment against Taylor would be initiated. The president called the opposition's bluff and made his decision, but the Senate responded by discussing impeachment.

Whig leaders thought they could control Taylor, but he resented any attempts to be manipulated. One day in February of 1850, a small group of congressmen, including some Southern Whigs, entered the White House. They threatened to leave the Union if the Compromise of 1850 was adopted and signed into law. The president shook his fist at them and said he would hang anyone who preached secession. Willing to keep the nation together with military force, if necessary, Taylor said, "I will take command of the Army myself!"[24] Taylor then chased them out of his office, shaking his fist at them as they scampered down the stairs. Hannibal Hamlin, a senator from Maine and a future vice president under Lincoln, was going up the stairs as the Congressmen were running down. Hamlin went in to see Taylor, who was pacing the floor "like a caged lion." The President asked Hamlin, "Did you see those damned traitors?"[25]

Would President Taylor have used armed force to keep the Union in tact? On a number of occasions he indicated so, but perhaps he was just "blowing smoke." A more realistic approach to respond to the crisis was a plan he revealed to Congressman Horace Mann. Dining with Mann at the White House, Taylor explained he would blockade Southern ports, thus crushing attempts without violence. Such a move, however, may have made matters worse.

Sometimes when Taylor got too frustrated with his job, he would go for a stroll or take a carriage ride through the streets of Washington where Pennsylvania Avenue was paved with rough cobblestones and lit by oil lamps while Congress was in session. He was occasionally seen walking with Old Whitey around the White House grounds.

There were other concerns as well and Taylor relished taking care of business which did not involve politics. One such incident took place in February when the President responded to a request from two young girls from Portsmouth, New Hampshire. Two sisters, Susan and May Hayes, had asked for a Valentine's Day card. Taylor sent two separate poems, along with an introductory note which read,

>"And all the Congress men shall come
>   To see my little lady
> And they shall say how do you do
>   Sweet Miss Rough and Ready."

The card was signed "Old Zack."[26]

One person President Taylor did not have to contend with was John C. Calhoun. He had been deathly ill from tuberculosis and on April 2, Taylor and his cabinet attended Calhoun's funeral service. Henry Clay gave the eulogy, stressing his affection for Calhoun. Certainly Taylor realized, however, there were others waiting to carry the banner of states' rights disunion advocated by Calhoun.

The result of Clay's Compromise of 1850 went unresolved during Taylor's term. The president had indicated he would veto the bill, and he grew angry at members of Congress who even discussed the subject at White House functions. Vice President Fillmore went to the White House and met with Taylor, informing him that he hoped the bill would not end in a tie vote, for if it did he (Fillmore) would have to vote in favor of it. This decision created distance between the two men, though they remained on friendly terms. But for other officials who disagreed with Taylor on this issue, the story was different. Fewer and fewer invitations were given out to dinners and socials by Taylor during his last couple months in office as the climate inside the mansion took on an atmosphere of dissension and gloom.

Despite the climate of anxiety the Taylors still tried to maintain a cordial White House with Betty Bliss and Varina Davis hosting a few socials. The president was not one to project gloom. Marine Band conductor Francis Scala observed, "Gen. Taylor was an old fashioned soldier who put on no airs whatever. In fact, he was rather gruff than otherwise...He was fond of older martial music."[27]

There was a controversy brewing, however, of which Taylor may not have been fully aware. Perhaps more than any other national leader, he was certainly cognizant of the increasing emotions on the subject of slavery. While living in the nation's capital of 36,000, Taylor was well aware of the thousands of blacks in the city. There were 8000 slaves and 2000 free Negroes among Washington's population. The fifteen "house slaves" he brought to the White House from his Louisiana plantation generated some criticism. Taylor tried to keep them "invisible," assigning them work upstairs in the private family quarters. Most of them slept in the eight attic rooms.

Assigning Negro slaves to do chores in the White House was not uncommon. Several presidents, including Washington, Jefferson, Jackson and Polk staffed the mansion with their personal slaves in an effort to save money and meet the demands of the office. But times were different now and passions grew deeper. Many Northerners in Washington, D.C. grew uncomfortable about the presence of slaves.

CHAPTER 11

President Taylor's America

As Zachary Taylor looked out into the sea of faces before him little did he or anyone else realize the full extent of existing problems or foresee the substantial changes which might take place. Nor was any American much aware of the promise and influence which lay dormant in American society.

Beginning around the time of Zachary Taylor's nomination for president by Louisiana Whigs in February of 1848, and ending with his death, the United States was witness to a number of significant events and changes. Taking a closer look at America during this time period will allow us to observe some of what Taylor and his countrymen saw.

According to Census Bureau information, the population of the United States in 1849 was 23,191,876. Four out of every five Americans lived on a farm or in small villages, and of the 8,000,000 people working, two-thirds of them were engaged in agriculture. Americans felt secure and entrusted their protection to 18,000 army and naval personnel. The average adult man earned five cents an hour in the factory and a man splitting logs earned $280 a year. These wages fluctuated depending on the state of the economy.

America's economic backbone was of course its workforce. The vast majority of workers earning a living in mid-century were men. Women remained at home bound by tradition to domestic duties. A closer glimpse at the types of jobs and the numbers involved reveal an America vastly different from today. This information on occupations, based mainly of the census of 1850, excluded all workers under fifteen years of age, and there were many thousands of them.

Among the plethora in various vocations were 2,300,000 farmers, 908,000 laborers, 130,000 cobblers and shoemakers, 100,000 merchants, 93,000 blacksmiths and skilled metal workers (called whitesmiths), 80,000 miners, 73,000 masons and bricklayers, 43,000 coopers making barrels and boxes, 31,000 weavers and an equal number of wheelwrights, 30,000 teachers (as well as 950 professors), 27,000 clergymen, 27,000 planters (95% in the South), 24,300 grocers, 24,000 lawyers, 22,000 innkeepers, 22,000 servants, 18,000 in lumbering, 17,000 butchers, 14,500 ship carpenters, 14,000 stone and marble cutters, 12,500 local and state officials, 11,500 brickmakers, 11,100 federal officials, 11,000 hatmakers, 10,600 peddlers, 9000 fishermen, 5000 railroad workers, 2600 professional musicians, 2200 rope and cordmakers, 100 stage actors (including a handful of women), 550 telegraph operators, and 90 male and female authors. Additionally, there were 18,500 whalers aboard 715 ships, reaping a harvest of $7 million annually.

Though wages may have changed slightly from year to year, work hours and working conditions did not. Most laborers toiled twelve to fourteen hours a day, six days a week, often under dangerous or oppressive conditions. Hazardous job environments existed in cramped, unventilated sweat shops. Girls working in textile mills were subjected to dangerous equipment and hours of monotonous drudgery. Several investigations brought little changes. Not wishing to be subjected to such trying conditions, hundreds of poor young ladies chose to be servants to affluent families while others, engaged in clothing manufacturing, took their sewing jobs home with them. For men, there was the blacksmith or iron-making trades, as well as working on canals and steamboats. Hunting and trapping were profitable to those willing to expose themselves to the risks of nature and Indians out West.

With little leisure time for the working classes, some Americans found time for entertainment and recreation. One sport, boxing, was gaining momentum. Though it initially failed to attract men of high society, large crowds turned out at sites where it was legal. One noted match drew thousands just out of the jurisdiction of New York City where two boxers, Lily and McCoy, fought bare fisted for an astonishing 119 rounds. The fight ended only when McCoy dropped dead in the ring after being knocked down for the eighty-first time. Another growing sport was horse racing. The sport became a popular local pastime but it too had not yet reached respectability in the East. Not until after the Civil War was it developed and organized.

In Boston, Philadelphia, and New York City proper society attended the theater, mostly to watch Shakespearean plays or light comedies. Among the nation's greatest actors included Junius Brutus Booth, the erratic English actor who settled in America and fathered Edwin and John Wilkes Booth. Other stars were Edwin Forrest, John Howard Payne, and the elegant Fanny Kemble. Less talented performers could find work, touring towns west of the Alleghenies and beyond.

Americans took pride in their stage performers. This was evident in the riot which took place in New York City in May of 1849. The cause of the unrest began in London when the American actor Edwin Forrest was snubbed by William Charles Macready, England's most popular actor and a rival of Forrest. Forrest made comments to English reporters degrading Macready. When Macready toured the American stage he was often booed and hissed at, besides being hit with vegetables and rotten eggs. For months newspapers on both sides of the Atlantic fueled the rivalry between the two Shakespearean actors.

When Macready appeared in a play at the Astor Place Opera House in New York City he was booed and forced off the stage. Patrons of the opera, headed by Washington Irving and Herman Melville, were embarrassed at the behavior of their fellow Americans and promised Macready their support, convincing him to appear again on stage, scheduled for May 10.

An angry crowd gathered outside and pelted the opera house with stones. The mayor, sensing there might be trouble, had not only assigned police to protect Macready, but provided militia out in the street. When police arrested offenders inside the theater a full-scale riot broke out. The militia fired into the mob, killing 30 and wounding 36 before order was finally restored.

Another 120 soldiers and civilians were injured. Perhaps the main ringleader in stirring up the crowd was none other than writer Edward Judson, aka Ned Buntline, who later became wealthy as the author of the dime novel. He was convicted of leading the riot and sentenced to one year in prison. Fortunately for William Macready, he was quickly hustled off to Boston by friends where he boarded a ship and returned safely to England.

Americans by mid-century were beginning to hear music written by Americans. Negro spirituals were often combined with folk tunes, resulting in a flurry of songs which were introduced by minstrels. Made up in blackface and colorful clashing clothes, white performers entertained in dance halls and saloons throughout the country. Minstrel "plantation melodies" were often accompanied with banjos, fiddles and tambourines, mixed in with outrageous jokes and dancing. As degrading as it seemed to many Negroes, even a few black actors participated in minstrel shows.

Two enterprising songwriters began their careers by the time Taylor had been nominated for president. Their melodies spread rapidly, and have to this day, become part of our musical legacy. One of these was Ohioan Daniel Decatur Emmett, who performed with Bryant's Minstrels and the Virginia Minstrels, writing tunes such as "Old Dan Tucker," "Turkey in the Straw," and "Jimmy Crack Corn" (or "Blue Tail Fly"). Less than a decade after Taylor's death, Emmett composed "Dixie," which became the signature song of the Confederacy, much to the composer's dislike.

The country's most gifted songwriter was a young man from Pittsburgh, Stephen Collins Foster. Writing both the words and melodies, his song "Open Thy Lattice, Love" was published when he was just sixteen. Soon, his songs were heard everywhere. On stage at Liberty Hall and Andrews' Eagle Ice Cream Parlor in Pittsburgh, and in music halls in Cincinnati where Foster worked as a bookkeeper at his brother's steamboat shipping company, many of his songs were introduced by E. P. Christy's Minstrels. Foster had already written the nostalgic "Old Folks at Home" and the rollicking "Camptown Races," but when his tune "Oh! Susanna" made its debut on September 11, 1847, it became an overnight sensation. By January of the following year the piece became the anthem of the gold prospectors rushing out to California. It was also being printed and sung in Mexico, Germany, Greece, France, Italy and India. Thousands around the world who sang and played the tune never heard the name of the author. More than twenty different publishers in America printed the song and not one gave credit to Foster.

Foster profited little from his compositions. He sold many of his earlier songs to minstrel troupes, whose names, and not Foster's, appeared on the sheet music. Also, many publishers printed their own versions of his songs, thus preventing the author from receiving any royalties. He eventually made a small fortune but spent his money more quickly than he made it. Foster went heavily into debt, borrowing from friends, his relatives and even his publishers. A poor businessman and subject to bouts of depression and illness, Foster separated from his family, becoming an alcoholic. His most popular tunes, the sentimental ballads "Old Black Joe," "My Old Kentucky Home," "Beautiful Dreamer," and "Jeanie with the Light Brown Hair" (written for his wife) came at a time when the nation teetered on civil war. Indeed, few composers were as original and prolific as Foster; he wrote the words and music to over 200 songs.

In 1864, penniless and raked with fever, he stumbled and fell against a ceramic wash basin in his New York City apartment, slashing his face and neck and losing a lot of blood. Stephen Collins Foster died three days after his accident. His unidentified body lay in the Bellvue Hospital morgue until it was claimed by a friend. Foster was not yet 39 years old.

Foster had his detractors, that much is certain. Some of them were jealous of his success while others criticized his work, especially the lyrics, as being gushy, overly sentimental or just plain silly. Decades after his death other critics felt his Negro dialect verses were "politically incorrect." Foster was no racist, nor was he an abolitionist. He was a songwriter who knew no class distinction and loved all people. He had an ear for melody and an uncanny ability to put it to paper. Stephen Foster was an American original, a genius who can be compared to Mozart or Beethoven. To this day his music remains a part of our American heritage.

Other forms of entertainment were also available. Museums were beginning to be constructed, and the most popular was Barnum's in New York City. When Phineas T. Barnum took Charles Stratton on a nationwide tour, he struck gold. Stratton was a two-foot tall adult from Connecticut who weighed only twenty pounds. Barnum named him Tom Thumb and even took him to Europe where he was introduced to royalty. The famous showman and his little friend made over a thousand dollars *a day*.

In early 1850 Barnum announced he would bring Jenny Lind to the states. Known as the "Swedish Nightingale," the singer was not yet world famous, but she was about to be. Barnum deposited $187,000 in a London bank, agreeing to pay Lind $1000 per concert, plus all expenses paid for her and her two servants. These were staggering terms and the following year Jenny Lind made a triumphant tour.

Another entertainer who made a name for himself was Dan Rice. He began his career as a jockey, riding in the Kentucky-Ohio circuit. As Rice grew to adulthood he got too heavy to race. The ex-jockey joined a circus and dressed as a clown. By the mid-1840s he was the most famous clown in America. For the next three decades Dan Rice toured the country's theaters and circuses as one of the highest paid comedians. A craving for alcohol, however, ended his career.

In the mid-19th century there was a flurry of inventions. One man in New York City, Walter Hunt, received a patent for his small contraption he called the safety pin. To satisfy a $15 debt owed to J. R. Chapin, Hunt spent three hours bending thin pieces of steel wire into various designs. Not seeing much of a future in his brainchild of the safety pin, he sold the rights to Chapin for $400. Hunt also worked on devising a repeating rifle without much success. Two other enterprising men were Linus Yale who designed a cylindrical lock and Waldo Hanchett who came up with the dental chair.

There were more important inventions and discoveries. Advances were made in farm tools and by 1850 Cyrus McCormick's factory in Chicago had sold nearly 18,000 reapers. Another milestone in agriculture, though not recognize right away, took place in 1851 when Lorenzo Langstroth of Philadelphia invented a moveable frame to abstract honey from bees. Prior to this, the bees had to be killed to obtain the honey and beeswax. Langstroth's innovation revolutionized the bee keeping industry, thus having a profound effect on agriculture.

Elias Howe and Issac Singer teamed up to produce a practical sewing machine. Changes in the designs of horsecars, rail locomotives and steamboats took place. Products made of natural rubber sold briskly. Major changes occurred in photography. The wet plate process, even with its limitations, was replacing the messy, time-consuming and complicated methods of using daguerreotypes (there were at least five daguerreotypes taken of Taylor and one of his wife).

Interests developed in sculpture and painting. Art unions were formed in Philadelphia, Boston, New York City and Philadelphia. These establishments promoted American artistic achievement and total membership surpassed 16,000. For some Easterners not interested in visiting museums to gaze at sculptures or portraits, other forms of entertainment could be found.

There were diversions for the young and privileged crowd. In big cities some men sniffed chloroform where "sensations of one week are crowded into two minutes." Others smoked Hashish which provided the user "a current of delirious thought...when I closed my eyes, a phantasmagoria of living and moving forms kept pace with this current of delirious thoughts."[1]

For the less adventurous, who were literate, there was always reading as an activity. But millions of Americans could neither read nor write; they were never taught.

Samuel Finley Breese Morse was one of the country's best known inventors. He was also a talented portrait painter, and on a return trip from France in 1839 he introduced photography to his fellow New Yorkers. Though the daguerreotype method of taking pictures was slow, messy and even dangerous due to the chemicals involved, the art form of photography flourished. Creating images on a copper plate without using a negative competed with the procedures first used by a couple of Englishmen who used glass negatives. By 1850 there were 70 photography studios in New York City.

Another phenomenon also had its roots in New York. It began in 1848 when one resident experienced strange, unexplained noises and movement in his house. This paranormal activity eventually led to the practice of spiritualism, which attracted scores of believers.

More than one-tenth of the population consisted of Negro slaves, totaling nearly 2.8 million men, women and children. Confined mostly to the deep South and Virginia, the states of New Jersey and Delaware also had black slaves totaling 3000 combined. About 30 per cent of the white families in the South owned Negro slaves, most of them with less than five. In some areas of the South, slaves far outnumbered whites. In Madison Parrish, Louisiana, for example about 7500 Negroes made up the population of 9000.

The average life expectancy among slaves was not known, but for an adult white male in 1849 it was 38 years, compared to 40 years for a woman. Families for both slave and free Americans were generally large and a couple with ten or more children was common because many youngsters died in childhood. And due to unsanitary practices used in childbirth, the rate of death for mothers was so alarming it was not uncommon for men to have had three different wives within their lifetime.

Despite efforts to abolish it, slavery remained the ugliest blight on the land. Each day for a slave was a sort of continuing warfare with the white master determined to extract a full measure of work. Since the early seventeenth century when Negro slaves were first introduced into Jamestown, Virginia, Southern whites realized such conditions posed a threat to their lifestyle. In the early 1800s Thomas Jefferson observed, "The whole commerce between master and slave is a perpetual exercise of the most boisterous passions; the most unremitting despotism on one part, and degrading submission on the other."[2]

Though not all Negro slaves were mistreated, nor hated their white masters (Taylor was quite benevolent to his), they were all considered inferior by the vast majority of whites. Teaching a slave to read and write in some Southern states during the antebellum period was punishable by death, though such laws were never enforced. And among the plantation slaves there was a stark difference between the field hands and the house servants. Many of the slave drivers on larger plantations were black, and they didn't hesitate to use their whip on a defiant or idle kindred.

Most of the slaves in the South did *not* live on large plantations. In 1849 approximately 1800 Southerners, or around one per cent, owned more than a hundred slaves. A white farmer or prosperous businessman typically owned two or three, but even those who did not own slaves favored the practice. Most all slave owners had to discipline their slaves at one time or another and this was where the difference lay. Disobedience and indiscretions often resulted in stern punishment or a slave being sold. In many cases, white overseers on plantations were sadistic in handing out discipline. Still others had black mistresses, as did some plantation owners.

No matter what conditions existed, the system bred hatred and contempt. A few lucky slaves worked extra hours, making perhaps fifty or a hundred extra dollars a year, and after twenty years were able to buy their freedom, usually at a cost between $1200 and $1500.

Very typical of circumstances on the plantation were those of a mulatto slave, Frederick Douglass. Like many of his contemporaries, Douglass lived in a dilapidated shed with a dirt floor, and no furniture or bed, other than a pile of straw or old rags. His food consisted of spoiled beef or rotted fish; he was given two linen shirts a year. Youngsters in bondage were fed corn, using oyster shells or pieces of flat boards to scoop it up from the ground where it had been tossed by their masters. Other youngsters simply ate what was left by the hogs around the trough. Slave children received neither pants nor shoes. Douglass eventually made a daring escape from Maryland disguised as a U.S. sailor aboard a train.

Slavery on the larger plantations, such as the ones owned by Taylor, was subject to different conditions. Usually slaves were summoned at sunrise and carried their breakfast with them to the fields in tin buckets consisting of cornbread, salted boiled pork and some vegetables. Around noon they returned to their quarters for a lunch break before returning to the fields, working until sunset.

Many of the slaves who attempted escape did so at night, often during a rainstorm so bloodhounds could not pick up their scent. Some traveled over a hundred miles to find sanctuary, knowing if they were caught the punishment would be brutal. In the year 1850, it was conservatively estimated that 2000 slaves escaped to the North, most of them fleeing from the border states.

By 1848 slavery spawned a growing resentment in the Northern states which reached a boiling point, and there were attempts in Congress to abolish it. Abolitionists for the past decade had published horror stories in trying to gain sympathy for the slaves. Among the more active groups in the underground railroad were the Presbyterians, Quakers and Methodists, who risked fine and imprisonment to assist runaway blacks escape to freedom in Canada. Some of the more prominent leaders in the underground movement were John Rankin, Lucy Stone, William Lloyd Garrison, Elijah Lovejoy, Levi Coffin and Harriet Beecher Stowe. A few abolitionists were Negroes: Sojourner Truth, Harriet Tubman and Douglass, but they had to be constantly aware of bounty hunters. As president, Zachary Taylor had little regard for both abolitionists and bounty hunters, as did most Northern whites at the time.

There were women like Fanny Kemble Butler who, though no abolitionist, provided accurate accounts of how blacks were treated. The beautiful, wealthy, talented actress/equestrian, had lived in both the North and South and chronicled the plight of slavery in her diary. Her written records, along with the diaries of several other educated men and women, provide us insight.

Prior to and during Taylor's administration concern ran deep among some Southerners of a slave rebellion. Previous attempts by Gabriel Prosser, Denmark Vesey and Nat Turner to overthrow their white counterparts all failed with scores of lives lost. There was plenty of prejudice to go around. Even free blacks in the North weren't safe. Employers throughout New England refused to hire Negroes for fear that their white workers would walk off the job. Slave owners would threaten a business owner with prosecution if they found his runaway working. In fact, some churches in New England were destroyed after abolitionists spoke there.

Negro children in the North went to their own schools in inferior buildings. In several New England communities where integration of classes was attempted, outrage often followed. In Canan, New Hampshire, a teacher allowed blacks into a classroom and found the building completely destroyed the next day. Fanny Kemble noted that Northern blacks were "pariahs; debarred from all fellowship save with their own despised race.... scorned by the lowest ruffian...free but they are also degraded, rejected, the offscum and offspring of the very dregs of society."[3]

Taylor was one of ten presidents who at one time during their lives owned slaves (this includes Grant who received two Negro slaves as a gift from his Missouri in-laws). Perhaps no large plantation owner in the entire South was more humane, but his slaves were still regarded as property. Slavery was an ominous sign as passions mounted and the South talked of secession. Taylor recognized the constitutionality of slavery, but he would not allow it to spread into the territories. In his inaugural address he announced that "the attachment to the Union of the States should be habitually fostered in every American heart." Warning those who called for rebellion against the federal government, Taylor said of the Union that "upon its preservation must depend our own happiness and that of countless generations to come. Whatever dangers may threaten it, I shall stand by it and maintain it in its integrity to the full extent of the obligations imposed and the powers conferred upon me by the Constitution."[4] This statement made clear the path ahead to pro-slavery advocates in both the North And South.

Talk of reform was in the air and it was not all about slavery. A handful of female "radicals" were stirring society with their talk of giving women the right to vote, along with abolishing slavery and alcoholic drink. Susan B. Anthony, who taught school for a decade, joined the temperance movement and after meeting Elizabeth Cady Stanton, dedicated herself to suffrage and women's rights. Lucretia Mott, a Quaker teacher, organized a women's rights convention in Seneca Falls, New York, where the Stantons lived. Her book *Discourse on Woman* was published in 1850. The ladies had some support from men such as George Francis Train. A wealthy merchant who also sought the presidency, Train lent women his active support, though he saw nothing wrong with slavery.

Sojourner Truth campaigned for both suffrage and the abolition of slavery. Some whites, including women, were uncomfortable with her. Truth attended a women's rights convention uninvited and appeared before the delegates. Upon being recognized, she was asked to speak. Shouts from the men echoed, "An abolition affair!" "Women's rights and niggers!" "Go it, darkey!" No doubt some of the men came to harass the strong-willed ladies but when Truth rose to speak the crowd listened. The former slave, in a slow, deliberate and eloquent speech, talked about the evils of slavery. Having been sold twice, she was raped by a white owner and after she was freed in New York, worked as a household servant. She told of how all thirteen of her children had been sold into bondage. Her remarks both stunned and electrified her listeners and she received a long ovation.[5] But Sojourner Truth, as well as most other escaped slaves, had to be on guard at all times. Bounty hunters roamed throughout the North attempting to capture escaped slaves and collect the reward money.

Many women who did not embrace the issues of suffrage or the anti-slavery movement helped the poor and oppressed through church missionary boards and charitable groups. Crusaders like Dorothea Dix became the spokesperson for the less fortunate. During the middle part of the nineteenth century she traveled nearly 11,000 miles, taking notes, lecturing and raising funds. She determined in all there were about 10,000 citizens who fit the categories of mentally retarded, physically disabled or insane. She appealed to intelligent, caring adults who possessed a high sense of moral obligation. Dix's efforts reaped some dividends: by 1850 ten states had built hospitals for the insane, even though President Pierce later vetoed a federal measure to lend aid. This reform and benevolence, gradual and sometimes inadequate, went hand-in-hand in the sense that both were directed at removing or improving some of the harsher elements of the public.

Another pioneer during this time period was English-born Elizabeth Blackwell. Her reform minded parents were religious, highly intelligent, abolitionists. Elizabeth and her eight brothers and sisters all received a superior education by private tutors. In 1849 Elizabeth graduated from Geneva College in New York, becoming the first female in America to receive a medical degree (her sister Emily also became a medical doctor). She toured Europe to study more about medicine; after teaching school in Kentucky for five years she became blind in one eye from a contagious disease while treating a child and gave up her pursuit of performing surgery. After several years of struggling in New York City, she gained the respect and trust of male doctors. Eventually she returned to England where she promoted the role of women as physicians. Through sheer determination and sacrifice, Elizabeth Blackwell broke down prejudice against women in the medical field.

For most Americans, religion was still an important part of their lives, despite the fact that only about 22% of the population in 1850 belonged to a particular denomination. The Protestant churches were well established and the Catholic church, due to large numbers of immigrants, was also growing. The Baptists, Methodists and Presbyterians in particular sponsored missionaries at home and abroad, and these "spiritual messengers" enjoyed support from many non-denominational groups as well.

Among the 18,000,000 or so members who attended church, not all were members of a particular denomination. Methodists had the greatest membership with more than 4,400,000, worshipping in 12,400 churches. There were about 2,300,000 Baptists (meeting in 8800 churches), followed by 987,000 Quakers or Friends, 700,000 Roman Catholics, 802,000 Congregationalists, 643,000 Episcopalians, 540,000 Lutherans (who often worshipped with Dutch Reformed members), 202,000 Presbyterians, and a handful of Jews praying in 31 synagogues in six large cities of the Northeast.

The role of mission boards, made up mostly of women, cannot be overstated. Since the early 1800s several Protestant groups sent hundreds of missionaries to the four corners of the earth. Some American missionaries in China, Burma, Ceylon, Turkey, Spain, Liberia and Mexico were joined by European brethren. These brave pioneers of the Gospel built schools and hospitals, both in the U.S. and in foreign lands. By 1850 tens of thousands of American and foreign students had been educated in mission schools.

Each missionary from the states was also an embodiment of American customs and lifestyles. Leading converts from darkness to light sometimes brought inherent dangers, particularly if racial superiority was attached to these Christian messengers as they tried to change the world. Many weren't prepared for the clash of culture and religion. In India for example, men who would never kill a sacred cow, dog or rat, did not hesitate in murdering a woman. One visitor from Great Britain witnessed an incident where a 17-year-old girl was suspected of being unfaithful to her 13-year-old husband. She was led to the front of her home by her father who twisted her long hair and held her up by the toes while her brother hacked off her head. Unwanted daughters, often a financial strain in many Asian societies, were killed by drowning, with overdoses of opium, or letting them be trampled by water buffalo.

By mid-century nearly 50 mission schools in the Sandwich Islands (Hawaii) had educated 20,000 students. Since the 1820s one of the biggest challenges for missionaries was keeping frisky American sailors away from young Hawaiian women. In at least two cases violence erupted when naval crews attacked Church missionaries. Realizing that owning a foothold in

Hawaii could prove a commercial bonanza, President Taylor announced, "We desire that the islands may maintain their independence and that other nations should concur with us in their sentiment."[6]

Still other concerned citizens felt compelled in helping immigrants. Among the groups needing the most relief were the Irish and eastern Europeans. They came to America by the hundreds of thousands and by 1850 it was estimated that 1.7 million had settled in the nation. Many Germans left their homeland as well when revolution throughout mainland Europe forced them to look for opportunities and calmer conditions. Masses of German immigrants settled in Cincinnati, Cleveland, Milwaukee and St. Louis, bringing with them their skills and ingenuity. In the West it was the Chinese who landed by the shiploads, taking whatever kind of work they could find. And of the approximate 20,000 Jews in the country, most of them settled in New York City while some plied their skills in Southern ports.

While this newly-arrived mass of humanity contributed to huge economic growth, it also gave rise to fear and suspicion resulting in the formation of nativist organizations such as the Know-Nothing Party. Active politically, the Know-Nothings, some of whom were Masons, sought to control immigration and make it more difficult for immigrants to become citizens. Most newcomers to the U.S. were looked upon with cynicism and scorn. Prominent New York businessman George Train witnessed immigrants being processed at a naturalization center, describing the "wretched, filthy, bestial-looking Italians and Irish...the very scum and dregs of human nature."[7] There were other events, however, which attracted greater attention from the American populace.

The California Territory had been ceded to the United States by the Treaty of Guadalupe Hidalgo after the Mexican War. The conquest of California came during the war when U.S. soldiers and sailors, led by John C. Fremont and Robert F. Stockton respectively, took control of the vast region. General Fremont had already led two surveying parties into California and with help from General Stephen Kearny, gained a firm foothold. Mexico, having lost the war, had no choice but to sign the peace treaty. But just as the Mexicans were about to sign the treaty, they heard some provoking news.

It was a bitter cold morning on January 24, 1848 at John Sutter's saw mill, situated on the American River near Sacramento. One of Sutter's employees, a carpenter/mechanic named James Marshall, was inspecting the channel below the mill and noticed two shiny objects near the shore. What proved to be chunks of gold set off one of the wildest and most exciting events in all of history—the California gold rush.

Oddly, gold had been found in California six years before when Francisco Lopez, working as a ranch hand in southern California, dug some up in a clump of wild onions. Over the next three years he mined $8000 worth out of the ranch property and sent twenty ounces of it to the Philadelphia Mint. It caused only a minor stir.

When word of Marshall's discovery reached the states, the migration of people to the West Coast was unprecedented. When the gold bug bit in 1848 gold fever took on epidemic proportions, both in the U.S. and in foreign lands. California's population exploded from 20,000 in 1848 to 200,000 in 1851. In fact for the first and only time in American history, *every state* decreased in population. Of the 90,000 prospectors who came to California in 1849, more than half of them were in their twenties.

Entire families packed up their belongings and headed west. Soldiers in distant outposts deserted the army by the scores and U.S. ships lost their officers and crews. The boom period in gold would peak after five years: in 1849 $5 million worth of gold was mined; by 1853 it had risen to $60 million per year. But mining and panning for gold the entire day, six days a week was hard work and a half ounce of it yielded only about eight dollars.

People in the East and Midwest could make the trip overland to California through the Rockies, the desert and Indian territory by horse and wagon, or by two different routes via ship, sailing around the tip of Good Hope or disembarking in Panama and crossing the isthmus to board another vessel. All three routes were filled with danger, but the long trip around the tip of South America, covering a distance of 19,000 miles from New York to San Francisco, was probably the safest. At least one man walked 2000 miles across the country by foot, taking three months to reach California. Hundreds of motivated, exciting and adventurous men left their families and were never heard from again. Stephen Foster, seemed to capture the spirit of the gold rush when he published his song, *Oh! Susanna*, which proved to be an immensely popular tune.

Perhaps typical of what happened in many American households was the experience of Hiram Dwight Pierce of Troy, New York. Pierce worked as a blacksmith, had served on the town council and was president of the Troy

Fire Department. His future appeared to be bright. By 1848 he was in poor health, despite a thriving business. He and his wife Sara had seven children and the Pierces were looking for more income.

In early 1849 Pierce took a train to New York City where he boarded a ship to make the arduous voyage to California, promising to send his riches back home. After landing in Panama he crossed the isthmus by foot and waited six weeks for a ship. Two months after leaving Troy he arrived in San Francisco.

Pierce found very little gold and there was no money sent to his family. He struggled just to survive, at times only making ten dollars a month. More than a year passed and he continued to make only enough to provide for bare essentials. Sara meanwhile was getting desperate. To make ends meet and feed her brood she rented out her husband's shop, borrowed money from relatives and did odd jobs. Her husband managed to scrape together a few dollars which he invested in a mining venture with several other prospectors. But this too failed and after another unsuccessful attempt at striking it rich, Hiram Pierce sold his shovel for two dollars, hawked some of his meager possessions, and returned home in 1851. He was so physically changed that friends failed to recognize him.

Pierce's blacksmith business declined, though his physical health seemed improved. Still determined to become wealthy, he again left for California where he tried farming and working part time in a mine. But these ventures proved worthless and Pierce returned to Troy for good. He died in 1866 in near poverty, but four of his children later moved to California.

The mass migration meant short supplies and high costs for some articles. Prices in Sacramento and San Francisco skyrocketed. One man bought a herd of sheep for 50 cents a piece, took them to San Francisco and sold them for $1600 each. Milk was sold at a dollar a quart and a 30-cent metal pan fetched $15. A hammer valued at one dollar commanded $40. A slice of bread was a dollar, two dollars if buttered. It was documented that extremely thirsty miners paid $100 for a glass of water which had been shipped in containers. And one woman in Nevada City was offered $10 for biscuits—that's $10 *a piece* (the amount of two week's wages back in Ohio). She soon started a bakery and profited handsomely.

Miners destroyed streams and animal habitats, dumping toxic chemicals into the water, killing fish and depleting oyster beds. Fish and oysters understandably resulted in high prices. The hide and tallow of a steer increased from $12 to $75. Strangely, the cost of bacon and shovels escaped the inflationary spiral. By the summer of 1850 supply and demand brought prices almost back to normality.

With the huge influx of people came other problems. Greed and hunger for gold spelled doom for others. Indians throughout most of California were run off their lands, or simply murdered. Chinese and Latinos who had staked earlier claims disappeared. Laws were passed by the white-dominated legislature to tax Chinese, Latino or Native-American prospectors, thus giving the white man a monopoly in gold hunting.

But the Indians suffered the most. White settlers freely raided their villages, killing the adults and taking the children as servants. The state legalized and subsidized their extinction. Within two decades more than 120,000 American Indians died, while many others simply left their homelands.

The scene in California was survival of the fittest. All people of color suffered greatly because there were no laws to protect them. But it just wasn't minorities who became targets. In Los Angeles County, with a population of 8000, there were 44 murders in a single year, many of the victims being white. Only one man was ever brought to trial for homicide and he was found not guilty. Vigilantes enforced justice swiftly and the fact an innocent man had been hanged didn't seem to bother anybody. One eleven-year-old boy was caught stealing $1100 and had both ears cut off.

The transformation in San Francisco was almost beyond belief. With an approximate population of 1800 in 1848, the city's numbers reached 25,000 by the end of 1849. Men outnumbered women thirteen to one. More than 3500 sailors jumped their ships which lay in the harbor and an estimated 40,000 immigrants landed in San Francisco before migrating to other parts of California. The city within its sandy hills was made up of hundreds of canvas tents, shanties and a few one-story frame houses. Garbage heaps and large patches of human and animal filth pockmarked every street. Lawlessness and disorder reigned while a vigilante committee inflicted swift and brutal justice.

Gambling, the grand occupation of all classes of society, was everywhere. Fortunes were won or lost on the turn of a card, the toss of the dice or the spin of a roulette wheel. There were only a very few higher class hotels, elegant restaurants or public buildings in the city. But another real danger was fire. In an eighteen month period San Francisco had eight major fires, finally forcing the residents to use brick, stone, and clay as building materials. This rough and tumble devil-may-care condition remained so until 1850 when *some* semblance of law and order, along with zoning regulations and building codes, brought civilization to the city. But one statistic continued to rise; the murder rate failed to slow and each year hundreds of people were killed.

For every prospector who struck it rich a dozen others did not. Many miners who did discover a bonanza lost their fortune because of gambling, prostitution, drunkenness and crime. Some men found their treasure in providing miners with necessities such as supplies, food stuffs, laundry service and clothing. The thousands of Chinese in particular were adept at finding jobs. They and less fortunate others realized one could make a comfortable living by what some have described as "mining the miners." Seventeen-year-old Levi Strauss, for example, found himself stuck with a surplus of tents he couldn't sell, so he made pants out of the canvas. Miners loved them, even though they were a bit stiff (Strauss later used denim and dyed the pants blue to hide the dirt and stains).

Since there was a scarcity of women, prostitutes from the states, Chile, China, and Mexico commanded high fees. Within a year after Marshall's discovery there was a need for lawyers, bartenders, bankers, and ship owners. And while waves of eager folks continued to trek to the West, many millions more remained in their home towns where there was plenty of opportunity to make a modest living. To some the risks involved in a long journey to a strange land were too great.

President Taylor was opposed to seeing slavery adopted in the territories, and emerging states like California would upset the balance of power in Congress between slave and free states. On the other hand, he was also aware that many Northern abolitionists wished to secede from a Union tainted with slavery. Tempers were rising and Taylor was discovering there was no middle ground on the issue.

Southerners in the House and Senate felt the people in the territories should at least be able to vote on whether or not they wanted slavery. Taylor, however, found a way to circumvent this opportunity. In April of 1849 he sent Thomas B. King of Georgia to California with instructions to encourage organizing a government which would apply directly for statehood, thus by-passing the territorial stage and preventing a mad rush of pro-slavery citizens into the region. This maneuver doomed slavery. In August during a speech in Mercer, Pennsylvania, Taylor stated flatly, "The people of the North need have no apprehension of the further extension of slavery."[8]

Travel in America in the late 1840s could be dangerous and time consuming. Train derailments, steamship boiler explosions, drownings at sea during storms, Indian attacks, stagecoach accidents and injuries on horseback caused more than 2000 deaths a year. In a four-year period during the mid-1840s 138 steamboats sank between Cairo, Illinois and St. Louis, resulting in numerous deaths and a total loss exceeding $3 million. If one wanted to travel from New York City overland to San Francisco, it took an average of 139 days. One safer alternative for many travelers in the East was by canal packet, but it was slow and uncomfortable.

There were other hazards as well. Disease took its toll. One gold seeker, Dr. Israel Lord, boarded a steamer on his way to California on May 6, 1849. Within two days eight passengers died, including a child and a Negro servant. All the deaths were attributed to cholera.

Despite these impediments, Americans continued to build their transportation system. By 1850 there were 10,000 miles of railroad tracks, though some Southern states used a different gauge of tracks, forcing rail passengers to switch trains. Steamboats were being constructed; one was 300 feet long and 46 feet wide. Buggies, stagecoaches, and Conestoga wagons were built and sold, though unpaved roads were little better than mere dirt paths. And in Boston, New York City and Philadelphia, discussions were underway to lay tacks for horse-drawn trolleys.

The greatest shipbuilder of the day was Donald McKay. Born in Canada, he moved to New York City where he worked for a decade and saved enough money to start his own shipbuilding business in Boston. A brilliant engineer and draftsman, in 1850 McKay constructed a clipper ship, *The Stag Hound*, soon followed by *The Flying Cloud*. The trip by ship from Boston or New York to San Francisco usually took an average of 159 days, but McKay's ships cut that time nearly in half. These two vessels were the fastest afloat, setting world speed records upon the high seas and wielding a tremendous influence on American trade and international commerce.

Long distance postage was initially expensive, until telegraph lines were stretched (often along railroad tracks) and the cost of mailing letters and packages decreased. It was said that letters should be sent only to notify a far-away friend or relative of a birth, death or wedding. Five and ten cent stamps, with the portraits of Benjamin Franklin and George Washington respectively, were issued, but it cost 25 cents, or a day's wages, for mailing a letter 400 miles or more. Less than a year after Taylor's death, postal rates were lowered and the Post Office issued a 3-cent lick-and-stick stamp

The importance of education in the mid-nineteenth century played a minor part for most people. One need not have a diploma or a degree to find a good paying job. Taylor himself had little classroom schooling and he had done fine. But there were those who felt their fellow countrymen should uplift themselves, expand their horizons by enlightenment and guidance, and the only way to achieve that was by academic exertion. Wealthier families hired private tutors or sent their children off to board in refined schools in larger cities.

Teaching in a one-room schoolhouse was usually a challenge. Most instructors were unmarried women or young men looking for work while they prepared for the law or business. Discipline was often severe and in several instances downright cruel. As many as 35 children ranging in age from five to twenty with varying intelligence levels might be crowded into a small classroom. Boys and girls were usually separated and more often than not materials were in short supply. The average school term lasted from November to March because children were needed at home to help with the crops and chores. There were many cases where children *wanted to go to school* but were not permitted by their parents.

Teachers were often not fully paid in common schools, since money was hard to come by for some people. By mutual agreement, teachers accepted barter for payment of teaching a child. Thus, subscription schools allowed parents to subscribe their children to a teacher in exchange for non-money items. This included things such as food, room and board, clothing, or fuel for the pot belly stove inside the schoolhouse. There were even agreements where parents had their child do jobs for the teacher, such as cleaning, hauling wood, or providing coal.

Two men played a major role in the development of education in America during the mid-1800s: Horace Mann and William Holmes McGuffey.

Mann was the son of a Massachusetts farmer and a Unitarian. He earned a law degree and taught school before being elected as a superintendent of public schools. Like Taylor, Mann was a Whig and in 1848 was elected to Congress on the anti-slavery ticket, replacing former President John Quincy Adams who died shortly after his collapse on the floor of the House of Representatives. As a member of the House Mann used his position as a forum to promote free education for every child. And though the president lacked formal education and disagreed with Mann on some political issues, both men recognized the need for public schools, though most of the burden in establishing them would have to be shouldered by the states and individual villages.

Horace Mann's reforms in Massachusetts became widely accepted. He started the first normal school to train future teachers, improved the curriculum, redesigned school furniture and established standards on discipline. Mann also helped the mentally ill. As the nation adopted his suggestions, a marked improvement in elementary education took place. After being defeated in a bid for reelection to Congress as a Free Soiler, Mann ventured to southern Ohio where he founded Antioch College.

Just as remarkable as Mann was a contemporary, William Holmes McGuffey. Born in western Pennsylvania, he taught school at the age of thirteen. Settling in Ohio, he became a Presbyterian minister and soon saw the need for better methods of learning. By 1850 his *McGuffey's Eclectic Reader* had sold more than 9 million copies. These first and second level books (there were eventually six levels) borrowed stories from a variety of sources like the *Bible*, Aesop's fables, Greek mythology and history. Children learned how to read, spell and pronounce words. More importantly, they learned values promoted in the readers.

Four generations of Americans had their character shaped in part by McGuffey, whose textbooks eventually reached sales of 125,000,000 in six different countries. His Christian nurturing was plainly evident and a theme of "Good is rewarded; evil is punished" was in every lesson. Readers were also convinced of McGuffey's adage, "Education is power; get yourself some." But for most Americans in 1850, public education was an end, not a beginning. A select few who had the initiative and the money could attend an academy or prep school to ready themselves for college. For the few women who pursued a higher education, small female seminaries offered courses in music, social refinement and literature.

Probably less than four percent of those in public schools ended up furthering their formal education. In just the state of Ohio at mid-century, less than 30 percent of those between the ages of five and twenty went to school. Not withstanding the low numbers, by 1847 there were 110 colleges in the country, many of them religious or denominational schools. Attending some of the elite schools in the East for some was out of the question. Tuition at Harvard, Yale, Brown, Princeton or William and Mary was prohibitive. Institutions of higher learning sprang up in less populated states like Tennessee and Indiana, though some of these colleges closed their doors within a dozen years when they ran out of funds. And being admitted to college was no guarantee one would make it through; estimates at Harvard in the middle 1800s revealed only a 20 percent graduation rate.

It's not certain what Zachary Taylor's views were toward college. Certainly many of his fellow Americans mistrusted colleges as undemocratic institutions which questioned authority and challenged the status quo. These same critics saw professors as lazy, arrogant and set in their ways, claiming they or their schools did little to promote moral values or foster patriotism. Fraternities served no purpose at all. One father removed his son from Columbia because, "the youth belonged to some mystic association designated by two Greek letters which maintained a sort of club room over a Broadway grocery store, with billiard tables and a bar."[9]

Typical of the smaller schools west of the Alleghenies was Mount Union College, in what is now Alliance, Ohio. Founded in 1846 by Methodist Orville Hartshorn, classes were first conducted in a third floor attic of a woolen mill. Beginning with six students, Mount Union prepared young men for the ministry or teaching. Within a decade its numbers grew to 441.

Another school, known for its liberal views, was Oberlin College in northern Ohio. In 1837 it became the first co-educational college in the nation. In 1850, Oberlin raised eyebrows again in announcing it would become co-racial. Dartmouth soon followed suit, becoming the first college in the East to admit blacks. But many whites, even those opposed to slavery, thought this policy was going a bit too far. It would take nearly three quarters of a century before most other schools followed Oberlin's example.

Those who could read began buying books by original American authors. By 1848 Rufus Griswold's volumes of *The Path and Poetry of America* had sold more than 300,000 copies at $3.00 a piece. Perhaps the most widely read novelist was Texan Mayne Reid, who published *The Rifle Rangers* in 1850 and *The Scalp Hunters* the following year. Reid's books were based on his adventures in the southwest and his experiences as a commissioned officer in the Mexican War. In addition, two sisters, Susan and Anna Bartlett Warner, writing under the pen names of Amy Lothrop and Elizabeth Wetherell respectively, became overnight sensations with their novel *The Wide, Wide World* (they would go on to write other best sellers and compose the hymn "Jesus Loves Me, This I Know").

Other writers had begun making a name for themselves: John Greenleaf Whittier, William Cullen Bryant, Nathaniel Hawthorne, James Russell Lowell, Edgar Allen Poe, Oliver Wendel Holmes Sr. and Ralph Waldo Emerson. Walt

Whitman, a Brooklyn newspaper editor, began working on *Leaves of Grass*, which took him 17 years to complete. He lost his newspaper job when he advocated abolition of slavery and uncensored freedom of the press. Herman Melville was just beginning his career and Frederick Douglass, former slave and abolitionist, had returned from England as a successful writer and lecturer. Establishing a newspaper in Rochester, New York, called *The North Star*, Douglass preached against the horrors of slavery. Henry David Thoreau was living at Walden Pond and with Emerson's support, wrote essays on civil disobedience and nature. Francis Parkman's accounts of the Oregon Trail and women authors Margaret Fuller and Sarah Josepha Hale enjoyed great popularity. Horace Greely's *New York Tribune* reached a circulation of 200,000 and the city of Chicago sported two dozen newspapers. Theodore Parker, described as a Transcendental minister, stirred minds with his sermons and writings critiquing American churches. In the ante-bellum South, however, intellectual and literary life was confined largely in the minds of cultivated ladies.

Life styles in America differed considerably from those in Europe. Nowhere was this contrast more apparent than in the eating habits. Men in the U.S. consumed enormous amounts of food, especially meat. And they ate quickly. The food served in taverns, saloons and hotels was often ill prepared or indigestible. Foreign visitors observed that Americans had to learn how to *enjoy* their food. Food poisoning and tainted drinking water were common. Indeed, one of the victims of these conditions was Zachary Taylor himself.

Related in part to the poor food and the sickness attached to it was the problem of sanitation. Households which didn't have an outhouse used chamber pots, the contents of which were dumped in streets or alleyways. This human excrement, along with garbage, simply lay in the roadways or alleys of large cities and villages alike. In some communities like Cincinnati and New York, the refuse was consumed by hogs which roamed freely.

Piles of horse dung dotted every thoroughfare. One man noted, "It dried in the summer sun to become high-flavored dust blowing into the mouth and lung. In wet weather it incorporated into the mud that was tracked everywhere. Women's long dresses and men's shoes carried the filth everywhere while the smell permeated the entire community.[10] And it was only after mid-century that babies began to have their diapers changed and washed each day and not allowed to dry while the baby wore them.

Added to these inept and unhealthy practices were the droppings from dogs and livestock of every kind along sidewalks and roadways.

The quagmire of human and animal waste was accompanied with stagnant or polluted water which lay in ditches along unpaved streets, spawning millions of flies and mosquitoes. The ultimate result of these conditions was disease. Life was cut short due to cholera, dysentery, malaria, typhoid and yellow fever. Cities had not yet begun to pay others to clean up the mess or haul away the debris. Also water systems were poor, or non-existent. Some residents used rain water from a cistern installed on their roof, letting gravity fill a tub or wash basin.

Serious illness or injuries were treated the same as they had been since colonial times. In the mid-1800s there were few advances in medicine. One wanting to become a doctor did not have to spend a great deal of time attending medical school, and only three states in 1850, Louisiana, Michigan and New Jersey, had laws concerning the licensing of regular physicians. Doctors still blistered and bled patients, applied hot compound of salve, gave large doses of calomel or antimony to induce vomiting, and administered a blend of assorted elixirs and timeworn remedies. More often than not these measures weakened the patient or killed them. The loss of teeth was also common, due in part to the mercury poisoning from traditional medicines.

While medical doctors were purging the sick, homeopathic doctors were concentrating on the other end, using small doses of homemade liquids and natural herbs as enemas to flush out one's insides. Using a holistic approach and rivaling medical physicians, homeopathy was based on nutrition, exercise, minimal medicine and human relationship. One homeopathic practitioner, Samuel Thompson of New Hampshire, sold 100,000 copies of his booklet on home cures.

Compound fractures often meant amputation, because most physicians didn't know how to properly set bones. Surgery was performed while the victim was awake, with patients enduring unspeakable pain. A shot of strong whiskey was sometimes given before an operation but that practice changed somewhat in 1846 when a Boston dentist, William Morton, administered ether to one of his patients. Four years earlier, Crawford Long, a Georgia doctor, had used ether vapors during surgery, but didn't publish the facts of his discovery until after Morton used it. Another physician, John P. Maynard of Dedham, Massachusetts, used clean gun cotton dissolved in sulfur ether, then brushed it on a patient's skin with cotton strips. This technique was the grandfather of what later became known as the Band-Aid.

Hospitals were also being built in larger cities and the few bathhouses which invited ailing citizens to receive a healing were affordable only to the wealthy. Though public baths had been banned in Philadelphia and Boston for a while, city laws were changed to accommodate those who had written permission from a physician. Another growing phenomenon was phrenology whereby "experts" could read a person's character and predict certain ills simply by feeling bumps on one's head. Certainly not all of these medical techniques could be considered improvements but the ones which were gained acceptance gradually over the ensuing decades.

If there was one commonality many American men and women shared with the British was the trend in dress and mores. Culture and fashion were influenced, unconsciously perhaps, by Queen Victoria and her husband Prince Albert. London was the center for styles of clothing and the royal couple's tastes in dress and decorum set the tone for ladies and gentlemen in the states. The exceptions to this effect were the poor and particularly the women who lived in the backwoods. In addition, the unshaven "Forty-niners" during the gold rush in California were pragmatic in adapting to the environment with their garb of baggy pants, slouch hats, high boots and red flannel shirts.

Styles for both men and women in America changed little during the 1800s. One marked deviation for men began in New England in 1840 when they began sprouting facial hair. Goatees and mustaches within a decade became commonplace. With few exceptions, however, men's fashions in clothing, form and deportment changed little.

Fashion for women could best be described as confining. Beneath their long dresses was a labyrinth of accompanying undergarments. Tight waistbands, tight stays, tight corsets, tight garters, tight shoes and even tight bonnet strings impeded breathing and circulation. Freedom of movement was sacrificed for style with some costumes so elaborate that women needed a maid to get dressed. Some models of proper etiquette which remained unchanged since the 1700s were the covering of bare arms and wearing high collars; the showing of a lady's ankles or leg (properly referred to as limbs) was considered scandalous.

One woman who challenged this traditional manner of dress and propriety was Amelia Jenks Bloomer. As the wife of a newspaper editor from

Homer, New York, she was actively involved in the temperance and suffrage movement. Bloomer discarded the idea of hooped skirts and donned pantaloons, or bloomers, under a shorter skirt. Other liberal thinking ladies adopted this style. Bloomer became a controversial figure as she lectured to curious onlookers, but because of her apparel she was ridiculed everywhere she went. The press and the public heaped so much criticism on her that within six years Bloomer and her small band of devoted followers stopped wearing the outfit.

If clothing inhibited a lady's movement, her lack of exercise compounded many a health problem (something she shared with the men folk). Exercise was not necessarily the same as work and few doctors or anyone else promoted the idea of rigorous physical activity. Child bearing, mundane housework, never-ending chores, birthing and raising numerous children and wearing restricted clothing all took its toll. Resigned to a life of labor, the average female felt trapped by her circumstances. Fanny Kemble, who traveled extensively throughout Europe, observed that most American women by the age of 25 looked overweight, faded and old compared to those in England.

One dilemma which had faced the nation ever since its inception was the treatment of Native Americans. Peace treaties were continually broken by encroachment from white settlers, and in some instances the army could not enforce treaty provisions because of the large number of squatters. Beginning in 1850 the federal government decided that the tribes' best interests would be served if they were designated to reservations for their protection not just from advancing whites but from raiding tribes as well. Government officials, including the commissioner of Indian affairs, urged that reservations be established with well-defined boundaries furnished with clothing, supplies and farm tools. Additionally, the government promised to provide comfortable dwellings, religious training and education. However, these assurances meant to help the Indians assimilate to the white man's culture often fell short.

The Indians understandably showed a stubborn determination to remain Indians. Providing them with the white man's way proved ineffective and few people in Washington understood the complexities of the problem. There was fighting between the Pawnee and Sioux while the Crows carried on a long-standing war the Blackfeet. Many Indians also suffered from a variety of diseases from whites. Wagon trains of settlers and isolated pioneer families were attacked and later, railroad and telegraph lines ran through Indian lands. By the time Taylor took office many of the Native-Americans confined to the reservation lived in abject poverty and squalor.

It can be said with accuracy that Zachary Taylor, during his short stay in the presidency, recognized the plight of the Indians and treated them fairly. On his own initiative and authority, Taylor appointed Indian agents to protect the rights of Native-Americans in the West, particularly in California. But as they saw their way of life gradually disappearing, along with the buffalo herds, the indigenous people of the Western tribes were caught in a no-win situation which would fester into the next two centuries.

One aspect of American society which fascinated many Americans was the surge in Utopian towns. Throughout the North and Midwest groups like the Shakers, Rappites, Fourier's Phalanxes (50 different communities), Oneida's Perfectionists, Ripley's Transcendentalists and Zoarites in northeastern Ohio broke away from mainstream of society to live their own lives. In Illinois alone two dozen such colonies existed, inhabited mostly by transplanted folks from New York and New England.

Idealistic enterprises based on socialism were met with both tolerance and suspicion, depending on the location of the commune and the makeup of its inhabitants. The great majority of Americans, however, looked upon such communities as visionary, quixotic and impractical. The inhabitants of most utopian towns adhered to rules which many Americans discounted as too restrictive. The life of simplicity in seeking spiritual nourishment raised few concerns, with one major exception.

The Church of Jesus Christ of Latter-Day Saints, better known as the Mormons, was founded by Joseph Smith in 1830 near Palmyra, New York. Gathering a band of loyal followers, Smith attempted to create their own community in New York. To avoid discrimination and run-ins with the law, they settled in Kirtland, Ohio, and Independence, Missouri. After unsuccessful attempts to live in these communities, the Mormons moved en masse to a new settlement in Illinois, naming it Nauvoo. Within eight years and more than 15,000 inhabitants, Nauvoo became the second largest city in the state, next to Chicago.

What had angered many Americans was the practice of polygamy by male Mormons. A farmer had a right to be angry if his daughter ran off to wed a man of a different faith, but if that man already had two or three other wives, an entire community might be enraged. This was not the only reason the industrious Saints spawned controversy. The federal government had problems with Mormons building their own banks, printing money, forming militias and later making separate treaties with Indians.

In Nauvoo, there was unrest among the Saints themselves, leading to serious disputes. Rumors circulated throughout Illinois that the Mormons would use their armed forces to take over other communities or resist any legal force sent to investigate. Joseph Smith, his brother Hyrum, and a handful of other Mormon leaders were arrested. On June 27, 1844 a mob stormed the jail and killed Smith and his brother.

Brigham Young, after considerable opposition from some of his own people, took over as leader. To avoid further bloodshed, in two large migrations he had the Mormons head west. Settling in the barren valley near the Great Salt Lake, the Mormons struggled to make a living in the desert. In 1848 the vast region of 85,000 square miles was ceded to the U.S. by Mexico following the war. But during the summer of the following year the Mormons' first harvest was almost destroyed by vast swarms of crickets until thousands of sea gulls arrived to fill themselves on the crickets. Eventually the Mormons succeeded beyond imagination.

During the gold rush, streams of travelers passed through Utah. These emigrants were treated with suspicion; government officials claimed they were harassed. In 1849 the Mormons sought to join the Union as the State of Deseret, based on terms by Brigham Young. Taylor and Congress opposed the conditions, wanting to create Utah under the authority of the U.S. flag. The president also objected to several Mormon principles and personally mistrusted Young. The feeling was mutual: upon learning of the president's death, a delighted Brigham Young remarked, "Zachary Taylor is dead and in hell, and I am glad of it."[11] It would be almost five decades later before Utah became a state when Mormon leaders agreed to give up their practice of polygamy.

The middle part of the 19th century in America was basically a time of war, an expansion of our borders through Manifest Destiny, a period of restlessness, and a continuation of time honored traditions. There were, of course, exceptions to this state of affairs. While several social and political issues intensified, other controversies were either settled or suspended. But one thing remained constant—the American people, with their faith and trust in their democratic form of government, along with their innate will, were heading into an era of unprecedented growth, civil war, and greatness.

CHAPTER 12

Sunset and Darkness

Washington, D.C., was an unhealthy city. Citizens who could afford it often vacationed away from the Potomac River and its adjoining creeks. Summers were especially trying; people dumped their garbage and dead animals into the dirt streets or the rivers and creeks, polluting the air and the surrounding groundwater. Raw sewage flowed into the waters. The smell was so bad that the White House windows often had to be shut on warm days. Worse yet were the millions of insects which proliferated from the stagnant waters and spread disease, keeping the Washington's population from growing. Despite these conditions, the president walked freely in the area outside the White House grounds and was accustomed to all the city's defects.

On July 4, 1850, President Taylor attended a morning school recital then headed to the Independence Day celebration at the uncompleted Washington Monument. After the dedication ceremony, he decided to stay and listen to two other speakers who gave lengthy remarks. Sitting patiently on the platform, Taylor felt dizzy and had a headache. The day was cloudless and extremely warm and humid. For more than two hours the president sat unshielded in the sun, freely drinking from the pitchers of ice water provided to the guests. He then strolled around the site and along the banks of the Potomac, further exposing himself to the sun. He returned to the White House around 4:00 p.m.

Thirsty and hungry, Taylor ate a large portion of cold oranges, wild berries, cucumbers, and frozen cherries, washing them down with ice milk. Shortly after completing the meal, he ordered another helping. One servant saw Taylor eat a dead fly that had landed on a cucumber. Within an hour, Taylor developed severe cramps. The president also complained of a fever and went to bed.

The next day, July 5, the president gathered enough energy to take care of some business. He took time to pen a thank-you note to a friend who had sent him some salmon. He signed the Clayton-Bulwer Treaty then wrote a personal letter to E. P. Prentice of Albany, New York, sending his regrets that he could not attend the annual New York State Fair. This was his last correspondence as he became violently ill.

Doctor Alexander Weatherspoon, an army surgeon, diagnosed Taylor with cholera. The doctor gave Taylor opium and calomel, a mercury-based laxative. The president apparently rallied and the next day even conducted some minor business. Though he seemed to be improving, the infection was spreading throughout his body. He felt strong enough to complain that most of the criticism which had been directed toward him was unjust. "My motives have been misconstrued," he said, "and my feelings grossly betrayed."[1]

On the afternoon of July 5, he ran a high fever and experienced agonizing cramps again. Other physicians were sent for, including Taylor's son-in-law Dr. Wood and Dr. Thomas Miller. Miller applied the standard treatment of the day by bleeding his patient's veins and blistering his skin. Over the next two days, Taylor grew weaker from diarrhea and vomiting. Convinced he was dying, the depressed Taylor was given quinine and more calomel. News bulletins were issued every hour to an anxious nation.

Despite rumors of Taylor failing, there was politics as usual. Because of his decision to supply troops to New Mexico to prevent a takeover by Texas, Taylor had incurred the wrath of others besides Texans. Using the Galpin scandal and the Treasury Department dilemma as an excuse, 91 Congressmen passed a motion to censure the President. By Saturday, July 6, Taylor was feeling better, but four doctors noticed a change for the worse in his color and demeanor.

Adding to Taylor's declining health, typhoid apparently set in. Orderlies were posted at the White House doors to answer questions from reporters and concerned citizens. On the 8th Taylor, repeating a complaint made three days earlier, told a male nurse at his bedside, "I shall not be surprised if this were to terminate in my death. I did not expect to encounter what has come to me in this office. God knows I have tried to do my duty. But I have made mistakes. My motives have been misconstrued and my feelings have been outraged."[2] A bulletin was issued announcing Taylor was improving and out of danger. But again, his condition took a sharp turn for the worse.

On the afternoon of July 9, Taylor lay on his deathbed. Representatives Horace Mann of Massachusetts and Thomas Bayly of Virginia announced to their colleagues in the House of Representatives that they had just received news the president was dying. Webster disclosed the news in the Senate, and Congress was adjourned. Around 4:00 p.m. another bulletin reported that the president was improving. Church bells began to peal upon hearing the good news, and toward sunset boys built celebratory bonfires in the streets. By 7:30, however, the crowd in front of the White House was informed that Taylor was sinking. Asked by the doctors if he felt comfortable, Taylor said, "Very, but the storm in passing has swept away the trunk."[3] The president drifted in and out of consciousness.

Members of the Taylor family and friends Jefferson and Varina Davis gathered around Taylor's bed while Vice President Millard Fillmore and the cabinet gathered in the president's bedroom for a final visit. Other military and government officials arrived at the White House throughout the evening.

Taylor vomited green bile and he was given another dose of quinine. Again he was bled and blistered. A little after 10:00 p.m. President Taylor spoke with perfect clarity, saying, "I am about to die. I expect my summons very soon. I have tried to discharge my duties faithfully; I regret nothing, but I am sorry I am about to leave my friends."[4] After a couple minutes he turned toward his wife and tried to speak but couldn't. At 10:25 p.m. the twelfth President of the United States died. Peggy, who had fainted twice during the ordeal, became hysterical. She put her head on her husband's chest to listen for a heartbeat. She felt for his pulse and begged him to speak. Both she and her daughter Betty were led away by the Davises.

Just before midnight Millard Fillmore, waiting in his room at the Willard Hotel was given the news as he opened the door: "Sir, the painful duty devolves on us to announce to you that Zachary Taylor…is no more…We have the honor to be, very respectfully, your obedient servants." Fillmore replied, "I have no language to express the emotions of my heart…I am overwhelmed with grief…I shall communicate the sad intelligence to Congress and appoint a time for taking the oath.[5]

Millard Fillmore was sworn in as the 13th President of the United States fourteen hours after Taylor's death. At noon on July 10, his tribute to Zachary Taylor was read to the House of Representatives. Senator Thomas Hart Benton of Missouri declared that Taylor's death "was a public calamity. No man could have been more devoted to the Union, or more opposed to the slavery agitation."[6]

Peggy Taylor refused to permit a mortician to embalm her husband's body, nor did she allow a plaster death mask to be made of his face. She had the body packed in ice before it was displayed in an open casket in the East Room. The lead casket was enclosed by another one of mahogany with silver decorations on it. Three times the ice was removed so Peggy could view the body in private. Flowers covered the casket as thousands of mourners filed past. The flowers had to be replaced as viewers took them for mementoes. The rush of viewers was so great that people began pushing and shoving each other. When White House attendants warned the crowd that guards would be called in, order was restored. Peggy was so grief stricken she did not attend any of the services, though her grandsons did. She remained on the second floor of the White House with Varina Davis at her side.

On Saturday, July 13 the funeral service began. Reverend Smith Payne from St. John's Episcopal Church read from the 15th chapter of *Corinthians*. Reverend C. B. Butler, chaplain of the Senate, also officiated. After a lengthy service during which prayers were read and Scripture verses recited, U.S. Marines carried the coffin from the White House while two little girls Taylor had known, Emilie and Virginia Eberbach, sang sweetly.

Shortly after 1:00 p.m. the funeral entourage began its slow progress along Pennsylvania Avenue toward the Congressional Burying Ground. Among the twenty pallbearers were Senators Webster, Clay, Cass, and Benton. General Winfield Scott, who was in charge of the ceremony, rode at the head of the procession, which contained more than 100 carriages and stretched for two miles. Taylor's two grandsons, John Bliss and John Wood, rode with Secretary of the Navy Preston. John Taylor Wood (1830–1904), later served as an officer in the Confederate army and was aboard the *Merrimac* in 1862 during its encounter with the *Monitor*.

The day was warm and clear, with a gentle breeze giving some relief to the onlookers. The president's remains were placed on a hearse, its four large wheels painted black. Above the coffin was an arched canopy draped in black velvet and white satin. Overlooking the canopy was a carved, gilded eagle, and at each corner of the hearse stood a golden urn. Eight white horses with feathered plumes on their heads pulled the bier, while a Negro servant dressed in white walked slowly beside each horse. People openly wept and waved handkerchiefs as the body passed by. Perhaps the saddest site was Old Whitey, who trailed his master's coffin. The empty saddle had the president's boots placed backwards in the stirrups.

An estimated crowd of 100,000 people, the largest one ever to occupy Washington, D.C., lined the streets several rows deep, or peered from windows and rooftops to witness the spectacle. Sentries kept the crowd at a distance at the cemetery. Reverend Payne gave a fitting eulogy. The infantry and artillery fired three volleys each. Taylor's remains were lowered and after that, according to the *Washington Union* newspaper, the "valiant warrior was left sleeping, the sleep that knows no waking."[7]

Peggy Taylor may not have taken part in the service, but she could *hear it* while it was going on. According to Varina Davis, she "trembled silently from head to foot as one band after another blared the funeral march of the different organization, and the heavy guns boomed in quick succession to announce the final parting."[8]

There was hardly a dry eye in the city. Some mourners looked for a sign from God. At 4:30 a.m. the next day, after a brief thunderstorm and a single bolt of lightning, the skies suddenly parted during the sunrise and a brilliant rainbow seemed to rest on the White House, extending into the Potomac River.

Throughout the nation, church bells tolled and memorial services were held in every city and hamlet. Cannons on town squares were fired in salute. In the capital nearly every building was draped in black. The White House was swathed in ebony mourning cloth inside and out as President Fillmore declared six months of official mourning. The new president invited Peggy to stay at the White House, but she declined and moved in with the Davises.

Taylor's remains were put in a temporary vault in the Congressional Cemetery. Expenses paid by the United States for the ceremony totaled $3088.09, which included shaving and dressing the body. Three months later, on October 25, 1850, the sealed coffin was taken to Pittsburgh, then moved by a steamer to Louisville, Kentucky, and placed in what is today the Zachary Taylor National Cemetery. On May 6, 1926, the Taylors were moved to a final resting place into a mausoleum there. The cause of death may never be exactly known, but there is a strong indication that Taylor died from a combination of causes: cholera, food poisoning, pneumonia, and a weak heart. Some doctors today believe Taylor may have also suffered a ruptured appendix.

Beginning on July 20, 1850, the Taylor cabinet resigned and President Fillmore named his own appointments, with Daniel Webster as Secretary of State. Fillmore, like most vice presidents before him, had been relegated to less-than-cabinet status by the president. He had not been included in Taylor's council and sat on the sidelines where his skills, knowledge and experience remained untapped. Though Taylor and Fillmore had their differences, Fillmore tolerated a wide latitude of opinion among Whigs on the slavery issue and continued a policy of restraint and non-confrontation, though he too (like Taylor) would not sanction the South challenging federal authority.

Peggy departed Washington and stayed in Baltimore for three months, then with Betty and Ann moved into Richard Taylor's cottage in East Pascagoula, Mississippi. Without her husband by her side, she lost the will to live. Margaret Smith Taylor died on August 14, 1852. Her obituary in the *New York Tribune* did not even give her full name, referring to her only as "Mrs. General Taylor." Daughter Betty Bliss was certain her mother would die first; she wrote after the death of the president, "We had thought of our mother's dying, for she is…seldom well. But our father…we never expected to die!"[9] Peggy Taylor's body was taken to Louisville where she was buried next to her husband.

Taylor's estate, according to appraisers Maunsel White and Company, was valued at nearly $200,000, not including his property at the Fashion Plantation. The estate included his income-producing Louisville warehouses, a small lot there, 105 shares of the Bank of Louisville, $1700 from the sale of furniture in Washington, stock in the Western Bank of Baltimore, 30 shares in the Northern Bank of Kentucky, half of Cypress Grove, $18,000 in cash, 106 Negro slaves and six house servants.

Not long after Peggy's death, Richard Taylor sold Cypress Grove and its 131 slaves for $77,000 while the Taylor plantation at Fashion and its 64 slaves remained in Richard's name. Thus, the money and property were equally divided among Taylor's children. The president's private papers and personal effects also remained in the possession of his son Richard. These were destroyed when Union troops sacked Richard's plantation at Fashion during the Civil War in 1862. Taylor's clothing, relics, guns, field cooking utensils, old hats and private papers were taken by the invaders. Only a few items were ever recovered. Even the Cypress Grove location was destroyed in 1927 by the great flood.

Even in death Zachary Taylor remained restless—141 years after his passing, a woman named Clara Rising wrote a historical novel suggesting Taylor had been poisoned by political enemies. Following the advice of forensic experts, she secured permission from several of Taylor's descendants to exhume the body and have it examined for arsenic poisoning. A handful of direct descendants witnessed the event as a team of specialists dug up the unembalmed body.

The hermetically sealed coffin still bore remnants of the silver cords and blue braiding used to drape over it during Taylor's funeral. The coffin, however, proved difficult to open. After attempts with a torch failed, a power saw was used. Most of the remains inside were skeletal but there were still some hair and fingernails. After a careful investigation lasting a few days, doctors were able to prove what most historians believed all along—that Taylor had died of natural causes.

CHAPTER 13

Inspection and Judgment

On President James K. Polk's last day in office, March 5, 1849, he told his close associates and confided in his diary, "General Taylor is, I have no doubt, a well-meaning old man. He is, however, uneducated, exceedingly ignorant of public affairs, and, I should judge, of very ordinary capacity. He will be in the hands of others, and must rely wholly upon his cabinet to administer the government."[1] This assessment of course came from a man who saw his own popularity suffer at the expense of Taylor's rise in national prominence.

Zachary Taylor was one of the greatest field commanders of the nineteenth century. As a military leader he was bold, unorthodox, and possessed a singleness of purpose. Though he was often short on supplies, outnumbered by the enemy, and lacking the approval or support of authorities in the nation's capital, his daring exploits proved successful. Besides being an intelligent farmer—as president he advocated a Department of Agriculture—Taylor must also receive credit for playing a major role in helping to settle the frontier. His construction of forts, bridges, and roads, and his negotiation with numerous Indian tribes in addition to his military exploits, encouraged population growth and made the frontier safer for settlers. Due to his efforts, tens of thousands of pioneers trekked to the West. In addition, Taylor is the only president to have participated in four wars. As he had often observed, "My house was a tent, and my home the battlefield."[2]

General Taylor was thrust into the limelight by a country that was tired of seeing professional politicians become president. It was also an era when partisan politics became embedded in presidential politics, even in wartime. According to his own statement, Taylor did not even vote for himself in the 1848 election. Though he was labeled a "Cotton Whig" because of his Southern leanings, he professed little faith in politics. As president, he refused to accept the doctrine of legislative dominance, something Senator Henry Clay had not expected.

During his time in office, Taylor failed to build support in Congress and neglected to communicate with lawmakers. This lack of cooperation between the executive and legislative branches of government resulted in problems. And like most of his predecessors, President Taylor put little faith in his vice president. He looked upon Fillmore as an *ex-officio* member of the cabinet and relied on his input only sparingly. Fillmore had battled with Weed and Seward, and lost, over patronage in the state of New York, and jockeying for position as to who had the president's ear. The patronage issue changed of course when Fillmore became president.

Taylor delegated some responsibilities to his cabinet which, in retrospect, he should have handled himself. But he did so with caution, picking and choosing the issue depending on its severity. He had a healthy mistrust of political tricksters and "their obvious forms of nonsense."[3] He also could have taken stronger action on a number of issues. In a country obsessed with the quagmire over slavery, Taylor did little to resolve the problem, perhaps hoping the predicament would either disappear or cure itself. One achievement largely overlooked, however, was Taylor's ability to keep the nation from being ensnarled in foreign disputes while maintaining prestige among European powers.

In June of 1850, just a month prior to his death, one influential Democratic editorial noted: "And what has he done? If he has not fed the fire or blown the coals of dissension,…he has stood looking on as an idle spectator by abdicating his authority to those who it would appear or afraid or ashamed of the responsibility of its exercise in anything but removing officers and settling old accounts. A man so brave on the battlefield as General Taylor should exhibit such a cowardly will in the cabinet."[4]

One eminent historian observed, "Now he was dead; his colorless successor commanded no enthusiasm and the Whig Party, without ideas or a commanding new leader, and with a deep split between the slave South and Seward's disciples in the North, held a forlorn position."[5]

Taylor's comrade-in-arms General Winfield Scott provided a fitting tribute following the president's death: "This old soldier and neophyte statesman had the basis of great character—pure, uncorrupted morals, combined with indomitable courage...With a good store of common sense, General Taylor's mind had not been enlarged by reading or much converse with the world...Kind, sincere, and hospitable in a plain way, he had no vices but prejudice, many friends, and left behind him not an enemy in the world."[6] Scott's comments differed greatly from ones made three years earlier when both men were being considered as presidential nominees and Scott said of Taylor, "Old Zack is a good old soul but don't know himself from a side of sole leather in the way of statesmanship."[7]

Taylor's achievements as a president have been overlooked by some historians. It is true he leaned heavily on the advice of others because he realized he lacked political experience. Political leaders at the time of his death differed much on Taylor's actions in office. Some believed that, had he lived, the nation would have witnessed a civil war. Others felt he was responsible for preventing it.

President Zachary Taylor knew his limitations. Before a large crowd during his inaugural address he had remarked, "I am conscious that the position which I have been called to fill, though sufficient to satisfy the loftiest ambition, is surrounded by fearful responsibilities." But Taylor grew statesmanlike in stature under his new burdens of office as chief executive. And though both friends and critics knew that anyone could advise him, no one could sway him to act against his conscience. Since he didn't live to complete his term, we will never know if he could have achieved greatness.

It may be argued that Taylor failed to develop a broad objective in his handling of foreign policy matters. He relied heavily upon his Secretary of State John Clayton, even in matters which were non-diplomatic. Clayton, as well as other cabinet members, used their position to promote their own ideas on patronage, as Taylor felt uneasy about firing minor officeholders for political reasons. On the other hand, the nation experienced an era of peace, if not total tranquility, during Taylor's term as president as he took a strong stand in protecting American interests abroad.

When the Union armies occupied and ransacked Taylor's plantations during the Civil War (because his son Richard was a general for the Confederacy), a number of documents and papers, along with family heirlooms, were either carted away or destroyed. Important letters and documents which may have shed more light on Taylor's life may never be found.

Zachary Taylor "is remembered for his consistent and unyielding opposition to the Compromise of 1850, a congeries of legislative measures designed to pressure a temporary peace on the slavery issue…the president stood firm against Southern threats of disunion."[8]

Though there are only a few busts and statues of Taylor in the country (one statue is located in Green Bay, Wisconsin), the people of the United States and the federal government have not forgotten him. His likeness can be found on commemorative coins and on at least three occasions he has been depicted on postage stamps, including a 5-cent one in 1875 and later on a 12-cent stamp in 1938. Tourists today can travel on the Zachary Taylor Parkway in Louisiana, visit the Taylor memorial in Galveston, Texas, or sojourn to the Fort Zachary Taylor State Park in Key West, Florida, where every November 24 the city celebrates Zachary Taylor Day. In 1942 a Liberty ship, the *S.S. Zachary Taylor* was commissioned and sailed the Atlantic during World War II. It was scrapped in 1961. In addition, some veteran organizations and the National Cemetery in Louisville, Kentucky, have also been named in his honor.

One contemporary who knew him well, educator and former Congressman Horace Mann, wrote, "He really is a most simple minded old man. He has the least show or pretension of any man I ever saw; talks as artlessly as a child about affairs of state, and does not seem to pretend to a knowledge of anything of which he is ignorant. He is a remarkable man in some respects; and it is remarkable that such a man should be President of the United States."[9]

One biographer of Taylor summed up his career in another perspective. John Eisenhower, a West Point graduate, World War II veteran, former ambassador and son of the 34th President, made the following observation in his book about Taylor: "Presidents are inevitably remembered far less for the abilities of the men occupying the office than for the magnitude of the events that happened during their administrations. Sometimes mediocre men are given undeserved status because significant events transpired during their presidencies, whereas very capable men are often overlooked because no great events happened during their terms in office. Taylor fell into the second category and therefore has been generally underrated as a president."[10]

Abraham Lincoln may not have realized his own potential in 1850, but he did recognize Taylor's invaluable service when he stated, "It did not happen to General Taylor, once in his life, to fight a battle on equal terms, or on terms advantageous to himself; and yet he was never beaten, and he never retreated…General Taylor's battles were not distinguished for brilliant military; but in all he seems rather to have conquered by the exercise of a sober and steady judgment, coupled with a dogged incapacity to understand that defeat was possible."[11]

Though temperamental, Taylor was man of integrity and a staunch supporter of the Constitution. He was a product of his times. Perhaps *New York Tribune* editor Horace Greeley summed it up best on July 10, 1850, when he described Taylor as "A Southern man and slaveholder, his mind was above the narrow prejudices of district and class and steadily aimed at the good of the nation as a whole."[12] Though his time in office was cut short, he left a legacy of great service to his country as a soldier and as president.

Zachary Taylor Chronology

1784   Born Nov. 24 near Barboursville, Virginia

1806   Joins the militia at age 22

1810   Marries Margaret Mackall Smith on June 21; promoted to rank of army captain

1811   Daughter Ann Margaret born on April 9 (died December 2, 1875)

1812   Defends Fort Harrison against Indians led by Tecumseh; promoted to major for gallantry

1814   Daughter Sarah Knox born on March 6, 1814; married Jefferson Davis and died a few months later

1815   Resigned from army and built a home near Louisville, Kentucky

1816   Reinstated as a major in the army; daughter Octavia born on August 16 (died July 8, 1820); assigned to Green Bay in the Wisconsin Territory

1819   Commissioned a lieutenant colonel; daughter Margaret Smith born on July 27 (died October 22, 1820)

1820   Malaria strikes the entire family; two small daughters die

1822   Taylor's mother Sarah dies

1824   Daughter Mary Elizabeth (Betty) born on April 24 (died July 26, 1909)

1826 Son Richard born on January 27, 1826 (died April 12, 1879)

1829 Taylor's father Richard dies in Kentucky on January 19

1831 Purchases 137 acres of land next to his plantation in Wilkinson County, Mississippi

1832 Promoted to colonel; receives surrender of Chief Black Hawk

1835 Daughter Sarah dies of malaria after three months of marriage to Jefferson Davis (September 15)

1837 Defeats Seminoles in battle at Lake Okeechobee in Florida (December 25)

1838 Promoted to brigadier general and overall commander in Florida

1840 Relieved of Florida command upon request; took charge of forces at Baton Rouge (May 6)

1845 Polk puts Taylor in command of the Army of Observation (3500 men) and sends him to Texas

1846 Mexican War begins on April 26; Taylor wins several battles

1847 Defeats Santa Anna at Battle of Buena Vista (February 24)

1848 Nominated by the Whigs for president; elected president

1849 Officially resigned from the army (January 23); inaugurated as president on March 5

1850 Purchases Fashion Plantation; died in Washington on July 9

Timeline 1848–1850 (beginning with Taylor's nomination for president)

1848

Feb. 22 A Louisiana convention formally proposes Zachary Taylor as a candidate for president

Feb. 23 President Polk submits the Treaty of Guadalupe-Hidalgo to the Senate

Jan. 24 Gold discovered in California at Sutter's Mill

May 22 Democratic Convention meets in Baltimore, nominating Lewis Cass of Michigan for president

May 29   Wisconsin is admitted as the 30th state

June 7   Whig Convention in Philadelphia nominates Taylor for president and Fillmore for vice president

June 10   New York City and Chicago are linked by telegraph wires

July 4   President Polk lays the cornerstone of the Washington Monument

July 19   First women's rights convention is held in Seneca Falls, New York (300 men and women attend)

Aug. 9   The Free Soil Party, meeting in Utica, New York, nominates ex-president Van Buren and Charles Francis Adams on their ticket

Aug. 14   Oregon Territory established by Congress

Nov. 7   Zachary Taylor is elected as the 12th president

Dec. 29   Gas lights are installed in the White House

1849

Jan. 23   Elizabeth Blackwell becomes the first female to receive a medical degree (Geneva College in New York)

March 3   Minnesota becomes a territory; the Department of the Interior is created

March 5   Zachary Taylor sworn in as president

May 17   Docked steamboat catches fire in St. Louis destroying 400 buildings and 25 steamships

June 15   Former president Polk dies in Nashville

July 12   Former first lady Dolley Madison dies in Washington

Oct. 7   Author Edgar Allan Poe dies in Baltimore at age 40

Nov. 13   California voters approve a state constitution

Dec. 6   Negro slave and abolitionist Harriet Ross Tubman escapes from Maryland

1850

Jan. 29   Senator Henry Clay introduces a compromise bill on the issue of slavery

March 7   Senator Daniel Webster introduces the Compromise of 1850 in a three hour speech

March 16   Hawthorne's *Scarlet Letter* is published (4000 copies quickly sold)

March 19   American Express Company founded by Henry Wells and William Fargo

April 15   The city of San Francisco is incorporated

April 19   The U.S. and Great Britain agree on terms in the Clayton-Bulwer Treaty

June 3   Delegates from nine Southern states gather at the Nashville Convention to defend slavery

July 9   Zachary Taylor dies in the White House

Chapter Notes

Chapter 1. Common Threads

1. Rick Beyer, *The Greatest Presidential Stories Never Told* (HarperCollins, New York, 2007), p. 59.

Chapter 2. Disobeying Orders

1. Jack K. Bauer, *Zachary Taylor: Soldier, Planter, Statesman of the Old Southwest* (Baton Rouge: Louisiana State University Press, 1985), p. 186.

2. David R. Collins, *Zachary Taylor—12th President of the United States* (Ada, Oklahoma: Garrett Educational Corporation, 1989), p. 79.

3. Holman Hamilton, *Zachary Taylor—Soldier of the Republic* (Norwalk, Connecticut: The Eaton Press, 1941), p. 231.

4. Hamilton, p. 226.

5. Collins, p. 80.

6. Oliver Otis Howard, *General Taylor* (New York: D. Appleton and Company, 1892), pp. 246–247.

7. Richard L. McElroy, *American Presidents and First Ladies, Vol. III.* (Canton, Ohio: Gillilan Enterprises, 2001), p. 40; Collins, p. 80.

8. McElroy, *Vol. III*, p. 50.

9. John S. D. Eisenhower, *Zachary Taylor* (New York, Time Books, 2007), p. 69.

10. Bauer, p. 205.

11. Holman, p. 244.

12. Taylor letter to Jefferson Davis, August 16, 1847 (compliments of Harold "Skip" Hensel).

Chapter 3. Ancestry and Boyhood

1. Cranston Jones, *Houses of the American Presidents* (New York: McGraw-Hill Book Company, 1962), p. 90.

2. William A. DeGregorio, *The Complete Book of U.S. Presidents* (New York: Dembner Books, 1984), p. 177.

3. Collins, p. 7.

4. Richard L. McElroy, *American Presidents* (Canton, Ohio: Daring Publishing Group, 1992), p. 48.

5. Collins, p. 9.

Chapter 4. The Military and Matrimony

1. Hamilton, p. 36.

2. Collins, p. 20.

3. Howard, pp. 36–37.

Chapter 5. A Series of Ups and Downs

1. Hamilton, p. 52.

2. Collins, p. 32.

3. Ibid., p. 35.

4. Hamilton, p. 59.

Chapter 6. Summoned Again

1. Hamilton, p. 64.

2. Mary Ormsbee Whitton, *First First Ladies 1781–1865*. (New York: Hastings House Publishers, 1948), p. 223.

3. Bauer, p. 37.

4. Hamilton, p. 69.

5. McElroy (*Vol. IV*), p. 42.

6. Hamilton, p. 73.

7. Collins, p. 41.

Chapter 7. Fighting, Farming, and Family

1. Bauer, p. 58.

2. Hamilton, p. 68.

3. Collins, p. 44.

4. Ibid., p. 48.

5. Hamilton, p. 101.

6. James Deem, *Zachary Taylor* (Berkeley Heights, New Jersey: Enslow Publishers, Inc., 2002), p. 24.

7. Silas Bent McKinley and Silas Bent, *Old Rough and Ready* (New York: The Vanguard Press, 1946), p. 99.

8. Bliss Isley, *The Presidents: Men of Faith* (Natick, Massachusetts: W. A. Wilde Company, 1961), p. 94.

9. Ibid., p. 95.

10. Webb Garrison, *A Treasury of White House Tales* (Nashville: Rutledge Hill Press, 1989), p. 205.

Chapter 8. The Mexican War

1. Eisenhower, p. 34.

2. McElroy, *Vol. III*, p. 107.

3. Page Smith, *The Nation Comes of Age Vol. IV* (New York: McGraw Hill Book Company, 1981), p. 227.

4. Eisenhower, p. 49.

5. McElroy, *Vol. II*, p. 107.

6. Howard, p. 109.

7. McKinley and Bent, p. 151.

8. Ibid, pp. 128–129.

9. H. Montgomery, *Major General Zachary Taylor* (Auburn, New York: Derby, Miller & Company, 1850), p. 241.

10. McKinley and Bent, p. 156.

11. Smith, p. 225.

12. Bauer, p. 208.

13. Frank Freidel, *Our Country's Presidents* (Washington, D.C.: National Geographic Society Press, 1981), p. 82.

14. Letter from Taylor to Reynolds, dated November 25, 1847, now in possession of Harold "Skip" Hensel of Metairie, Louisiana.

15. Freidel, p. 80.

16. Encyclopedia Brittanica, *Annals of America, Vol. 7* (Chicago and London: William Benton Publishers, 1968), p. 422.

Chapter 9. Politician Candidate

1. Douglas G. Brinkley and Stephen E. Ambrose, *The Mississippi and the Making of a Nation: The Louisiana Purchase to Today* (Washington, D.C.: National Geographic, 2002), p. 40.

2. H. Montgomery, p. 374.

3. Ibid., p. 384.

4. McKinley and Bent, p. 216.

5. Letter from Taylor to Haslett dated March 26, 1848, now in the possession of Harold "Skip" Hensel of Metairie, Louisiana.

6. Edward Allen, *Horace Greeley* (Chicago, Brittanica Books, 1962), p. 77.

7. Robert J. Rayback, *Millard Fillmore: Biography of a President* (Buffalo, New York, Buffalo Historical Society and Henry Stewart, 1959), p. 184.

8. Letter from Taylor to Wiley dated August 5, 1848, now in possession of Harold "Skip" Hensel.

9. McKinley and Bent, p. 216.

10. Collins, p. 93.

11. Paul F. Boller Jr., *Presidential Campaigns* (New York and Oxford: Oxford University Press, 1996), p. 85.

12. Holman, p. 99.

13. Paul F. Boller Jr., *Presidential Wives: An Anecdotal History* (New York and Oxford: Oxford University Press, 1988), p. 95.

14. Glenn D. Kittler, *Hail To The Chief!* (New York: Chilton Book Company, 1968), p. 61.

15. Boller, *Presidential Wives: An Anecdotal History*, p. 97.

16. Carl Anthony, *First Ladies* (New York: William Morrow, 1990), p. 147.

17. Collins, p. 92.

18. Garrison, p. 117.

19. B. S. McReynolds, *Presidential Blips: Dips, Flips, Lip, Pips, Quips, Rips, Slips, Tips, and Zips!* (University City, California: B S Book Publishing, 1998), p. 226.

20. Bauer, p. 251.

21. Edward Allen, p. 99.

Chapter 10. Chief Executive

1. Glenn Kittler, *Hail to The Chief!* (New York: Kittler), p. 63.

2. McKinley and Bent, p. 226.

3. Ibid., p. 228.

4. James M. McPherson, *"To the Best of My Ability"—The American Presidents* (New York: A Dorling Kindersley Book, 2000), p. 355.

5. Kittler, p. 63.

6. Ibid., p. 64.

7. Robert C. Post, ed., *Every Four Years* (New York, Smithsonian Books & W. W. Norton, 1984), p. 144.

8. Robert Ketchum, *Faces from the Past* (New York: American Heritage Press,1970), p. 73.

9. Collins, p. 107.

10. James Ford Rhodes, *History of the United States, Vol. I* (New York: Harper & Brothers Publishers), p. 102.

11. Boller, *Presidential Wives*, p. 36 and Richard L. McElroy, p. 83.

12. McElroy, *Vol. IV*, p. 42.

13. McKinley and Bent, p. 265.

14. Ibid., p. 264.

15. Page Smith, p. 1065.

16. Betty Boyd Caroli, *First Ladies* (New York and Oxford: Oxford University Press, 1987), p. 48.

17. Boller, *Presidential Wives*, p. 97.

18. McElroy, *Vol. II*, p. 44.

19. Collins, p. 108.

20. Ibid., p. 100.

21. Taylor letter to Jefferson Davis, August 16, 1847 (compliments of Harold "Skip" Hensel).

22. Lorant, p. 202.

23. McKinley and Bent, p. 282.

24. Ibid, p. 283.

25. William Seale, *The President's House: A History* (Washington, D.C.: White House Historical Association, 1986), p. 287.

26. The Magazine *Antiques* (New York, New York, February, 1983), p. 290.

27. Elsie Kirk, *Music at the White House* (Urbana, Illinois: University of Illinois Press, A Barra Foundation Book, 1986), p. 64.

Chapter 11. President Taylor's America

1. Page Smith, p. 790.

2. Ibid., p. 18.

3. Ibid., p. 640.

4. Roger Matuz, *The Presidents Fact Book* (New York: Black Dog and Leventhal Publishers, 2004), p. 210.

5. Page Smith, p. 724.

6. Ibid., p. 1066.

7. Ibid., p. 740.

8. David M. Potter, *The Impending Crisis* 1848–1861 (New York: Harper and Row, Publishers, 1976), p. 87.

9. Smith, p. 857.

10. Eisenhower, p. 140.

11. J. C. Furnas, The *Americans: A Social History of the United States 1587–1914* (New York: G. P. Putnam's Sons, 1969), p. 457.

12. Roger Matuz, p. 206.

Chapter 12. Sunset and Darkness

1. Freidel, p. 80.

2. James Ford Rhodes, p. 176 and McKinley and Bent, p. 286.

3. Henry Montgomery, *The Life of Major-General Zachary Taylor* (Philadelphia: Porter & Coates, 1851), p. 429.

4. Oliver Otis Howard, *General Taylor* (New York: D. Appleton and Company, 1892), p. 373.

5. Hamilton, pp. 393–394.

6. DeGregorio, p. 184.

7. Hamilton, p. 398.

8. C. Brian Kelly, *Best Little Stories from The White House* (Nashville, Cumberland House Press, 1999), p. 271.

9. Boller, p. 97.

Chapter 13. Inspection and Judgment

1. Elizabeth Frost, ed. *The Bully Pulpit: Quotations from America's Presidents* (New York, Facts on File Publications, 1988), p. 239.

2. Kittler, p. 60.

3. McPherson, p. 96.

4. Encyclopedia Brittanica, *The Annals of America, Vol. 8* (Chicago and London: William Benton, Publishers, 1968), p. 66.

5. Allan Nevins, *Ordeal of the Union: Fruits of Manifest Destiny* (New York: Charles Scribner's Sons, 1947), p. 3.

6. G. S. Weaver, *The Lives and Graves of Our Presidents* (Chicago: Elder Publishing Company, 1884), p. 342.

7. Nevins, p. 229 and DeGregorio, p. 184.

8. Miller and Nelson, p. 141.

9. Richard Kenin and Justin Wintle, *Dictionary of Biographical Quotation* (New York: Alfred A. Knopf, 1978), p. 726.

10. DeGregorio, p. 184.

11. Elbert B. Smith, *The Presidencies of Zachary Taylor and Millard Fillmore* (Lawrence, Kansas: University of Kansas Press, 1988), p. 158.

Other sources for this book include the following works:

James Truslow Adams, *The Epic of America* (New York: Triangle Books), 1931.

Thomas A. Bailey, *Presidential Saints and Sinners* (New York: The Free Press), 1981.

Allan W. Eckert, *The Frontiersmen* (Boston: Little, Brown and Company), 1967.

James D. Horan, *Mathew Brady: Historian with A Camera* (New York: Bonanza Books), 1955.

Richard Kenin and Justin Wintle, *Dictionary of Biographical Quotation* (New York: Alfred A. Knopf), 1978.

William S. McFeely, *Grant: A Biography* (New York: W. W. Norton & Company), 1981.

Elbert B. Smith, *President Zachary Taylor: The Hero President* (Hauppauge, New York: Nova Science Publishers, Inc.), 2007.

Robert C. Toll, *On With The Show* (New York: Oxford University Press), 1976.

David C. Whitney, *The American Presidents* (Garden City, New York: Doubleday & Company, Inc.), 1969.

John Hoyt Williams, *Sam Houston* (New York: Promontory Press), 1998.

Garry Wills, *Inventing America* (Garden City, New York: Doubleday & Company, Inc.), 1978.

PART II

BENJAMIN HARRISON: Hoosier Hero

Introduction

SOMEWHERE IN THAT CLUSTER OF BEARDED AND MUSTACHIOED CHIEF EXECUTIVES, between Lincoln and William Howard Taft, lies one of the country's most underestimated and less known leaders. His name is Benjamin Harrison. He is usually ranked by presidential scholars and historians as a slightly above average president. And to those lovers of American history and devotees of White House minutia who recognize his name, they know that he had a grandfather who also served as president, be it ever so briefly.

A closer look at this man, our 23rd President, will reveal a person of unique character and bearing. Harrison was ambitious, austere, formal, independent, resolute, demanding, rock-solid honest, calm, and at times, uncommunicative and humorless. Harrison was a brilliant attorney, gallant soldier, devoted husband and father, active patriot, and innovator and a true conservationist. He was among the first chief executives, next to Lincoln, to recognize abuses in the environment and take steps to preserve our national and natural heritages, despite violent protests from corporations, mining and lumber interests, and farmers. In addition, Harrison denounced the excesses of the monopolies and business trusts, and initiated steps to curb their corrupt power and influence.

Viewed by some scholars as a weak president, it is true that Benjamin Harrison was satisfied not to go beyond his legal duties in working with the other branches of government. He headed an administration which was sound and relatively free of scandal, for only a trace of corruption touched any of Harrison's cabinet or his federal departments, though the same may not be said of several members of Congress at the time.

Harrison was the first chief executive to preside over a national budget of $1 billion. The first part of his term was identified with the "Billion Dollar Congress." And when critics and Democrats used this nickname to deride Harrison and the Republicans in the House, Speaker Thomas Reed retorted, "This is a billion dollar country!"

Little is remembered today that Harrison was also the author of two books, one of them a best seller entitled *This Country of Ours*. It is a most remarkable work on the American system of government. First published as articles in the *Ladies Home Journal*, Harrison said he wrote it "to give a better knowledge of things that have been too near and familiar to be well known. We stumble over things that are near our toes." Probably only the works of professor Woodrow Wilson and statesman Thomas Jefferson equal its depth and influence.

Harrison was *not* a man of contradictions. He was consistent and true to his ideals. He had, like all of us, flaws in his character and these defects most likely cost him politically and in terms of popularity (not that the latter mattered much after he became president). He safeguarded those things he cared for and lived a exemplary life to establish a lasting reputation as a leader.

Benjamin Harrison's tenure in the White House was not one of fondest memories for him. Seeing the death of his wife, father-in-law, other relatives and close friends, and the near fatal illness of several youngsters in his family, he may have felt his presidency was too great a burden. Just three weeks after leaving office, Harrison wrote a friend, "The White House was a hard place on the nerves for children as well as grown people. If I had been there much longer I am sure I should have broken down."

Harrison's first Secretary of State James G. Blaine described him as "a man with whom nothing is gained by argument or urgency at the wrong time." Henry Adams, direct descendant of John Adams and a Pulitzer-prize-winning historian, noted that Benjamin Harrison was "perhaps the best president the Republican Party had put forward since Lincoln's death." These views differ greatly from those of Theodore Roosevelt, who had nothing but contempt for Harrison.

This is his story.

CHAPTER 1

Following in Grandpa's Footsteps

IT WAS A SUNNY DAY IN MID-NOVEMBER OF 1840. LITTLE BEN HARRISON, JUST seven years old, was walking along the streets of Cincinnati, Ohio, holding his grandfather's hand. Grandpa was William Henry Harrison, who had just defeated Martin Van Buren to become the ninth President of the United States. This was William Henry Harrison's second attempt at the presidency, having been defeated in 1836 by Van Buren.

Harrison's presidential campaign slogan "Tippecanoe and Tyler Too," along with symbols of the log cabin and the raccoon, generated great excitement. Cincinnati admirers and well-wishers stopped President-elect Harrison several times to congratulate him. As the crowd grew larger, young Ben walked over to an apple stand, filled his pockets, and took a bite from an extra apple. The woman in back of the stand said nothing until the Harrisons began to leave. She then yelled, "That boy did not pay me!" William Henry Harrison turned in surprise, walked over to the woman, and placed a coin in her hand. Benjamin was not punished, however, because at his North Bend, Ohio, home anyone could have as many apples as they wanted for free. The Harrison orchards provided enough apples to hand out to the throngs of visitors who often stopped there. Benjamin said to his grandfather, "I didn't know apples ever cost money, Grandpa."[1]

The ninth president was in office only one month. After giving a two-hour inaugural address of 48 pages, in blustery, freezing weather without wearing an overcoat or hat, 69-year-old William Henry Harrison caught a cold. His condition worsened when he insisted on doing some shopping and got caught in a rainstorm, in which he got completely soaked. Refusing the advice of a servant to change into dry clothes, he continued to sit before a fire.

A combination of pneumonia, poor medical treatment and the constant crush of office-seekers prevented him from getting the rest and cure he so badly needed. Harrison died just after midnight on April 4, 1841. He was buried in Washington until June when his remains were removed to his beloved Ohio home. His wife Anna, who had been making preparations when she learned of her husband's death, never served in the White House.

William Henry Harrison's estate was located at North Bend, about twelve miles southwest of Cincinnati. He owned 2,800 acres of land and a sixteen-room mansion he called "The Big House." A six hundred acre farm owned by his son, John Scott Harrison, adjoined their property. John's home was located on a five-mile strip of land near the mouth of the Big Miami River, which flows into the Ohio. Where the Big Miami on the north side of the land met the Ohio River on the south, is where the property ended. The western edge of the property bordered the state of Indiana. John Harrison settled on a 600-acre stretch of land on the peninsula he called "The Point" and built a two-story brick house. The house had a large dining room which faced the broad Ohio River. Nearby was a small graveyard surrounded by fields and dense forest. Unfortunately the house was torn down in 1959.

The lush green valleys and gently rolling hills of southwestern Ohio provided its inhabitants with many opportunities. Rich soil and numerous creeks and rivers, combined with a growing season of seven months, made it possible for farmers to do well. The environment lent itself to manufacturing and trade, and two generations of Harrisons took advantage of this location.

Ben's father, John, had served two terms as a member of the U.S. House of Representatives. He came to dislike the nature of politics and turned once again to his mainstay of farming. He raised sheep, cattle, hogs, chickens, and turkeys. He grew corn, wheat, and hay. His orchards yielded peaches and apples. John Scott might be seen taking a boatload of livestock and goods down the river to sell in New Orleans. Some of his corn crop was sold to whiskey makers in Lawrenceburg, Indiana, just five miles away.

The Harrison family of the early 1800s was land rich but cash poor. Markets for their products were often unpredictable. Fluctuating farm prices, frequent floods, droughts, and the constant sickness of a large family forced John Harrison to take out loans, using his property for collateral. On more than one occasion the Harrison family faced bankruptcy. Evidence of this appears in a letter John wrote in 1850 to his brother-in-law John Cleves Short, requesting a loan of three thousand dollars and putting up four hundred acres of land as security. Describing his unpaid bills as "unpleasant embarrassments," he further explained, "Some months ago I mentioned my troubles to Judge Hart and he advised me to sell my farm and come to the city and live—sell my farm, I really would, but what could I do in the city? I could not feed myself much less my children. Besides I am miserable enough here and I should be more so there."[2]

This ongoing struggle for survival was hidden from young Benjamin Harrison, for he spent his early days as a boy both working and having fun, though there were few luxuries. He often assisted the black servants who worked in the household by stacking wood, carrying water, cleaning dishes and even helping the women as their spinning wheels turned constantly to make clothing. Benjamin was up by 5:00 each morning to do his chores. Feeding animals, tending crops, milking cows, making tallow candles and husking corn meant long hours of hard work. According to one friend, Benjamin "used to go to the mill on a sack of wheat or corn and balance it over the horse's back by getting on one end of it, holding on to the horse's mane while he was going up the hill."[3]

But there also was time for some play. Ben liked to run and swim. Always accompanied by an adult, he also loved to fish and hunt (especially ducks and squirrels). With other boys, Ben played childhood games such as poison, prisoner's base, town ball (a form of baseball), and old witch. One playmate recalled, "Ben had the usual number of stone bruises and stubbed toes and the average number of nails in his foot."[4]

Young Ben Harrison spent many happy hours at The Point and at his grandparents' home nearby. The chubby, blond-haired boy recalled years later this idyllic life on the farm. Though he was destined for greatness, there were no early indications to suggest it, in spite of the fact that his grandfather was president. Ben's ambition as a young man was to become either a minister or lawyer.

He grew up in the shadow of his famous grandfather, William Henry Harrison. Years later, during his term as a United States Senator, Benjamin Harrison had a specially-framed parchment mounted on his Indianapolis home library wall. It was a document confirming the election of William Henry Harrison as President of the United States, dated 1841 and signed by Vice President Richard Johnson. This, along with other family keepsakes and photographs, served as a constant reminder of the family heritage.

Chapter 2

Ancestry and Youth

From the time he could remember, Benjamin Harrison took pride in learning about the background of his ancestors. He had a right to be proud, for his family tree was made up of a list of imposing characters. If every family has a hero and a horse thief in its lineage, and the Harrisons were no exception, then there were indeed a couple rogues in his heritage.

Through his paternal great grandmother, Anne Carter Harrison, Benjamin was a descendant of King Henry III of England (1207–1272). The Carters emigrated to Virginia where they became wealthy landowners. Also on his maternal side of the family were the Bassets of Virginia and the Irwins of Pennsylvania, but not much is known of these families. The Harrisons were also distant cousins to Richard Taylor, whose son Zachary became the 12th U.S. President. In addition, Benjamin Harrison was a fifth cousin to John Tyler, fourth cousin to Lyndon B. Johnson, and distantly related to William Howard Taft and Calvin Coolidge.

Another of Harrison's distant relatives was Thomas Harrison, a resident of Staffordshire, England, and a military leader who became a member of Great Britain's House of Commons in 1649. During a civil war Oliver Cromwell gained control of the parliamentary army and after four years of fighting, arrested King Charles I. Harrison commanded the guard which brought

Charles I to London for trial and he voted for the king's execution. Charles I was beheaded in 1649. General Harrison initially supported Cromwell but after Cromwell's death, he fell out of favor with both Cromwell's son Richard and later, Charles the II, who assumed the throne in 1660. Harrison, an outspoken Presbyterian, was imprisoned four different times and was finally tried for treason on suspicion of taking part in various plots to overthrow the king. On October 13, 1660, Thomas Harrison was hanged, drawn, and quartered at Charring Cross. Eventually, each of Thomas' six grandsons moved to America where they all served in the Revolutionary War.

Also on his paternal side of the family, the 23rd president was preceded by six other Benjamin Harrisons. The first one, the president's great, great, great grandfather, came to America around 1632 and settled in the Tidewater region of Virginia. He served as a clerk in the Virginia Council and became a wealthy landowner. His son Benjamin II (the president's great, great grandfather) served in the House of Burgesses off and on from 1680 to 1698, and later in the Virginia Council until 1712. His son, Benjamin III became attorney-general of Virginia in 1702 and continued as a land owner and planter.

Benjamin Harrison IV, the president's great grandfather, served as a colonel in the state militia and was elected county sheriff and to the House of Burgesses. On July 12, 1745, during a violent thunderstorm, Benjamin and two daughters were killed when lightning struck their house at Berkeley Plantation. His son, Benjamin V inherited a vast estate and slaves.

Berkeley, incidentally, became known for other events. President Abraham Lincoln visited the estate twice, conferring with General George McClellan and reviewing troops. And it was at Berkeley where "TAPS" was composed in 1862.

It was Benjamin Harrison V who added a star quality to the family genealogy. Born in Charles City County, Virginia, he too served in the House of Burgesses, from 1748–1775. On February 7, 1775, Harrison, under the command of Colonel William Crawford, led a squad of militia into Pittsburgh where fighting had broken out between Virginians and Pennsylvanians over a land dispute. Harrison used a sledge hammer to break down the door of a jail, freeing three Virginia prisoners.

As Great Britain continued to tax the colonists, Harrison denounced the Stamp Act and other British policies. And as a member of the Continental Congress, he was one of seven Virginians to sign the Declaration of Independence. He resigned from Congress to take a seat in the Virginia

House of Delegates. When he ran for reelection in 1784 he was defeated by John Tyler, father of the future tenth president. He decided to run again, this time from a neighboring district, was elected, and served until his death in 1791.

The youngest son of Benjamin V, William Henry Harrison, entered the Sydney-Hampton premedical school at age 14 (his brother Benjamin VI was a paymaster general with the Continental army during the Revolutionary War). While attending the medical college at the University of Pennsylvania in Philadelphia, William learned of his father's death. That same year he dropped out of school and joined the army, later moving to the area around Fort Washington in Cincinnati, Ohio. William Henry Harrison was an outstanding soldier and married Anna Symmes, the daughter of a judge. Together they had ten children, one of them being John Harrison, the father of the 23rd president.

Benjamin Harrison entered the world on August 20, 1833. Born to John Scott Harrison and Elizabeth Irwin Harrison, he was the fifth of his father's thirteen children and the second of ten children from a second marriage. Ben was born in "The Big House" of his grandparents, and named for his great-grandfather. His day of birth was significant in that August 20 marked the thirty-ninth anniversary of General Anthony Wayne's victory over the Indians at the Battle of Fallen Timbers in 1794. One of Wayne's best soldiers at that battle was Ben's grandfather, William Henry Harrison.

By his father's first marriage, Ben Harrison had two older half sisters who lived to maturity. These were Elizabeth "Betsey" Eaton and Sarah "Sallie" Devin. Both were born to John Scott's first wife Lucretia Knapp Johnson, who died in 1830. Ben had three full brothers and two other sisters who lived to adulthood. His brothers included Irwin, Carter, and John Scott Jr. His sisters were Mary Jane "Jennie" Morris and Anna Morris.

Ben also had numerous aunts, uncles and cousins living nearby. One of his uncles, John Cleves Symmes Harrison, was charged with embezzling $12,000 and had been dismissed from his Indiana land office by President Andrew Jackson. He died in 1830, heavily in debt, leaving behind a widow and six children. Another uncle, Benjamin, had been wounded and captured by Mexican forces during the 1836 Texas War for Independence. Briefly held as prisoner, he became a doctor, and died in 1840 at the age of 34. Two of Ben's aunts married cousins and their families also lived at North Bend, Ohio.

Ben's early education came from a number of private tutors who instructed the Harrison children in a small one-room schoolhouse built on the family homestead. In addition, his mother taught her children the *Bible*. The Harrison clan was well ingrained in the customs of Presbyterianism. The nearest house of worship was a small Presbyterian church in Cleves, a few miles away. When they couldn't attend church, services were held in the Harrison home where family and friends gathered for *Bible* reading, prayer and hymn singing. The family hymn sessions on many Sundays lasted for five or six hours. No outdoor activities were allowed, and even writing letters was forbidden. Prayer and hymn singing were an important part of Harrison's life. This family ritual of religious training had a profound effect upon Benjamin's character. Later in life he remarked, "I am sorry to say it is greatly neglected in many homes nowadays."[1] And later, as President of the United States, Harrison conducted no official business of any kind on Sundays.

Early on Ben showed a compassion and understanding beyond his youth. From sunrise to sunset he worked hard and didn't have to be told twice about doing something. He frequently helped the Negro cook with chores and preparing meals. But Ben's education went beyond religion and formal schooling.

The fair-skinned boy spent days on end observing nature, watching the barges, flatboats, rafts and steamboats travel past his home, and reading books in his grandfather's library which, incidentally, contained no works of fiction. While still a college student, Ben declared that reading fiction, "weakens the mind, and if carried to excess, will destroy it."[2] His views on this subject would change, for a decade later he became "hooked" on reading novels. At his mother's insistence, he read John Bunyan's *The Pilgrim's Progress*. Harrison also learned about people when many visitors, including politicians and dignitaries, came to the John Harrison farm.

Ben's first tutor was a young, attractive governess, Harriet Root. She fondly recalled years later, "Ben was the brightest of the family, and even when five years old was determined to go ahead in everything...Ben was terribly stubborn about many things. He would insist upon having his own way not only with me, but with his mother."[3] After a couple slight misunderstandings, she and her pupil got along very well. Subsequent teachers included Joseph Porter, a Mr. Skinner, and Thomas Lynn. It was only when Benjamin reached the age of fourteen that he attended a school outside his home.

From 1847 to 1850 Ben attended Farmer's College, also called Carey's Academy, named after Dr. Freeman Carey who was the son of the school's founder. The college was a preparatory institution located six miles north of Cincinnati in Walnut Hills. To send Ben and his older brother Irwin to school, John Harrison had to borrow money. Ben soon fell under the spell of some mischievous upperclassmen and took part in raiding the adjoining orchard and vegetable garden. After a couple raids, Ben was found out and apologized for his actions. He also proved a disappointment to his parents by failing to write them regularly and, to make matters worse, he took to smoking cigars. But under the instruction of Dr. Robert Bishop, a Scottish Presbyterian minister and former president of Miami University, Ben Harrison developed a lifelong passion for geography, philosophy, and politics.

Bishop was demanding but sympathetic and he passed along some valuable advice to his young student: "Education is getting possession of your mind, so you can use facts as a good mechanic uses tools."[4] Bishop had a reputation as an excellent teacher and soon captured the attention of Harrison by using political lectures in place of traditional classroom curriculum. Reading official Congressional papers and speeches from legislators, Bishop developed analysis and discourse while emphasizing a strong classical style of presentation. Harrison was also introduced to books of fiction, and became interested in novels by Thackeray, Dickens, and Sir Walter Scott. In September of 1850 Ben was admitted as a junior to Miami University in Oxford, Ohio, after a letter of recommendation from Dr. Bishop.

Benjamin Harrison's first year at Miami was a sad one. His mother died in childbirth and his baby brother Findlay also died when Harrison was just seventeen. He immersed himself in his studies and became a frequent guest in the home of Dr. John Witherspoon Scott, one of his former science professors at Farmer's College. Scott had also founded a women's college, later named the Oxford Female Institute. Dr. Scott's two pretty daughters, Lizzie and Caroline, or Carrie, eventually attracted Harrison's attention. Both were enrolled in their father's school. Eighteen-year-old Carrie was especially drawn to Harrison. During this time, Harrison also developed a deepening interest in history and government, and he made an interesting observation when he noted, "The manner by which women are treated is a good criterion to judge the true state of society. If we knew but this one feature in a character of a nation, we may easily judge of the rest."[5]

Located not far from Cincinnati, Miami University was called the "Yale of the West." The college consisted of six professors, 250 students, and had a library of 6,200 volumes. The rules at Miami were strict. No dancing or card playing was allowed. Attending daily chapel was mandatory. All two hundred and fifty male students had to be in their rooms by 7:00 p.m. and authorities in charge of discipline visited the student rooms often for inspection. Ben decided he preferred living off the campus and for a while stayed in a public boardinghouse. He also continued his habit of smoking cigars, much to the disappointment of his father. But Ben was earnest in his studies.

Farmer's College had prepared him well. He also wrote home on a regular basis, and was soon recognized as a top student, proficient enough in Latin and mathematics that other students came to him for help. Showing attributes as a future leader, Harrison co-founded the Phi Delta Theta fraternity and served as its president. The members showed a keen interest in writing and debate. One of his friends, John Herron, became president of another fraternity at Miami; he also became the father of Nellie Taft, wife of William Howard Taft. Years later Herron was appointed a district attorney by Harrison. William Howard Taft, incidentally, became solicitor-general in 1890 under Benjamin Harrison. Another classmate was John Alexander Anderson, son of the college's president and a future U.S. Congressman. Ben also attended several revival meetings, a couple of which were conducted by Dr. Joseph Claybaugh, a Presbyterian minister. It was Claybaugh who drew young Harrison toward the ministry.

During his two years at Miami, Harrison managed to avoid trouble. Refusing to carouse or drink, he earned a reputation as a no-nonsense student. David Swing, a fellow student who later became a minister and campaigned for Harrison, noted, "Ben…was an earnest grave fellow and had no time or taste for going in any form of mischief as in moonlight serenades…He was either reading the speeches of Edmund Burke or the essays of Macaulay, or was making a weekly call on the daughter of Dr. Scott…He had a lofty mind and a wonderfully pure heart."[6]

One trait which developed in Ben's character was a genuine regard for those less fortunate than himself. His compassion for others was instilled in him by his parents. In a letter received from his father, Ben was advised to refrain from alcohol and demeaning others. He was told, "We should never seek to make a witty remark at the expense of the feelings of a less gifted friend or acquaintance."[7] When one of his classmates admitted that he had an unhappy home life, Ben took his friend back with him to North Bend to spend summer vacation.

Young Ben was going through some physical changes. Having blue eyes, light brown hair and a fair complexion, he possessed a noble face. He would grow only another inch and, perhaps to make himself look a bit older, he sprouted reddish-brown whiskers.

Oxford Female Institute was just across the street from the university, but the young men of Miami were kept away because Dr. Scott locked the gate early each evening. Carrie pleaded with her father to let the young men visit, and thus a new social policy was adopted—under the watchful eye of school officials. The gates were opened during certain hours of the day. Benjamin and Caroline renewed their acquaintance, seeing each other on weekend evenings. The relationship soon blossomed into love. Harrison's classmates nicknamed him "the pious moonlight dude."

The young couple was not above mischief. On occasion they would meet secretly or go riding in a buggy without the consent of Carrie's parents. Carrie loved to dance, though her school forbid it. She was quite attractive with dark blond hair and blue eyes. A year older than Harrison, she was fun loving, refined, free spirited, and intelligent. Caroline was also talented in music and painting, but like many females of her day, disliked the domestic duties expected of married women in the mid-nineteenth century.

Ben Harrison continued to excel in his course work. In the literary society group Harrison later got the opportunity to put his skills as a public speaker to work. Perhaps he would follow in the path of his idol, Patrick Henry, a great orator of the American Revolution. Some of Harrison's speeches and debates dealt with the temperance movement, which advocated abstaining from alcohol. He also urged his peers to practice their speaking skills. Graduating third in his class, he was selected by the college to deliver the third address at commencement. Entitled "The Poor of England," his lengthy speech dealt with the causes of poverty in Great Britain. He was somewhat humbled, however, when he saw his name was accidentally listed on the program as "Harris."

Harrison had a voracious appetite for studying and work. His long hours of study resulted in weight loss, and his lack of sleep and physical activity even alarmed his classmates. Ben received a letter from home urging him to slow down his pace. Harrison was also having trouble deciding upon a vocation—it was either the church, the courtroom, or teaching physics in the classroom.

Though lawyers were considered by many as rogues and hypocrites, Harrison also realized there was not much money to be made in the clergy or education. He concluded, "The legal profession has not yet arrived at that dignity and moral excellence to which it could be brought."[8] He honestly believed he could provide a high moral tone to the practice of law. Some of his professors were disappointed when they learned he had chosen law, but one of them, J. M. Woodawl, wrote him a very cordial letter, ending it with "May God give you light in every duty."[9] Following a long conversation with his father, Ben Harrison decided to move into his married sister Betsey's home and study in a law firm.

CHAPTER 3

Law Practice and Marriage

AFTER HIS GRADUATION FROM OHIO'S MIAMI UNIVERSITY IN 1852, BENJAMIN HARRISON became secretly engaged to Caroline Scott. The couple decided to postpone the wedding while Benjamin studied law in Cincinnati and she completed her courses at Oxford. Realizing she could earn some money, Carrie taught music at the Oxford Female Institute and later at a girls' school in Carrollton, Kentucky, for a term. When they were able to meet, Carrie brought Ben to many social functions. Her passion for dancing was not shared by her suitor. When Ben insisted on sitting down, Carrie found another partner.

Ben Harrison stepped off the steamboat and took up residence in Cincinnati, which at the time was a city of forty thousand people. He saved about three hundred dollars a year by living with Betsey and her husband Dr. George S. Eaton. He studied law with the firm of Storer and Gwynne. One of the firm's partners, Bellamy Storer, was a former Whig congressman and a Harrison family friend. Ben Harrison studied hard, even taking some law books with him to the symphony to help pass the time. He dedicated himself to his work. He wrote to his sister, "I do the same thing every day… eat three meals…sleep six hours, and read dusty law books the rest of the time." He also confessed to being a "drudge" and "a poor seeker of pleasure."[1]

Ben missed Carrie terribly. They wrote each other often, and when he learned she had fallen ill while substitute teaching at her father's school, he went to visit her. Benjamin Harrison and Caroline Lavinia Scott were married on October 20, 1853, at the home of the bride. Dr. Reverend John W. Scott performed the ceremony. The couple honeymooned at the Harrison family home in North Bend.

In 1854 Harrison was admitted to the Ohio bar. He had come to dislike the atmosphere of the "Queen City" of Cincinnati. The crowded conditions and lawlessness, the stench from the slaughterhouses, and the billowing smoke stacks from riverboats and thousands of house chimneys left a haze hanging over the city. The young attorney described Cincinnati as a "smoky, dusty town," and an "abominable compound of coal dust and mother earth...it almost blinds you."[2] Seeking a healthier environment for his wife, Harrison knew some friends in Indiana and made some inquiries. Opportunity there seemed brighter, and Benjamin Harrison set off in search for a house and a job.

In the spring of 1854, after selling his Cincinnati property for $800, accepting $500 from his father and borrowing $300 from an aunt, Ben and Carrie moved to Indianapolis, a growing city of sixteen thousand along the banks of the White River. All of the couple's possessions were shipped in one large crate for 91 cents in freight charges.

Their first home was a sagging three-room shack on East Vermont Street. Looking for a more suitable place, the Harrisons moved into the lower part of a two-story house, paying seven dollars a week in rent. Harrison recalled later, "My wife and I took as our dwelling a little house of only three rooms...I remember we had six knives and six two-pronged forks, six plates and similarly slim equipment all around. My wife did her own work, and we have both said since we were never happier in our lives."[3] A fire destroyed this home and the couple was forced to go house hunting again. Soon Carrie became pregnant.

Harrison was having trouble finding clients, and he began looking for additional work. Through more contacts, Harrison found part-time work as a court crier at a salary of $2.50 per day. Harrison's duties in this minor post involved introducing judges in the courtroom and making announcements. He got a break when Major Jonathan Gordon, the prosecuting attorney for Marion County, asked for his assistance on a burglary case.

He had agreed to stand in for County Prosecutor Gordon, who was seeking a conviction for a burglar in nearby Clermont. While arguing his first case, the young lawyer was obviously a bit nervous. A single candle stood on a table in a dark and dusty Indianapolis courtroom where Harrison held his notes. It was daylight outside, but one could barely see inside the room because of cigar smoke and a leaky stove. He vainly shifted the candle back and forth to get more light. After stopping and stammering for a couple of minutes, Harrison threw the notes away. It was at this point that the novice attorney realized he could think clearly and speak quite well without using notes. He won the case and the justice of the peace awarded Harrison a $5 gold piece.

Harrison was soon being introduced to some important people, thanks to his influential cousin William Sheets. Both Ben and Carrie gradually came to know prominent citizens in the city due to Sheets' large circle of political friends. His confidence, as well as his stature, grew. His family grew as well when on August 12, 1854, Carrie gave birth to a son, Russell Benjamin Harrison.

By 1855 conditions were bad economically. The United States experienced a financial panic when stock prices tumbled, factories closed, prices rose dramatically, and banks failed. Thousands of unemployed people faced starvation. Harrison set up a law practice in the state bank building, but found it difficult to make ends meet. He wrote a friend, "Indeed I would almost work for nothing, just for the sake of being busy."[4] When Carrie and Russell became ill, he sent them back to southern Ohio to recuperate.

Life was austere and Harrison recalled the times were a challenge. Constantly in debt, Harrison later looked back on these years and remarked, "They were close times, I tell you. A five dollar bill was an event. There was one good friend through it all—Robert Browning, the druggist. I shall always recall him with gratitude. He believed in me. When things were particularly tight I could go into his store and borrow five dollars from the drawer. A ticket in its place was all that was required. Such friends make life worth living."[5] With few clients and a lack of steady income, Harrison knew better days were ahead. He noted, "I have long since made up my mind that with God's blessing and good health I would succeed, and I never allow myself to doubt the results."[6] The struggling barrister's luck, however, was about to change.

Harrison was proving to be one of the best lawyers in Indianapolis, specializing in divorce and criminal cases. The novice lawyer's sound logic, eloquent speech, quick analysis, and fine memory could sway judges and juries. William Wallace, a successful attorney, asked Harrison to become his law partner. Wallace was running for local office and needed some help. The law firm was opened in a front room of Temperance Hall on Washington Street. Their small business flourished. Before 1855 had ended Harrison used his cousin's and father's political connections to secure an appointment as Court of Claims Commissioner. For this position he earned $4000 a year. He now had two sources of income and became so busy that Carrie saw little of him.

Many political changes had taken place in America by the time Benjamin Harrison became politically active in Indiana. Originally there were no political parties during George Washington's presidency. Later, the Federalist Party and the Anti-Federalists, or Democratic Republicans, disagreed on how to interpret the Constitution and just how much power the federal government should have. They also bickered over the issues of slavery and states' rights. The Democratic Party later came together under the tutelage of powerful leaders such as Martin Van Buren of New York. This resulted in the 1828 election of Andrew Jackson as president.

Northern and southern factions fragmented the Democrats, and the newly formed Whig Party emerged. The Whigs, led by Senators Daniel Webster of Massachusetts and Henry Clay of Kentucky, became firmly established in 1836. Two of their presidential candidates, William Henry Harrison in 1840 and Zachary Taylor in 1848, were elected to the White House. Benjamin's father, Congressman John Scott Harrison, joined the Whigs.

Both the Whigs and the Democrats were at odds within their ranks as northern and southern members differed on the issues of slavery and tariffs. In 1854 the Kansas-Nebraska Act was passed by Congress and signed into law by President Franklin Pierce. This law declared that the issue of slavery in the new territories should be decided by the people living there. It overturned the Missouri Compromise of 1820, which had created a boundary line dividing slave and free states. People of both the North and South were angered. Settlers from both regions rushed into the Kansas and Nebraska Territories to establish these two future states as either slave or free. Riots and murder broke out in bitter fighting known as "Bleeding Kansas." The Whigs, however, could not agree on the issue of slavery. Nor could they find common ground in regard to the Kansas-Nebraska Act.

Another political organization, known as the Know-Nothing Party, was formed in the 1850s. Followers of this party promoted the idea of "true

Americanism," and they disliked foreigners and Catholics. They formed secret societies and practiced mysterious rituals. Many unhappy Whigs joined their ranks, including Harrison's father, John Scott Harrison. By 1854 the Whigs had become nearly non-existent and the Know-Nothings, officially known as the American Party, gained popularity. Several of its members were elected as governors and congressmen. But in the years just prior to the Civil War this political organization also lost ground. Millions of immigrants and even some native-born whites mistrusted and feared the American Party. In 1860 many former Whigs and Know-Nothings joined the Constitutional Union Party, whose platform rested on adherence to the Constitution.

In 1854 discontented Whigs, Democrats, and Know-Nothings from the northern states held meetings in Wisconsin and Michigan. They agreed on a strong central government and limited states' rights, which angered the South. Calling themselves Republicans, the group also opposed the expansion of slavery. In 1856 the Republicans held their first national convention in Philadelphia. They nominated western explorer John C. Fremont as their first presidential candidate. Fremont, a Catholic, lost the election to Democrat James Buchanan.

In 1856 Benjamin Harrison joined the Republican Party and campaigned for Fremont. His father, meanwhile, supported Millard Fillmore, the American Party candidate. These political differences created a strain in the relationship between father and son. Harrison's father warned him to stay out of politics, describing it as "a drug which should never be found in a gentleman's parlor...and fit only to scent the beer house."[7] These words must have sounded strange coming from a man who had served two terms in Congress. Benjamin ignored the advice.

In due time, father and son reconciled. Harrison wrote his father many letters and visited him on weekends at The Point, where John Harrison had retired after four years in the House of Representatives. Carrie did much to soothe any bitter political feelings existing between the two.

As the grandson of a Whig president, Harrison's name was well known to voters. At a Fremont rally in Indianapolis he was given a lengthy introduction as the grandson of William Henry Harrison. Though proud of his ancestry, the 5' 6" attorney stood straight up and announced to the Republican gathering, "I want it understood that I am the grandson of nobody. I believe that every man should stand on his own merits."[8]

The following year, 1857, he was elected as City Attorney at an annual salary of four hundred dollars. He became known for his habit of wearing gloves but had not yet acquired the moniker of "Kid Gloves Harrison." It was also during this time that Harrison tried to give up smoking cigars, but after a few months he fell back into the habit.

From 1858 to 1860 Harrison served as secretary of the Republican State Central Committee. He was in charge of collecting campaign funds and distributing them for expenses. This job put him into contact with many influential Republicans. His passion for politics, however, was postponed on April 3, 1858 when his second child, Mary Scott Harrison, nicknamed Mamie, was born. Carrie had a difficult labor but fully recovered after a few weeks of rest.

At last Benjamin Harrison was enjoying a period of relative prosperity. The Harrisons became active in the First Presbyterian Church, where Benjamin served as a deacon and elder. His involvement in the local Young Men's Christian Association (YMCA) and in the activities of the new Republican Party kept him busy. In 1860, Harrison declared himself a candidate for Reporter of the Indiana Supreme Court. After a spirited fight at the state convention, he won his party's nomination for the position. This job involved writing detailed reports of the state's supreme court decisions.

After a tough campaign where he gave 80 speeches and addressed crowds in every section of the state, the 27-year-old Harrison defeated his Democratic opponent by nearly ten thousand votes. He had also campaigned for the Republican candidate for president, Abraham Lincoln. Lincoln won the state of Indiana by fifteen thousand votes and was elected as the sixteenth President of the United States.

Harrison's future looked bright and secure. He kept busy, working long hours handling legal cases and writing the detailed reports of the State Supreme Court. He even set up a small office in the basement of the Presbyterian church where he taught Sunday school. There he finished his volumes of court proceedings. But a dark cloud was hanging over the nation. Civil War was about to erupt between the North and South, and Benjamin Harrison would play an important part in it.

CHAPTER 4

Off to War

Upon President Lincoln's election in November of 1860, several southern states decided to leave the Union. The eleven seceded states called themselves collectively the Confederate States of America. In April of 1861, Confederate forces fired upon troops stationed at Fort Sumter in Charleston Harbor, South Carolina. President Lincoln asked for seventy-five thousand volunteers to put down the rebellion. A tremendous wave of fervor swept through the North and West. Tens of thousands of men volunteered to fight, not to free Negro slaves, but to punish the South for insulting the flag.

Harrison, though a loyal Unionist and Lincoln supporter, was in no hurry to join the army. Carrie was pregnant again and, despite a steady income, Harrison continued to borrow money from friends to make ends meet. The Harrisons' child was born dead in June of 1861. Benjamin and Carrie were intensely distraught for months. In December, Harrison's law partnership with William Wallace was dissolved. Wallace had decided to run for Clerk of Marion County and needed time to organize and conduct his campaign. Harrison, however, was not too disappointed because, as he put it, Wallace "had not done a lick of work" in months.[1]

Harrison continued to practice law and formed a new partnership with a local attorney, William Pinkney Fishback, nicknamed "Pink." He had been a classmate of Harrison's at Miami University and the two became close friends. In spite of the war, their law firm flourished. With additional income from writing several volumes of the *Indiana Reports*, Harrison could afford a bigger home. These legal papers were explanations of decisions by the court and prescribed reading for lawyers in Indiana who needed to keep up with the ever-changing laws. He also took steps to ensure some income for his wife and children in the event that he was called to war. The detailed information required to publish his court reports took a great deal of Harrison's time, and he worked to finish the next volume.

In early 1862 Harrison purchased a two-story home at Alabama and North Streets. He needed room not only for his family, but for his brother and nephew who were living with him at the time. Harrison knew it was likely that he would be offered a command in the military that was being raised to put down the southern rebellion. And with his friends and relatives joining to fight, he no doubt felt obligated to serve. His brothers Irwin and Carter joined up with the 11th Indiana Volunteer Regiment and the 51st Ohio Regiment respectively. Henry Scott, his brother-in-law, was also in the army, serving in Virginia. Another brother-in-law, John Scott, later volunteered and was seriously wounded at the Battle of Murfreesboro in Tennessee.

The Union armies were losing battles on a regular basis during the first year of the war, and in 1862 President Lincoln called for an additional three hundred thousand men to serve. Indiana Governor Oliver Perry Morton had trouble raising volunteers in his state, telling Harrison and William Wallace, "Gentlemen, there is absolutely no response to Mr. Lincoln's last call for troops...Something must be done to break the spirit of apathy and indifference which now prevails." Harrison told him, "Governor, if I can be of any service, I will go."[2]

On July 14, 1862, a new wave of recruiting officers, including Benjamin Harrison, were appointed in each Congressional district of Indiana. Men were to be enlisted for either three years or "during the war." Volunteers were given seventy dollars, and this gesture, combined with a new patriotic zeal, resulted in a wave of support for the Union. Governor Morton asked Harrison to command Company A of Indiana's 70th Volunteer Regiment and appointed him a second lieutenant. As he and the governor were walking down the steps of the state capital, Harrison recruited his first soldier—his friend and former law partner, William Wallace.

Harrison bought a military hat, procured a fifer and drummer, and returned to his law office where he hung a flag outside his window. The new officer traveled the state seeking recruits, giving speeches, and reminding his fellow Hoosiers that a Confederate army was approaching Indiana. He appealed to future soldiers, "Boys, think quick, and decide as patriots should in such an emergency. Fathers, cease to restrain the ardor of your sons, whose patriotic impulse prompt them to aid our country in its hour of trials."[3] Within two weeks during July of 1862, he had eighty-five men, and within two weeks more the number had grown to 250. Harrison selected his re-enlisted brother-in-law, Henry Scott, as his First Lieutenant.

Harrison found a replacement for his court reporter's duties and arranged for "Pink" Fishback to manage their law firm. He persuaded "Pink" not to enlist so the law firm, and its steady income, could continue. By early August the 70th Indiana Regiment was full, eventually numbering a thousand soldiers due to the recruiting efforts of several officers. On August 8, Benjamin Harrison was commissioned a full colonel. The citizens of Indianapolis gave Harrison a rousing send off, presenting him with a fancy dress sword and a regimental banner. On August 12 Colonel Harrison received orders to join Union forces in Louisville, Kentucky, where Confederate General Braxton Bragg's army lay nearby. At 7:00 the next morning Colonel Harrison, astride his horse, led more than a thousand of his troops through the streets of Indianapolis amid a cheering throng. The regiment, with its new Enfield rifles, boarded a train bound south.

The 70th Regiment crossed the Ohio River at Jeffersonville, Indiana, and disembarked in Louisville, Kentucky. It marched proudly through the city streets where most of the citizens looked on in silence, except for a score of black slaves who could not restrain their joyous cheers. No sooner had Harrison's army camped than it was ordered the next day to board another train and go to Bowling Green, Kentucky. The men marched in a steady downpour of rain and boarded dirty boxcars. Confederate General John Hunt Morgan was reportedly in the region and Harrison was being sent to locate and capture him.

Expecting the unexpected, Harrison ordered his officers and men to load their muskets. Some soldiers loaded their weapons incorrectly. One officer noted, "As we jolted along at night through the enemy's country, with raw recruits lying on their loaded guns, it might be difficult to decide whether the danger was greater from within or from without."[4]

Colonel Harrison faced several problems. His army was inexperienced and had not had enough time for proper training. To resolve these issues, Harrison put his energy into making the Indiana 70th "march, think and act as one."[5] He drilled his troops for several weeks and spent days reading books on strategy and military history. No drinking was allowed in camp and Harrison encouraged his men to attend religious services he personally conducted. Rumors, however, soon spread to other regiments that the Hoosiers were generally unfit, uncivilized and unrestrained.

Complaints abounded and discipline, particularly in one company, was lacking. This undercut the colonel's authority and he had three of that company's officers and most of the renegade squad arrested and thrown into the guardhouse. The three subordinate (or insubordinate) officers apologized profusely. On another occasion several recruits were jailed after they sneaked out of camp to visit the Louisville prostitutes who had camped nearby. From that moment on, Harrison had no trouble with his men misbehaving or disobeying orders. Word quickly spread that Harrison was not to be trifled with and he wrote Fishback that his men "are beginning to know me now."[6]

Were recruits from Indiana any different than those from Ohio or New York? Some believed so. One New York enlisted man believed Indiana soldiers were "utterly beyond discipline…The men are good, stout, hearty, intelligent fellows and will make excellent soldiers, but they have no regard for their officers and, as a rule, do as they please."[7]

No doubt some of Harrison's soldiers saw a contrast in his behavior. One moment Harrison would conduct prayer with his officers and in another, he would lightly indulge when the whiskey or bourbon was passed around during off-duty hours. His fondness for cigars remained and only rarely did Harrison's men see him get angry or hear him cuss. Thus, any vices he possessed were minor.

In August of 1862 Carrie and the children paid a brief visit to the army camped near Bowling Green. This was her first, and she and some other wives spent their time mending clothes for the troops. For a few days Harrison forgot about the rigors of war. But Confederate General John Morgan and his raiders were still on the loose.

General Morgan put fear into the Union. With an army of 2400, Morgan was headed north. Along the way he destroyed bridges and railroads, robbed some banks and plundered farms. This bold, elusive leader vowed to attack cities and villages across the Ohio River. Morgan's intent was to take the war to the North, burn shops and factories, steal livestock for food and supplies and create panic among its people. When Morgan crossed the Ohio he made life miserable for townspeople in southern Ohio and Indiana.

Harrison's army failed to locate him. The wily Morgan created barricades for Harrison's pursuing troops, destroying sections of railroads, burning bridges and felling trees to block the roads. Back in Indianapolis, rumors circulated that Harrison and his men had been defeated by Morgan and taken prisoner. It would take another seven months to capture the elusive leader when Rutherford B. Hayes closed in on him between the villages of Lisbon and Salineville, Ohio; Morgan was sent to prison in Columbus but escaped to renew his attacks.

President Lincoln gave command of the Union armies to General George B. McClellan. The hopes of the North were restored, but only for a while. McClellan's inaction ultimately cost him his job. Meanwhile, Harrison's army in the West, under the command of General Don Carlos Buell, proved a nuisance to the Confederates. There was little good news coming from the fighting in Kentucky and Tennessee, except that one leader, Ulysses S. Grant, had demonstrated bulldog tenacity when fighting the enemy. General Buell, like McClellan, was eventually replaced by President Lincoln because of his reluctance to act.

Harrison was homesick, as were his soldiers. On September 26, 1862, he wrote Carrie, "How precious home seems to us all now that we are strangers to all of its comforts! The tender affection you have ever felt for me, and which I so often crossed with wounds, is now the source of my strongest longing." He missed his family deeply, especially the little arms and lips of his children, "Dear Gifts of God, a wife and two dear babes."[8]

On September 30, 1862, General Buell ordered Colonel Benjamin Harrison and his forces to occupy Russellville, Kentucky. Through some local citizens, including runaway slaves, Harrison learned that a rebel army of four hundred men was camped near the town. Sending part of his forces around Russellville to cut off their retreat, Harrison and his men attacked the Confederates, catching them completely by surprise. In the skirmish, Colonel Harrison lost only one man, compared to rebel casualties of thirty-five killed and wounded. The enemy scattered, leaving behind a large supply of food, weapons, forty-two horses, sixty saddles and other supplies. The Colonel spent the next few hours rounding up a dozen prisoners, some of whom were hiding in homes or barns.

Harrison's confidence in himself and his army grew. But he also realized his limitations. He hoped that friends and family would not expect too much of him. Later in the war he wrote his wife, "I am not a Julius Caesar, nor a Napoleon, but a plain Hoosier colonel, with no more relish for a fight than for a good breakfast ..."[9]

Meanwhile, back in Indianapolis, Democrats and southern sympathizers known as Copperheads tried to discredit Harrison. Rumors were spread that Harrison was not only a coward, but cruel to his men. The Copperheads' main political goal was to oust Harrison's appointed deputy from the position of Supreme Court Reporter. The Democrats put up Michael Kerr for the position.

Lincoln's announcement that he would free the slaves with the Emancipation Proclamation generated hostile reaction throughout central and southern Indiana, where there was no shortage of Democrats who hated both blacks and abolitionists. Due to a well coordinated political effort by the opposition, Harrison's replacement for court reporter was soundly defeated in the November elections of 1862. This was a personal blow to Harrison. In addition, the Democrats won control of both Houses of the Indiana legislature, and took seven of the eleven U.S. Congressional seats. Kerr completed writing the reports of the State Supreme Court that Harrison had begun. Kerr then published the volume and received the royalties. Harrison wrote his wife, "I would like to give Mr. Kerr a caning [beating] better than anything I know of."[10]

Copperheads were also trying to undermine Colonel Harrison's command. Their anti-war propaganda began to have an effect on Harrison's troops. Soldiers were constantly encouraged to desert, receiving newspapers and letters denouncing Lincoln and the war. The morale of the army became such a concern that Colonel Harrison called for a meeting with the entire regiment. He asked General Eleazar A. Paine to address the men. After a couple of other speakers, it was Harrison's turn to comment, and he gave a rousing speech. Following Harrison's talk, Paine walked over to a captain, slapped him on the back, and remarked, "By George, Captain, that Colonel of yours will be President of the United States someday."[11]

Carrie made a brief visit to Harrison's camp and raised his spirits, making life a bit more tolerable. But another enemy had been at work throughout the war—disease. During the winter more men were lost due to sicknesses like dysentery, pneumonia, measles, and typhoid than to enemy bullets. In addition, mules and horses were constantly dying and supplies grew scarce. Harrison got ptomaine poisoning from eating tainted pork. Critics accused him of being indifferent and insensitive as morale began to ebb among his troops. Nor did Harrison's practice of wearing gloves escape the attention of his subordinates.

During the first half of 1863, Harrison and the 70th Regiment saw little action. General William S. Rosecrans assigned him to guard supply trains in Tennessee. Harrison later described this dull task as "scavenger duty," as there were many of the enemy who sought to rob the Union's supplies. After the Union defeat at Chickamauga, near the Tennessee-Georgia border, Lincoln made some changes in command. In March of 1864 Ulysses S. Grant was appointed General of the Army. Grant assigned his friend William Tecumseh Sherman as head of the Division of the Mississippi. Joseph Hooker, who was relieved of his command in the East, was put in charge of the 20th Army Corps, one of Sherman's divisions. One of Hooker's brigades was led by General William Ward, which included Harrison's 70th Indiana Regiment. With the Union Army reorganized and supplied, it crept ever closer to the key Confederate cities of Richmond, Virginia, and Atlanta, Georgia.

It was during the winter of 1864 that Harrison received some bad news. His grandmother, Anna Symmes Harrison, died on February 25 at age 88. She had outlived nine of her ten children and was buried next to her husband at North Bend. Carrie, on the other hand, was quite busy. Besides raising a family and managing the household, she plunged into the war effort as leader of the Ladies Patriotic Organization and the Ladies Sanitary Commission, participating in community drives to collect clothing and supplies for the fighting men. She also volunteered at two city hospitals to nurse wounded soldiers.

In May of 1864 General Sherman began his invasion to defeat the Confederacy. His immediate goal was to crush General Joseph Johnston's army in Tennessee and Georgia and force it back into Atlanta. But Johnston's men were firmly entrenched at Resaca, Georgia, blocking Sherman's advance. Harrison, realizing the fighting might be intense, prepared for his stiffest battle. He wrote to Carrie, "I must write you tonight as we look for battle tomorrow, and God only knows who shall come safely through it. I am in my usual good spirits, though not at all insensible to grave responsibilities and risks which I must bear tomorrow."[12]

The Battle of Resaca, the first major engagement of Sherman's Atlanta campaign, began on May 14, 1864. General Ward ordered Harrison to move against the fortified rebel position on a hill overlooking the road to Resaca. Harrison's men were about to face their toughest test yet.

Generals Joe Johnston and John B. Hood had formed a defensive line to protect supplies and railroads destined for Atlanta. This high ground was manned by sharpshooters under the command of Hood. At this spot and most other emplacements, a thousand slaves had spent a month constructing rebel fortifications, which looked impregnable to some Union men. Harrison's brigade consisted of soldiers from five regiments: the 70th Indiana, 79th Ohio, 102nd Ohio, and the 105th and 129th Illinois. Harrison had all officers dismount their horses and advance on foot toward the rifle pits and four 12-pounder rebel artillery. His men charged down the side of a hill they occupied, rushed through a brushy pine thicket, then ran across a half mile of open ground toward the rebels.

Upon reaching the bottom of the hill, Harrison was angered when a message from General Ward informed him the wrong order had been given. Ward ordered Harrison to take his men *back up* the hill they had just descended. At this point Harrison and his troops were pinned down by murderous gunfire. Bullets from enemy rifles sprayed dirt in his eyes as he hugged the ground. Sending his men back in small groups, Harrison retreated with only a few casualties. In the evening he returned to the field to remove his dead and was fired on by Union soldiers. Harrison asked a lieutenant, "Have you your head on your shoulders yet?" Back came a quick reply, "Yes, sir!" Harrison told him, "Run then, as fast as you can and tell all those fellows in the rear that they are killing us, and to stop firing for God's sake."[13]

The Yankee attack had been repulsed, but the next day, May 15, there would be no retreat for the Union army at Resaca. Colonel Harrison was directed by Ward to capture another cluster of well-entrenched enemy rifle pits which were positioned behind a four-foot high wooden wall. Harrison ordered knapsacks placed in a large pile as a detail was assigned to guard them. Astride his horse, the colonel waved his sword in one hand and pistol in the other, leading his men against a volley of gunfire. They broke through the Confederate lines, using their fixed bayonets upon orders from Harrison. The rebels were shot or bayoneted as they defiantly stuck by their cannons. In the midst of battle, Harrison rode his horse into the assault, grabbed a rebel artilleryman by the collar and ordered him back into the lines of captured prisoners. His efforts, and those of his soldiers, dislodged the Confederates and a victory was won. Johnston's army waited until nightfall and retreated closer to Atlanta. The following day Harrison buried his dead, as well as the enemy soldiers who were killed. The 70th Regiment lost 26 killed and 130 wounded, compared to twice that amount for the Confederates. In addition Harrison had captured 1200 small arms and the enemy cannons.

General Hooker told him his action was "very brilliant and successful."[14] Known affectionately now as "Little Ben" to many of his men, Harrison was making a name for himself. Sitting down in his command tent, Harrison wrote Carrie and remarked on his accomplishments which had received public attention in published reports, "We must not however think too much of the praises of the newspapers, nor forget to thank God who sustains me belongs all the honor."[15]

On May 26–28 Colonel Harrison was again in the thick of battle at New Hope, Georgia, when he ordered a bayonet attack. Mounted again on his steed, the diminutive colonel yelled, "Men, the enemy's works are just ahead of us. But we shall go right over them! Forward! Double Quick! March!"[16] In the assault against sixteen cannon and five thousand rebels, the Federal forces in blue suffered heavy casualties but once again forced Johnston to retreat.

Less than three weeks later, on June 15, the tired and battle-worn 70th Regiment was thrust into action one more time at Golgatha Church, Georgia, near Kenesaw Mountain. The fighting was intense. Harrison wrote his wife, "We stood there fighting an unseen foe for an hour and a half without flinching, while the enemy's shells and grapes [grapeshot, or cannon charges] fell like hail in our ranks, tearing down large trees and filling the air with splinters. Two or three of my men had their heads torn off close to the shoulders and others had fearful wounds."[17]

Near the end of the battle, the surgeons of the 70th Regiment got separated from the army. So when Harrison entered a deserted house that was being used as a hospital, he rolled up his sleeves, and went to work. He ordered tents torn up to make dressings. When he ran out of cloth, he tore off his shirt and used it for more bandages. Though he had not studied medicine, the colonel performed emergency surgery, removing shrapnel and large splinters from arms and legs. When the surgeons finally arrived, they found both of Harrison's bare arms covered in blood from shoulder to fingertip. Months before he had been seen several times dismounting his horse to let a wounded comrade ride in his place. Such gestures endeared Harrison to his men, and he in turn was beginning to develop a strong attachment to them. He wrote his wife, "I wouldn't like to leave my Regiment to the command of another in a fight. I have got to love them for their bravery and for the dangers we have shared together…"[18]

By early July of 1864, the Union army was approaching the outskirts of Atlanta. On July 7, Harrison's army was within ten miles of the city and could see its church steeples in the distance. Sherman had split his army as Generals John Schofield and James B. McPherson (who was shortly thereafter killed) moved east, extending their lines several miles. General Johnston had been relieved of his command by President Jefferson Davis and Hood took control. A major portion of the rebel army arrived late in checking General George Thomas' advance and this may have cost the Federals a victory.

On July 20 Harrison's men were camped at Peachtree Creek, just two miles north of Atlanta. Located along a low-lying creek bed, Harrison was caught off guard as many of his men had stacked their rifles and headed off to pick blackberries or jump in the creek for a swim. It was around 3:00 p.m. when gunfire broke out as General Hood began his attack. Hood figured that Harrison's particular position was a weak spot in the Federal line, and indeed it did represent a gap in the Union forces. As enemy gunfire began Harrison gathered his men, jumped on his horse and dashed forward, yelling his command, "Come on, boys! We've never been licked yet, and we won't begin now! We haven't much ammunition, but if necessary we can give them the cold steel!"[19] In a wild melee, soldiers from both sides used their bayonets. When both forces ran out of ammunition, they engaged in hand-to-hand combat or used their rifles as clubs.

Harrison was nearly killed as the Confederates were driven from the field. General Hooker told him, "Harrison, by God, I'll make you a brigadier for this fight!"[20] Losses in killed and wounded for the Union Army totaled about 1700 while the enemy lost nearly 4000 (this included captured prisoners). After four hours of fighting the men in blue gained the victory, capturing seven regimental flags. They then climbed to the top of a hill and fired the first artillery shells into the city of Atlanta.

But getting *into* Atlanta was another matter. The cost in human life had been substantial. Peering through his binoculars, Harrison noticed a large system of breastworks and barriers. Trenches, gun emplacements, ramparts and a labyrinth of obstacles surrounded the city. Like they had done in other surrounding areas, more than a thousand Negro slaves worked for a month constructing the fortifications. Little did Harrison or anyone else know that most of the fighting to seize the city was over, as rebel forces abandoned their positions and moved north.

In another letter to Carrie, Harrison reflected on the sacrifice he and his soldiers were making. He observed, "In nature there is no life except the seed be cast into the earth and die, and so is our national life, shall yet yield its fruit in a purer, higher and surer national life...May God help us who stand for our country in the coming conflict..."[21]

It was during this military campaign that Harrison earned the everlasting nickname "Kid Gloves," a sobriquet which critics would later use to describe him. The habit of wearing fine, soft leather gloves made of goatskin was a tendency Harrison practiced later in greeting people in the White House. While serving in Georgia, Harrison suffered from a severe case of poison ivy. The infection spread to his face, fingers and eyes. His hands were so sensitive that for years thereafter he wore gloves for protection. More than one future political opponent accused "Kid Gloves Harrison" of having an aversion to shaking hands with people. The later efforts of Democrats to convince laborers and voters that Harrison didn't like to touch others or feared getting his hands dirty, failed. Working class people who knew Harrison admired him. Indeed, few politicians enjoyed meeting the public with a hardy handshake more than Benjamin Harrison.

In mid-summer Harrison learned his wife was very sick. However, on August 20, his birthday, he received two letters from her saying she was much improved. Though she had visited him twice briefly while he was stationed in Kentucky, Carrie was desperate to see him. During the months of battle the colonel expressed regrets and guilt about not having spent more time with her when he was at home. He wrote her from camp, "I now see so many faults in my domestic life that I long for an opportunity to correct. I know I could make your life so much happier than ever before." Harrison later promised Carrie, "I hope to be a better husband and father."[22]

On September 1, after two months of vicious fighting, Atlanta finally fell as the Union army marched through the streets. Harrison's troops entered the next day, and witnessed men in blue looting and setting fire to the city. After the fall of Atlanta, Harrison's soldiers occupied the city and General Sherman granted Harrison a much-needed furlough. Harrison had been in the field two years without a leave. He happily boarded a steamboat for home, not just to visit his family but also to campaign for Lincoln's reelection. On his trip up the Ohio River, while conversing with some of his fellow passengers, rebel bullets came crashing through the vessel, scattering civilians and military personnel alike, except for Harrison. He raced to the top deck and, with a pistol in each hand, began firing towards the southern shore until the boat was out of range. Upon reaching Indianapolis, he soon learned that area newspapers had dubbed him "The Hero of Peachtree Creek."

Upon returning to duty on October 31, 1864, Benjamin Harrison was promoted to brigadier general. President Lincoln signed the order, citing him for his "ability...manifest energy and gallantry in command of brigade."[23] He was ordered to Tennessee where he took command of a brigade to block a Confederate advance. He found raw, undisciplined recruits, most of whom were European immigrants who couldn't speak English. Within a short time the general whipped them into shape but they saw limited action in the defense of Nashville.

The new general and Sherman became close friends, having served side-by-side in planning strategy to capture Atlanta. Harrison was convinced the war was nearly over. But like many others who anticipated the rebellion's end, the tired Harrison was uncertain of what he would do after the war. Good news arrived when he found out he had won back the Indiana State Supreme Court Reporter position. His friends had placed his name on the ballot and once again, Harrison appointed a deputy to serve in his place until he could return from the war. Still, he expressed some doubts about his future and wrote Carrie, "If my ambition is to soar anymore after I come home, you will have to give it wings."[24]

There was still more fighting to come. In late 1864, the Confederates, led by General Hood, launched an attack on Nashville, Tennessee, in an attempt to regain the city. Harrison was under the command of General George Thomas, known as the "Rock of Chickamauga." The 70th Regiment was camped in the mud and freezing rain, and Harrison personally distributed hot coffee to the shivering soldiers standing guard. The call for combat came when the enemy launched an offensive. General Hood's army was driven back, though Harrison's men played only a minor role. Capturing several artillery pieces after a brief skirmish, Harrison praised the stubborn rebels for fighting barefoot on the frozen ground.

Hood retreated southward so fast that he could not be caught. Harrison's men were then ordered to board trains in Nashville and head to Murfreesboro to try and cut off Hood's retreat. On December 21, 1864, Harrison loaded his troops in boxcars, sixty men inside and twenty men on top of each car. It was a grueling trip; several men suffered frostbite and had difficulty climbing down from the cars. Harrison never caught up with Hood; freezing weather and mud slowed each army and on New Year's Day 1865, both sides went into winter quarters. Harrison described this theater of operations as severe and arduous even though there was little combat.

Sherman granted Harrison another short leave. Harrison hoped to return in time to rejoin Sherman and accompany him on his "March to The Sea." But in January of 1865, while visiting Carrie's sister in Honesdale, Pennsylvania, Harrison and his family contracted scarlet fever. They had to be quarantined for two weeks. Harrison's spirits rose when he was told to rejoin Sherman. Against the advice of his doctors, Harrison took a steamer from New York City to Hilton Head, South Carolina, in late February.

Hilton Head was an important base of operations for the Union blockade of Savannah and Charleston. There were thousands of ex-slaves, battle-ready troops, and wounded Union soldiers there and Harrison's leadership would be needed, or so he thought.

On March 4, socked in by fog, Harrison and a few men from the anchored steamer went oyster fishing. The new general learned how to locate and shuck them, eating more than thirty oysters (a delicacy he continued for the rest of his life). After the fog lifted the little steamer headed for Blair's Landing a few miles away.

General Harrison was reassigned to Camp Sherman and relegated to administrative duties. Sherman's whereabouts were unknown and Harrison's skills were needed to run the camp, which consisted of several thousand troops. The influx of reinforcements meant increased problems. Harrison grew frustrated and quite unhappy there, and complained that his biggest problems, next to disciplining stragglers and ferreting out wandering bands of rebels, was battling gnats, sand fleas, and mosquitoes.

One major concern Harrison had was with the sutlers in his army. Some considered sutlers similar to locusts who descended on crops, or like leeches which sucked the blood from humans. These industrious entrepreneurs offered soldiers things they couldn't normally obtain. Articles such as tobacco, gingerbread, pies, nuts, raisins, and playing cards could be purchased at the sutler's tent or shack. Some sutlers, including the ones attached to Harrison's army, charged outrageous prices. When Harrison complained to his superiors, however, he was told nothing could be done.

He could, however, do something about deserters. One day, some Union bounty hunters, after being paid, made a small raft to escape Harrison's camp. Of the eight men who left, one drowned and in less than a day, the other seven came back exhausted, unable to make it through the swamp. Harrison had these men paraded for two hours carrying heavy logs in front of their comrades.

On April 10 he set sail on the steamer *Champion* from Hilton Head to Wilmington, North Carolina, to finally join Sherman. When Harrison arrived he was met with the news that General Lee had surrendered to Grant at Appomattox Court House in Virginia the previous day. This touched off two days of celebration, including a parade and party sponsored by General Joseph Hawley, who later became a colleague of Harrison as a U.S. Senator from Indiana. Harrison still hadn't located Sherman but one image forever stayed in his mind during this time. He recalled seeing thousands of ragged, hungry Confederate troops marching toward what was left of their homes. His men provided food and shelter to their defeated comrades. The Civil War was over but Harrison's examples of kindness, and malice toward none to his fellow Confederates, did not initially extend to Southerners who later served in Congress.

On April 15, 1865, just five days after the end of the Civil War, President Lincoln was assassinated by southern sympathizer John Wilkes Booth. Harrison arrived in Wilmington in time to help conduct a memorial service for the slain president. Similar services were held throughout the country. In his eulogy, General Harrison told his comrades, "Qualities of heart and mind combined to make him a man who was the love of mankind. He is beloved. He stands like a great lighthouse to show the way of duty to all his countrymen."[25]

Within a short time, Harrison was back in good spirits, having been reunited with Sherman. His weight was up to one hundred forty-five pounds and he had not felt better in three years. He received orders to march his army to Washington, D.C., to take part in a parade of troops known as the Grand Review. Beginning on April 30, it took nine days just to march from Raleigh to Richmond. While passing through Virginia, General Harrison and his men encountered large numbers of ragged Confederate troops. Again, they provided them with rations, shelter, and clothing. His army also observed the skeletons of hundreds of soldiers killed on several battlefields.

On May 23, 1865, General Harrison joined tens of thousands of Union soldiers to march in the Grand Review, the largest parade ever held in the nation's capital. President Andrew Johnson, the Cabinet, members of Congress and a host of dignitaries sat in a reviewing stand in front of the White House. General Grant rode his horse up Pennsylvania Avenue amid thunderous applause before taking his seat beside the new president. Then came General George Meade's Army of the Potomac, 80,000 strong. The lines of soldiers stretched for seven miles; the cavalry alone took an hour to pass. The next day Sherman's Army of Tennessee and Georgia passed in review for six hours. Among the proud troops was General Benjamin Harrison. He would not have missed the parade for anything, yet he yearned to return home. He wrote Carrie, "I would not prolong my separation from you and the children one hour to see it."[26]

Harrison longed to return to his wife, "the temple of my heart at home," and promised Carrie he would become "a more domestic and sociable man."[27] Three weeks later, on June 8, 1865, he was discharged from the Army. Harrison returned to Indianapolis, where he received a hero's welcome.

During the Civil War, Harrison gained the respect of his men. His regiment had suffered heavy casualties, with 40 percent of his forces killed or wounded. As a tough and fearless leader, Harrison had faced death many times, but he always remained unruffled, steady, and alert in the face of battle. His men feared and admired him, but they also loved him. More than once Harrison gave a wounded comrade money so the soldier could return home. He never accepted repayment. Warm feelings toward Harrison only intensified with the passing years. His fellow soldiers, particularly those of the 70th Regiment, came to have a deep and abiding affection for their "Hoosier Hero."

Harrison had witnessed much as a leader of men during war, and the bonds he made with his fellow soldiers and officers would last a lifetime. Trying to understand all the misery and destruction he had seen, Harrison knew firsthand the folly of war. And though he was no stranger to the poverty and discrimination found in the cities of the North, he was convinced that his fellow Americans living in the southern states had grievously erred in believing that an economy built upon slave labor could ultimately succeed. Though the institution of slavery created *some* feelings of love and respect between the races, it also caused fear and hate because most white masters broke the spirit of those in bondage. Harrison once noted, "All those fires of industry which I saw through the South were lighted at the funeral pyre of slavery."[28] Years later he used this phrase in his inaugural address.

Perhaps Carrie saw that her husband was destined for politics, something which she particularly disliked. She had her husband's reassurance, however, that he was not interested in seeking public office. Though he had no objections to becoming a successful attorney, he promised he wouldn't run for Congress because "it would take me away from home so much."[29] Carrie took him for his word; after all he was a man who kept his pledges.

CHAPTER 5

Veteran and Politician

Harrison and Sherman rode their horses in the Grand Review parade in Washington on May 24, 1865. The march of tens of thousands of men in blue was a spectacle the capital had never witnessed, and one Harrison would never forget. While camped outside the city the trial of Lincoln's conspirators took place. Lew Wallace invited Harrison to the trial but he declined. On June 8, 1865 the general was mustered out of the army and became a private citizen.

He traveled by train to North Bend, took a steamboat to Lawrenceburg, Indiana, then boarded another train for Indianapolis. Laden with presents for his family, upon entering the city he was greeted by a large enthusiastic crowd. On Friday June 16, Governor Morton honored four Indiana regiments at a huge banquet. He called upon Harrison to speak and the veteran officer reminded his audience that he spoke for all soldiers, living and dead, who sacrificed to preserve the country. His stirring tribute moved some to tears.

Settling in and adjusting to civilian life took some time. Harrison busied himself with legal matters and spent hours each day immersed in paper work in his law office and home library. Visitors to the Harrison home saw few reminders of the war. No display of weapons or spoils of the Civil War adorned his fireplace or library walls. His silver scabbard which sheathed his sword had inset pearls, but the use of it in battle rubbed them out of their settings, leaving only small holes. This, along with his pistols and other paraphernalia, were stored away.

One obligation Harrison didn't mind was aiding veterans of the war. Just a few weeks after his return he helped two men of his regiment find jobs. David Ramsdell and Moses McLain had both been wounded and each had an arm amputated. Their former commander procured positions for them as county officials.

Many soldiers returning home found a mountain of debt waiting for them, but Harrison was not one of them. As Supreme Court Reporter he found a way to generate income while he served in the army. He had tried making some money by selling his reports before, but he added a new twist to promote sales. The reports were written and edited under his supervision until he could return home from the battlefield. In return for collecting fines and organizing the court's decisions, Harrison was permitted to sell his newly-published report book to attorneys throughout the entire state. Any profits made were his to keep. To promote higher sales, Harrison offered to pay the book's postage mailed to attorneys outside the community. In 1864, Harrison's legal publication sold out in three weeks, giving him a handsome profit of $1500.

Harrison returned home to discover a problem with his report book. The federal department of Internal Revenue in Indianapolis declared that Harrison owed a tax on the sale of his books. He refused to pay it, claiming that his published accounts of the supreme court were official state business and therefore exempt from federal taxes. The tax department disagreed and the case went to court where a judge ruled in the government's favor. Harrison paid the tax but appealed the ruling. A higher court reversed the decision and Harrison got his money back. This incident served to harden his view that tax collectors were immoral, but a necessary evil.[1]

Benjamin Harrison settled down to a life of calm and practicality in "a home brighter and happier" because of his wife and children.[2] The thirty-four year-old ex-officer was anxious to spend some time with his family and go back to work as well. He bought a new carriage and enrolled his children Russell and Mamie in private schools. The General, as he was called by his family and close friends, attended to his clerk duties. He composed the next volume of reports for the Indiana Supreme Court, making several hundred dollars profit on each edition. His yearly income the first two years after the war averaged around twelve thousand dollars, an impressive sum for the 1860s.

Harrison's work habits differed from those of many of his peers. He concentrated fully on a given task—any interruption was met with scorn unless it was very important. He was intense and often so engrossed in his work that as he walked in the street he failed to notice friends or exchange hellos. To some, this was simply arrogance or conceit. Gossip or small talk annoyed him. The General disdained stupidity and a subordinate who made too many mistakes was discharged. One lesson Harrison was learning in civilian life was how to delegate authority and routine work to others, but it was a habit in which he was not always successful.

Harrison's courtroom manner differed from his fellow barristers. He was level headed and never lost his cool. His poise was unshaken, and when cross examining a witness on the stand, he remained polite and seldom raised his voice. These idiosyncrasies remained unchanged throughout his lifetime.

On the political front, Harrison disagreed with Lincoln's Reconstruction plan of kindness and tolerance towards the rebellious states that now sought readmission to the Union. With Lincoln's death, however, the former Confederate states had little hope for a peaceful reconciliation. Harrison felt those in the South responsible for the war, as well as their Copperhead allies in the North, deserved to be punished. Nor should they hold public office. The South, he believed, should be rebuilt under the watchful eye of the federal government.

The Radical Republicans gained control of both the Senate and the House after Lincoln's death. In what became known as "waving the bloody shirt," the Radicals often reminded the public of the treacherous South and the great sacrifice Union soldiers had made to the country. Many Northern Democrats and Copperheads, particularly those holding public office, were equated with former Confederates. Harrison sided with the Radicals on most issues, though he was not in favor of granting immediate voting rights to blacks. And like many of his fellow citizens, Harrison was beginning to distrust the new president, Andrew Johnson.

In July of 1865, Harrison headed a welcoming committee to greet two special visitors to Indianapolis. One was his friend William Tecumseh Sherman. Two months later, Ulysses S. Grant paid a call. In each instance, the generals were met at the depot by a large crowd and were paraded through the streets, escorted by veterans. Receptions, banquets and other festivities ensued, making each of the three-day events a memorable one.

Harrison planned and gladly took part in these activities, often "waving the bloody shirt" himself.

In addition to writing his Supreme Court volumes, the General took on more clients. In April of 1867 he suffered a physical breakdown from overwork and was confined to bed for a week. Carrie nursed him back to health. He decided not to seek reelection to his Reporter seat. In the fall, he headed for the lakes of Minnesota to get some rest and relaxation, far from the reaches of any mail or telegrams. Duck hunting and fishing became his priorities.

The General found time for politics after his vacation. He campaigned for Radical Republican candidates and in 1868 "took to the stump" to speak on behalf of fellow Hoosiers. One of these men was Schuyler Colfax of South Bend. The Republicans nominated Colfax as former general Ulysses S. Grant's running mate for the election of 1868. Grant and Colfax were elected by a wide margin.

In December of 1868 Harrison made news as prosecutor in a sensational double murder case. A man and his young wife had been killed on the outskirts of Indianapolis. The victims were shot, and the murdered woman's body was discovered half naked and badly burned. There was money involved as well, the slain husband having recently withdrawn $7,500 from the bank.

Evidence indicated that two men and a woman were involved in planning the crime. Harrison, representing the state, sought a conviction for one of the accused, Mrs. Nancy Clem. The trial ended in a hung jury. A new trial was set for January of 1869. Mrs. Clem, the thirty-five-year-old wife of a respectable grocer, sat through a trial of nearly two weeks during which one hundred fifty witnesses testified. Some of the money was traced back to Nancy Clem, who hid it in her sister's chimney. She used part of the money to bribe witnesses who provided her an alibi. In his final argument before the jurors, Harrison gave an eight-hour summation. After three days of deliberation, the jury returned with a verdict of guilty for second-degree murder. Nancy Clem appealed her case and the Indiana Supreme Court reversed the conviction and ordered a retrial. Harrison was the prosecutor again at the second trial. He won again and Mrs. Clem was sent back to prison.

Nancy Clem's two male accomplices had also been tried and convicted, but one was pardoned in 1878. This man later confessed to the murders before committing suicide. After another appeal by Mrs. Clem, the State

Supreme Court heard arguments once more, and set her free. Harrison's expert handling of the case, however, drew high praise from the newspapers. The Hoosier lawyer felt vindicated when Nancy Clem was later arrested for perjury. And through Harrison's efforts, she was sent to prison for four years.

In June of 1870 Pink Fishback dissolved his partnership with Harrison to devote all of his time to his role as editor of the *Indianapolis Journal* newspaper. Harrison replaced him with Cyrus C. Hines, a Civil War veteran and attorney three years older than Harrison.

Harrison gained further notoriety in the Milligan case. L.P. Milligan was an attorney and Indiana Democrat who had opposed the Civil War. Outspoken and bright, Milligan and his crony Copperheads had criticized Lincoln, urging an end to the fighting, even if it meant surrender. They called themselves the "Sons of Liberty" and were looked upon by many as a private militia force because of the large number of weapons they claimed.

In order to silence opposition during the Civil War, President Lincoln had temporarily suspended the writ of habeas corpus. This gave the U.S. military more power in dealing with civilian problems. Milligan and his Copperhead associates were arrested, tried by a military court, and found guilty of inciting treason and aiding the enemy. Milligan and his ringleaders were sentenced to be hanged in 1865. His friends, some of whom were influential in the government, had urged Lincoln to pardon him. The President was inclined to release Milligan, but after he was killed by John Wilkes Booth, Milligan's situation looked hopeless. President Andrew Johnson ordered the execution to proceed.

Through her contacts in Washington, Mrs. Milligan appealed directly to Secretary of War Edwin Stanton, who had once studied law with her husband. Stanton went to President Johnson and secured a reduced penalty of life in prison for Milligan. The U.S. Supreme Court, however, ruled unanimously that the army panel of judges which convicted Milligan was illegal because he should have been tried in a civilian court. It further ruled henceforth that no military court could conduct trials against civilians. Milligan was set free.

In 1868 Milligan sued the military for damages and false arrest, demanding $100,000 in damages. He also claimed prison guards tried to poison him during his stay at the Ohio Penitentiary in Columbus. President Grant appointed Harrison to defend the government in the case. Harrison knew Milligan, having met him while both worked as lawyers in Indiana. He hated Milligan's politics, if not the man himself, and prepared his case against him.

The trial was held in Indiana's Huntington County Common Pleas Court. Milligan's team of lawyers was led by Indiana Democrat Thomas Hendricks, later vice president under Grover Cleveland. Harrison was masterful in his oral presentation. He knew he could not win the case by having the decision reversed, but he was bound to see that monetary compensations were kept to a minimum. The twelve jurors, after listening to testimony for more than a month, returned their verdict in late May of 1871. The decision technically favored Milligan, but instead of receiving his $100,000, he was awarded just five dollars. Harrison and thousands throughout the country were elated. Now, with his star on the rise, he was being mentioned as a possible candidate for governor of Indiana. In an article by Fishback's friendly *Indianapolis Journal*, Harrison was proclaimed as an attorney "with no superior at the bar in Indiana."[3]

Five years later, in another high profile federal case, Harrison argued for a defendant involved in the Whiskey Ring scandal. Whiskey was actually safer than milk or water, which were often tainted. It was also cheaper than coffee or tea, and there were hundreds of distilleries throughout the country. Corruption surfaced when a group of federal excise tax agents accepted bribes from distillers trying to avoid paying a high tax. Most of the arrests and indictments, 238 of them, took place in the Midwest in the Ohio and upper Mississippi Valley regions. One of the individuals accused was Hiram Brownlee, the son of a prominent Indiana family.

Brownlee supposedly accepted a $500 bribe in Evansville. Harrison agreed to defend Brownlee when the case came before Judge Walter Q. Gresham. The government's case rested primarily on the testimony of one of the bribers, Josh Bingham, who had turned states' evidence. The central theme of Bingham's testimony was his description of Brownlee accepting the money. Bingham explained he gave Brownlee the $500 while the accused was dressing for a wedding and donning a formal hat and white kid gloves. Harrison focused on this detail and produced witnesses who saw Brownlee attend the wedding bareheaded. Altogether, there were 110 convictions and many of those sent to jail had close ties to the Grant administration. Harrison, however, won his case but had annoyed Judge Gresham who felt that Harrison, an active proponent of temperance, was a hypocrite during the liquor-related case.

When the Indiana Republican Party, or Grand Old Party (GOP), held its 1872 state convention, Harrison made little effort to actively promote his own cause. He hoped to be selected as the candidate for governor, but he relied on others to recommend him. Harrison was up against other hopefuls who sought the governor's seat, including other Civil War veterans and experienced politicians. Area newspapers, including Fishback's *Journal*, clamored for Harrison's nomination. But neither the papers nor the general public did the nominating.

Oliver Perry Morton, the former governor and friend of Harrison, was a U.S. Senator who controlled Indiana politics. Harrison's men sought his support and asked for an endorsement. Instead they received Morton's *blessings*. Being the clever politician that he was, Morton did not want to make a commitment to Harrison for fear of offending other candidates. Harrison lost the nomination in a close vote. His backers realized that Morton not only refused to give Harrison his support, but also believed he had secretly worked against him. Senator Morton's hold on the state GOP, and his ambition to live in the White House, remained an obstacle to Harrison. The aging Senator saw "Little Ben" as a political rival and threat.

Despite his setback, General Harrison continued to campaign for U.S. Grant and other candidates. Harrison was personally disturbed by the corruption of the Grant administration but didn't make his views public. And when his circle of friends urged him to oppose Morton's reelection to the Senate, his politically astute father advised him to avoid risking Morton's wrath and simply wait.[4] In the fall election Democrat Thomas Hendricks was elected governor, but Indiana and the nation reelected Grant for another term as president.

In 1873 Harrison enrolled Russell as a cadet at the Pennsylvania Military Academy in Chester. He showered much of his attention on his teenage daughter Mamie, but he forbid her to take dancing lessons. Carrie secretly arranged lessons in the home of a friend and even invited boys to participate. If Harrison ever suspected this challenge to his authority, he never made it known.

When another partner left Harrison's law firm, he was replaced by William Miller. A brilliant, hard-working attorney from Fort Wayne, Miller established a close relationship with Harrison. The new firm of Harrison, Hines, and Miller proved to be quite successful, especially when the Financial Panic of 1873 took hold in September. Business for Harrison and his associates boomed due to the number of bankruptcies and foreclosures.

By 1875, the Harrisons had a new home, built on a lot on North Delaware Street which Harrison had purchased seven years earlier. They spent considerable time planning and supervising its construction. The two-story brick Victorian mansion built in the boxy Italinate style took a year to build and cost twenty thousand dollars. Built on a 150-foot lot, its plush interior was complemented by Harrison's library, fitted with a gigantic walnut bookcase. A dining room with a cascading chandelier could seat up to twenty. Upstairs were large beds with oversized headboards. Always conscious of exercising, Harrison kept a rowing machine and a wooden weight-lifting set in the sitting room. Later, an L-shaped veranda replaced the shallow porch.

On March 1, 1876, Carrie's mother died in Pennsylvania. After returning from the funeral, Harrison learned that his father, John Scott Harrison, was seriously ill. He traveled from Indianapolis to The Point in North Bend and stayed with him until the crisis passed. John Scott's letters from The Point to his son continued. He closely followed his son's career and offered plenty of advice and encouragement—including repeated warnings to stay out of politics.

Benjamin Harrison, however, was "bitten" by the political bug and ignored his father's warnings. Once again, he decided to make a run for the governor's seat. At the 1876 state convention, many delegates felt Harrison was the best candidate for governor. But Senator Morton and his loyal lieutenants proved once more to be a stumbling block. Harrison again failed to get the nomination. However, on August 4 the Republican nominee, Congressman Godlove Orth, withdrew from the race because of alleged involvement in some scandals of the Grant administration. The State Central Committee, meeting in Indianapolis, chose Harrison to replace Orth. Harrison received hundreds of letters and telegrams from well-wishers, including congratulations from Senator Morton. But Harrison had little time left to organize an effective campaign.

Harrison used the time he had to campaign aggressively, crisscrossing the state for two months. In mid-September he and other leaders welcomed the veterans of the Grand Army of the Republic (GAR) at their annual encampment outside Indianapolis. Senator Morton was on hand to serve as host to the veterans and their former officers, one of whom was Congressman James A. Garfield. In his welcoming speech, Morton proudly "waved the bloody shirt," reviving old passions and hatreds towards the Democrats.

A three-mile parade of veterans in blue, led by Garfield on horseback, was cheered by thousands of Indianapolis citizens. After the festivities, Harrison and Garfield took a buggy ride together and visited each camp, renewing old friendships and reminding their soldiers to support "loyal" candidates.

The Democrats nominated a farmer, Congressman James "Blue Jeans" Williams for governor. Tall, homely, humorous, and a fine campaigner in his stovepipe hat, Williams was a colorful figure who was well liked. He mocked and taunted Harrison in his speeches, reminding listeners, "Give Harrison a kid glove client and a two thousand dollar fee and......"[5] Hoping to take advantage of the scandals in the Grant administration, the Democrats worked feverishly for Williams. Harrison was favored to win, but many independent Republicans and Democrats joined in support of another candidate, former Republican Anson Wolcott. Wolcott represented the Greenback Party, which promoted the idea of printing and distributing large amounts of paper money. If the national government followed this practice, they reasoned, there would be prosperity, especially for farmers. Harrison, however, believed that such action might lead to runaway inflation and thus hurt everyone.

During the Civil War the government had issued more than $400,000,000 in greenback treasury notes unbacked by gold or silver. Other efforts in 1874 to pump an extra $44 million worth of greenbacks into the economy failed when President Grant vetoed the proposal. Harrison addressed the controversy when he told an audience during the campaign, "It is better to have a little less currency than we need than it would be to have more; for when we have an excess, speculation is stimulated to an excessive degree, and the currency becomes depreciated..."[6]

In a close contest, "Blue Jeans" Williams defeated Harrison for governor by five thousand votes, or about one per cent. Party leaders admitted that four-fifths of the thirteen thousand votes cast for Wolcott came from the Republican side. Two reasons for the defeat may have been the backlash of several scandals which plagued the Grant administration and an economic downturn. Despite his loss, Harrison went to Chicago where he had been invited to give a speech on behalf of the Republican presidential nominee, Rutherford B. Hayes. He also spoke to large crowds in Philadelphia, Newark, Bloomington, Illinois, and Indianapolis.

Rutherford B. Hayes, a gallant Civil War commander and Governor of Ohio, was chosen by the Republican Convention delegates because no other candidate could capture the nomination. His Democratic opponent,

Governor Samuel Tilden of New York, was an honest and popular reform-minded man. Tilden appeared to be the winner on election night, but the Republicans challenged the results, claiming massive cheating and fraud at the polling places in three southern states.

This disputed election of 1876 was settled by a special fifteen-man commission, consisting of eight Republicans and seven Democrats, appointed by Congress. After weeks of heated debate, charges and counter charges, and even the threat of bloodshed, the parties agreed on a number of compromises. They finally declared Hayes the winner of the presidential election, just in time for his inauguration.

In the spring of 1877 Harrison and Carrie vacationed in the East, taking the opportunity to visit Mamie, who was then in her second year of college, and Russell, who was completing his last term at Lafayette College in Eaton, Pennsylvania. During this trip, the Harrisons witnessed a disturbing sight as they traveled by train.

Labor unrest among workers, particularly railroad employees, was being fueled by hungry bellies, low wages, and mistreatment by rail company owners. This led to violence in major cities like Baltimore, Philadelphia, and Chicago between unruly mobs and local militias, which often consisted of police or sheriff departments. Nothing was resolved. In desperation, railroad workers called for a national strike. In Pittsburgh, mob violence erupted and federal troops were sent in to restore order and keep the trains running.

The Harrisons watched some of these events unfold during their train trip back home. Within a few days the wave of dissension spread to Indianapolis, where thirteen soldiers guarded the federal arsenal. Residents feared that if the strikers got control of the weapons and ammunition stored inside, the city might find itself in the middle of a revolution.

When the Harrisons arrived home on Friday, July 13th, they were relieved to learn there had been little violence in Indianapolis. Rumors were spreading, however, that a mob planned to overtake the arsenal. Fear and panic gripped the populace as the situation boiled to a fever pitch. The strikers disrupted rail transportation and destroyed some property. Federal troops were not available to prevent unrest because they had been sent to other strike-ridden areas.

City officials had to resolve the problem. At the request of the mayor, a crowd of concerned citizens met July 24 at the Indianapolis federal courthouse. Judge Walter Gresham and others got involved in a heated discussion as to what course of action they should take. Harrison rose to speak. He made three suggestions: that the concerned citizens should form their own emergency militia, that they should reinforce the protection of the arsenal, and that a committee be created to hear the grievances of the strikers. Most in attendance agreed. Harrison helped command the civilian volunteers, many of them veterans who had served with the two men in the Civil War. After securing the arsenal, Harrison spent nearly every waking hour over the next three days meeting with groups of strikers, militia, and citizens. He made a direct appeal to the mob gathered at the arsenal, explaining to the strikers that any violence would only hurt their cause. He also promised them he would help reach a fair settlement with railroad owners.

Peace prevailed. Rioting was kept to a minimum with only a little property destroyed. Some of the strike leaders were arrested and held on charges of disturbing the peace and contempt of court. Benjamin Harrison appeared with them in the courtroom and pleaded with the judge that the strikers not be punished. The men were set free. Harrison was establishing himself as a man who could resolve differences.

After campaigning for Rutherford B. Hayes in 1876, Harrison received word he would be offered a cabinet post, but to get it he would have to seek and obtain the support of Morton, and he was not about to do either. Morton, however, was not in good health. On November 1, 1877, Senator Oliver Morton died of complications after a stroke. Harrison, in spite of his differences with Morton, agreed to head an effort to erect a statue of him. It was placed in front of the Indiana statehouse. After Morton's death, Hoosier Republicans looked to Harrison for leadership.

In December of 1877, Harrison received news that his niece Mollie Eaton, and his brother-in-law, Henry Scott, had died. In the spring, tragedy struck again. On May 18, 1878, Harrison's twenty-three-year-old grandnephew August Devin died suddenly and was buried in the family plot overlooking the Ohio River. More disturbing news came a week later when Harrison, on the eve of the state convention, received a telegram informing him that his father had passed away. John Scott Harrison was seventy-three years old when he collapsed in his bedroom while preparing a lecture on Christianity. The funeral was set for May 29. Hundreds of family and friends came from miles around to pay their respects. While accompanying the coffin to the burial site, Benjamin's brothers noticed that August Devin's grave had been disturbed. Upon examining the coffin, they discovered his body was missing.

The family covered John Harrison's grave with dirt and a ton of cemented rocks and hired two watchmen to guard it. They began their own investigation while Benjamin returned to Indianapolis, vowing to punish those responsible for the body-snatching. His brothers Carter and John obtained a search warrant to look for Devin's body at the Ohio Medical College in Cincinnati. After a careful search they were about to leave when they found a cloth-covered body with a noose around its neck, hanging on a hook concealed in a dark open air shaft. To their horror, they discovered the corpse was not Devin, but their father. His body had also been stolen, even though guards had been assigned to protect it.

Harrison described in a public letter the sight of his father's body "hanging by the neck like that of a dog, in a pit of a medical college."[7] The janitor of the medical school was arrested for taking part in the theft of the body. An outraged Harrison arrived in Cincinnati where, much to his disgust, the dean of the college defended the actions of the janitor, arguing that the three hundred medical students needed corpses for proper instruction. After further questioning, the names of two other men were implicated. The janitor was released on bail and a trial was set.

A few weeks later Harrison again traveled to Cincinnati, this time to file a $10,000 lawsuit against the medical school. In the meantime, Devin's body was located at a morgue in Ann Arbor, Michigan. Newspapers throughout the country provided lurid details and the lawsuit initiated by the Harrisons was settled out of court. A more positive result came in 1880 when, because of this incident, the state of Ohio passed a new law increasing the penalty for grave robbing.

With their son Russell grown and living in Montana, Harrison and Carrie found themselves living in an almost empty nest. Daughter Mamie had finished school and was back home, but kept a busy social agenda writing her fiancé and attending many church and community activities. Immersing himself in his legal work, the General also found time to join a local literary club, where he took an active role. His wife devoted much of her time to cultivating the grapes and strawberries growing behind the house, which meant jars of delicious jellies and jams for family, friends, and neighbors.

In June of 1879, President Hayes named Harrison as one of seven members of the Mississippi River Commission, which was formed to improve the condition of that waterway. Harrison was defending a client in a murder trial at the time and declined the appointment. After a personal appeal from President Hayes and an invitation to the White House, Harrison accepted the post. He served twenty months, working with engineers and authorities to draw up plans to improve waterway shipping and help prevent the devastating floods along the river. He worked diligently and played a key role in submitting recommendations in his detailed report. Harrison, however, grew weary from his legal and political work, combined with his travels and duties on the Mississippi River Commission. Nevertheless, it fell upon him to try and unite a badly divided Republican Party in Indiana.

Many Republicans felt Hayes had failed as president. As the 1880 Republican convention approached, Harrison was chosen as chairman of the Indian delegation. President Hayes had declined a second term, since party leaders had assured him he would not be renominated. On June 2, a crowd of 18,000, including 756 Republican delegates, jammed into the Chicago Interstate Exposition Building. For eight days the delegates argued on issues, set rules, developed a party platform, and got down to the business of choosing a candidate. Harrison and his block of Indiana delegates pledged their support for Senator James G. Blaine of Maine. Though considered arrogant and proud by some, Blaine, "The Plumed Knight," was a forceful leader and gifted orator.

A major dilemma developed when U.S. Grant made it known he was seeking a third term for the presidency. Grant's supporters, nicknamed the Stalwarts, were led by an abrasive, sarcastic and cocky Senator from New York named Roscoe Conkling. Senator John Sherman of Ohio, brother of Harrison's friend William T. Sherman, also sought the Republican nomination. Several attempts were also made to nominate Benjamin Harrison, but he quickly suppressed these efforts.

As chairman of the Indiana delegation, Harrison made it clear that if no candidate could get enough votes, Indiana would throw its support to James A. Garfield. The battle at the convention dragged on. Finally, on the thirty-sixth ballot, the weary, hot, and frustrated delegates selected Garfield as their standard bearer. Garfield had pledged his allegiance for Sherman but Sherman could not garner much support. The pro-Grant faction, bitter to the end, were only mildly pleased when one of their own, Chester Arthur of New York, was nominated for vice president.

Garfield's Democratic opponent in the election of 1880 was a well-respected Civil War hero from Pennsylvania, Winfield S. Hancock. Harrison admired Hancock but took a very active role in Garfield's campaign. Harrison stumped for Garfield in many cities, both in and away from Indiana. After speaking at a rally in Bloomington, Indiana, Harrison was leaving the podium when an ex-Confederate blocked his path off the stage, called him a liar, and aimed a pistol at him. Bystanders grabbed the gun, wrestled the assailant to the floor and dragged him from the hall. Harrison was unharmed and continued his calendar of appearances.

As a state leader, Harrison worked diligently to deliver Indiana to Garfield. He also addressed a large crowd in New York City, appearing with Chester Arthur. Garfield won Indiana by about sixty six hundred votes out of 470,000 cast, squeaking out a narrow victory and getting all fifteen of Indian's electoral votes. To show his appreciation, president-elect Garfield offered Harrison a cabinet post.

Democrats leveled charges of fraud in the Hoosier State. Indeed, palms were greased and the state's political machinery was well lubricated by the Republican National Committee. The Democrats had tried similar tactics but got out-spent and out-cheated. At a GOP banquet in New York City in January of 1881, Vice President-elect Arthur, speaking with tongue-in-cheek, could hardly contain his laughter in thanking Republican campaign workers for their efforts in Indiana. Arthur's audience included some reporters and his remarks drew chuckles. Harrison was certainly aware of the allegations by Democrats but he was not implicated in any unethical activities.

CHAPTER 6

Senator and Presidential Candidate

THOUGH IT WAS NOT PUBLIC KNOWLEDGE, HARRISON HAD WRITTEN PRESIDENT-ELECT Garfield a letter just after the election of 1880, informing him that he planned to run for the U.S. Senate. This was the reason he might refuse Garfield's offer of a cabinet post in the new administration. The Indiana Legislature was going to elect a new senator because Joseph McDonald, the Democrat incumbent, was retiring. To Harrison, there appeared to be little opposition, with the exception of Walter Gresham, a Republican federal judge from Indianapolis whose independent views were often compared to those of a Democrat. He and Harrison had tangled several times in the courtroom and Gresham was not shy in letting others know his mistrust for Harrison. Gresham's duties on the court, however, prevented him from mounting a campaign and he withdrew from the race after three weeks.

The Indiana Legislature was scheduled to choose a senator on January 18, 1881. Harrison's loyal camp had little difficulty convincing the legislators that their man was the best choice. On the evening of January 15, however, the campaign was sidetracked when Carrie Harrison slipped on the ice outside a neighbor's home. She fell and struck her head on the pavement. Amazingly, Carrie was not cut, but she was badly bruised and needed a couple days to recover. On January 18th, Benjamin Harrison was elected the next U.S. Senator from Indiana.

On January 22 Harrison traveled by rail to Mentor, Ohio, to meet with Garfield, who still offered him a Cabinet post. Harrison stayed overnight as the two discussed a wide-ranging number of topics. Harrison boarded a train for Indianapolis and a week later, visited Garfield again, this time with a small delegation of Indiana Republicans. Harrison and his loyal supporters had made up their minds—he was going to the Senate.

After attending Garfield's inauguration on March 4, 1881, Harrison went to work. Taking his assigned seat, he spent most of his first year in the Senate saying little and observing his colleagues. Many fellow senators were millionaires, and Harrison soon learned that their power was wielded in the Senate committee rooms.

Benjamin Harrison's term as a United States Senator may not be described as exceptional or outstanding—he simply did his job. He authored and sponsored several important pieces of legislation, faithfully attended committee meetings, thoroughly investigated a number of wide-ranging problems, answered all of his mail, debated his colleagues with eloquence, voted mostly along party lines and, on occasion, demonstrated an air of independence and political courage in dealing with his fellow Senators.

Harrison's peers were impressed with his command of information and his use of words. One of his law partners back in Indianapolis was Harry Eaton, his brother-in-law. Eaton made this observation of Harrison: "Often he has taken the transcript of a case on the evening of his arrival from Washington and studied it that night, then going into court the next morning master of all the details and able to make a powerful argument."[1]

One issue the new senator faced was patronage—the practice of rewarding campaign workers with government jobs. Since the days of George Washington, the president and members of Congress had been besieged by supporters looking for jobs. In what was known as the "spoils system," office-seekers badgered their Congressman for a recommendation to the president, whom they hoped would then appoint them to a government position. Many applicants who lacked letters of recommendation simply went to the White House without any references to gain an interview with the president. The spoils system was dreaded by presidents because it took up much of their time. If Senator Harrison was frustrated about patronage, he would someday discover it would become even more of a dilemma.

Most of the available federal positions existed within the post offices throughout the country. Hundreds of Indiana men now sought out Harrison for written recommendations. Even old friends of his grandfather, William

Henry Harrison, wanted jobs or special favors. The pressure on Harrison to dole out patronage made him realize he was "not cut out for a Boss" and preferred instead selecting the best two or three people for a position.[2] In most instances, however, the senator relied upon the judgment of his friends in Indianapolis to screen local job seekers before they were recommended to him. By 1883 it didn't matter which method of selecting Harrison employed because when President Chester Arthur named Gresham as postmaster-general, Harrison's influence shrank.

Another problem Harrison dealt with was pensions to Union Civil War veterans. A surplus of several million dollars existed in the Treasury in 1881 and pension-hungry ex-soldiers wanted it. Senator Harrison eventually introduced hundreds of individual pension or family relief bills. Most of these were approved by President Garfield and his successor, Chester Arthur. This issue too, like the one concerning patronage, would cause him grief and much more anguish within a decade.

On July 2, 1881 President Garfield was shot by a deranged office-seeker. Senator Harrison left Indianapolis to offer his help and support to First Lady Lucretia Garfield. Ironically, Harrison had met the assassin, Charles Guiteau, just three weeks prior to the shooting. Guiteau had come to Harrison for a recommendation for an appointment as an ambassador, but Harrison sensed something odd about Guiteau and refused to give it, as did several other high ranking officials.

Garfield suffered terribly from the shooting. Failure to locate the bullet and an infection from contaminated instruments resulted in Garfield losing one hundred pounds before he finally died on September 19, 1881. Arthur was sworn in as president. Perhaps one positive result of the tragic shooting was the passage of the Pendleton Civil Service Act of 1883. This law awarded a significant number of government jobs based on merit and testing instead of influence, though many positions in civil service remained unaffected by the Pendleton Act.

In other matters, Harrison defended a high tariff to protect American industry. Senator Harrison also voted against the Chinese Exclusion Act of 1882, which gave the federal government the power to regulate and limit the large numbers of Chinese immigrants coming into America. This issue was of major concern to white laborers on the West Coast where they had to compete with the Chinese for jobs. Harrison was unhappy with the wording of the bill but despite his opposition, the Chinese Exclusion Act became law when Arthur signed it in 1882. On another matter, Harrison supported regulating the power of railroads to remove Indians and settlers from land adjacent to the railroads' right of way.

In 1882 Carrie became so ill she required surgery. She spent her recovery in a New York City hospital and later in Indianapolis. Her husband felt the strain of her illness and his own overwork. The Senator wrote his brother, Carter Harrison, "I am worked to death here and am getting tired of the long session."[3] In addition to his Senate work, Harrison spent much time campaigning for Republican candidates. He was in great demand as a speaker and during 1882 gave speeches for candidates in Ohio, Indiana, and Iowa. Proud of his party's record, Harrison told one crowd, "While the Republican Party may not always be right, it has been more nearer right than any party which has existed."[4] The Senator's efforts in campaigning paid off. The GOP gained four seats in the Senate.

In January 1884, Harrison attended the Nebraska wedding of his son Russell, who married Mary Saunders, daughter of a Nebraska Senator. Returning to the Senate, Harrison made news when he spoke out against the lynchings and acts of cruelty committed against blacks in the South. He admitted he was at a loss as to what could be done to end the terror. It was during this time that Harrison was urged by friends to consider a run for the presidency. A number of newspapers promoted his candidacy. *The New York Times* described Harrison as "a clean candidate...very strong."[5]

President Arthur, in poor health, had alienated GOP leaders and his nomination at the 1884 convention was in doubt. Harrison did not actively seek the nomination, preferring instead to help select his party's nominee. Postmaster-General Walter Gresham and Maine Senator James Blaine both wanted the nomination and sought Harrison's help. An angry Gresham backer who asked Harrison for support wrote a friend, "Senator H will never be President, nor do I believe will he ever get the support of Indiana in convention. He is too cold-blooded and too cold-hearted to secure the support of a warm-hearted party. He has done very little since his election for his friends who placed him in his present position..."[6]

Senator Harrison, however, threw his support to James G. Blaine, who was nominated by the Republicans. Blaine lost the election to Democrat Grover Cleveland. It was a vicious, mud-slinging campaign in which Cleveland was accused of fathering an illegitimate child and Blaine was charged with not being legally married. The day after the election, Harrison gave away his daughter Mamie when she married Indianapolis businessman Robert McKee, who later co-founded the General Electric Company.

Over the next two years Senator Harrison introduced and supported a number of bills to earmark federal funding for education, establishing civilian government in Western territories, setting aside land out West for preservation, and helping farmers fight against high railroad shipping rates. In the summer of 1885, Harrison, a member of the Senate Indian Affairs Committee, went on a six-week tour of the West, visiting Indian reservations. He took along several government officials, a reporter, and family members. He stopped in Montana to visit his son Russell. After touring the West coast, Harrison returned to Washington where he sponsored three bills to improve conditions for Native Americans.

A personal problem nagged Harrison during this time—his son's financial crisis. Russell Harrison lost several thousand dollars in his Montana business ventures. Russell's gold mine, cattle ranch and newspaper had all failed. Russell borrowed money from his father's friends, making trips to New York City and Washington to get it. He speculated in the stock market and spiraled into more debt. Russell appealed to his father for help, receiving advice but no money. Investors demanded their money back, and Russell borrowed more to pay them.

This entire episode tainted his father's reputation, and it would take a few years before Russell wrangled free of his failed business practices. Eventually, however, Russell would prove himself a success. He worked as his father's personal secretary at the White House. As a mechanical engineer, newspaper publisher and lawyer, he also served as a lieutenant colonel of volunteers in the Spanish-American War, seeing combat in Cuba. In addition, he was appointed inspector-general in Cuba (until he came down with yellow fever) and provost martial for Puerto Rico. Ultimately Russell was elected to both houses of the Indiana legislature before his death in 1936 at age 82.

In the fall of 1886, Harrison campaigned again for GOP candidates, speaking out against President Cleveland and the Democrats. Once more, his labors proved effective. The Republicans won seven of thirteen Congressional seats, but Democrats had made some gains back in Harrison's own district in Indiana. Harrison was hopeful he would be reelected as Senator but realized he might not make it. He confided to close friends that he would "shed no tears" if he lost his seat and that he would "greatly enjoy the opportunity to attend to my own business and let politics alone."[7] When the Indiana Legislature met in 1887, there was an equal number of Republicans and

Democrats. After sixteen exhausting ballots, the lawmakers, by a single vote, chose David Turpie to replace Harrison.

Despite the setback, Harrison still had three more months as a Senator. By the time his term was over, he could look back on his Senate career with a sense of achievement. Though he was never part of the inner circle of powerful Senators, he nevertheless attracted the attention of wealthy admirers such as Wharton Barker of Pennsylvania, a friendship which paid political dividends later. A handful of Harrison's fellow Republican colleagues were tainted with graft or scandal and some of these same men would prove troublesome after he became chief executive.

Harrison had sponsored hundreds of pieces of legislation, though many of his pension bills failed to pass in the House. He advocated the creation of the Interstate Commerce Commission to curb the power of the railroad industry. Harrison became known for his mastery of information and his hard work in committees, not for his brilliance on the Senate floor. His reports were meticulous and he knew their script verbatim, seldom using notes when he spoke. His voting record supported labor, much to the dismay of his Republican colleagues. He also worked in behalf of Native-Americans who needed a spokesman in Congress.

Any feelings of politics vanished when, in March of 1887, his daughter Mamie gave birth to a son. The child was named Benjamin Harrison McKee and proved to be a great joy not only to the Harrisons but inevitably to the American public as well.

Ex-Senator Harrison returned to his private law practice. In the spring of 1888 the Harrisons vacationed at Deer Park in Maryland, amid talk of a "Harrison for President" movement. The GOP was searching for a candidate to defeat Cleveland, and Harrison gave his permission to allow supporters to organize a campaign. Harrison was the guest speaker at a George Washington birthday celebration, sponsored by the Michigan Society in Washington, when he told a large dinner audience, "I am a dead statesman, but I am a rejuvenated Republican."[8] The words caught on and Harrison supporters began referring to themselves as "Rejuvenated Republicans."

Two of Harrison's friends, Eugene Hay and Louis Michener, became his campaign managers and they quickly set about making contacts, raising money and planning strategy for the convention. In June the Republican delegates met in Chicago's Exposition Hall when tens of thousands from the public vied for the 7000 seats inside. Prior to the convention, Harrison instructed his managers, "Remember, no bargains, no alliances, no trades.

I may like to be President, but if I am to go to the White House, I don't propose to go shackled."[9] This advice was ignored as Harrison's backers made several deals to secure the nomination. It is a credit to his supporters that they pushed their man's candidacy but conducted a strategy where few opponents were offended. The Harrison men were poised and ready to seize the nomination if opportunity came.

The 1888 GOP Convention proved to be quite exciting. Leading candidates for the nomination were Ohio Senators John Foraker and John Sherman, Maine's James G. Blaine, Judge Walter Gresham, Michigan's Senator Russell Alger, Iowa Senator William B. Allison and New York's railroad magnate Chauncey Depew. Another possible nominee was a rising star from the Midwest—Congressman William McKinley of Ohio. It was McKinley who was chosen to nominate John Sherman, while rejecting pressure from other delegates to declare himself a candidate.

After five ballots there was no clear winner. James Blaine, visiting Andrew Carnegie in Scotland, realized he could not win and telegraphed his supporters to switch their votes to Harrison. Sherman, suspicious that McKinley wanted the nomination, had to be reassured that the Ohio Congressman made a valiant effort to get him on the ticket. Sherman knew he could not win and he too released his delegates to Harrison. Finally, on the eighth ballot, Harrison was nominated. The delegates then chose Levi Morton as Harrison's running mate. Morton was a New York banker, a former Congressman, and a U.S. Minister to France. When Harrison heard the news of his nomination, he nearly fainted and had to lie down. That same evening Harrison's front yard was partially destroyed when a souvenir-hungry crowd took pieces of his white wooden fence.

President Cleveland was easily renominated by the Democrats. Cleveland's vice president, Thomas Hendricks, had died in office, so the Democrats chose seventy-five-year-old Allen Thurman of Ohio as Cleveland's running mate. A Copperhead during the Civil War, Thurman proved ineffective as a campaigner in the 1888 race.

Tariffs were the main issue of the 1888 presidential race. President Cleveland wanted import taxes reduced to encourage free trade, especially with England. Harrison, on the other hand, advocated high tariffs, even if it meant paying higher prices for American-made goods. He suggested during the campaign that "a cheap coat might conceal a cheap man under the coat."[10] To balance their stand on higher tariffs, the Republicans proposed a decrease on domestic, or internal, taxes.

Harrison decided to follow the example James Garfield had set and conduct a "Front Porch Campaign." He invited the public to come and meet him. Groups from fifty to thousands made visits to Harrison's Indianapolis home. A local band, The Harrison Marching Club, escorted groups from Union Station and took them on the mile and a half trip to hear the candidate. Between July 7 and October 23, candidate Harrison made more than one hundred speeches to some three hundred thousand visitors. Signs and symbols appeared, some of the same ones used in his grandfather's presidential campaign nearly fifty years earlier. Cider barrels, log cabins, a huge wooden ball, replicas of eagles and raccoons, and a torchlight parade were all reminiscent of the William Henry Harrison/John Tyler campaign of 1840. These signs and symbols were meant to link candidates with the Ohio pioneer life and the backwoods. They helped identify Harrison with the common man and were used to attract voters.

The candidate's campaign was better organized and more carefully scripted than Garfield's 1880 operation from Mentor. A committee arranged the visits and reviewed proposed introductory speeches *twice*. Several times a day, at the appointed hour, Harrison would appear and talk for about twenty minutes. Afterward, he edited his speeches and sent them out by wire to the Associated Press the following day.

Harrison showed signs of fatigue—one reporter feared the candidate would "suffer an utter collapse before the campaign is half over."[11] On two occasions during the campaign Harrison took time off to go fishing for a few days. And to prevent further invasion of his home and destruction of his yard, the campaign committee decided that sizeable crowds would assemble at University Park. Harrison would then walk a mile to greet each large delegation. After the candidate told one big gathering he regretted his home was not large enough to accommodate them, a man yelled to Harrison, "There will be more room in the White House!"[12]

The wealthy John Wanamaker served as Harrison's finance chairman. He summoned ten prominent Philadelphia businessmen to his home and each agreed to contribute $10,000. Wanamaker added $50,000 of his own money while Mark Hanna of Cleveland raised $100,000. Close to $4,000,000 was raised, about four times what the Democrats could muster. With all the expenses in conducting the campaign, funds were also used to buy votes.

The Grand Army of the Republic and other soldier groups turned out in large numbers. Harrison told one group of approximately 3000 veterans, "The comradeship of the war will never end until our lives end. The fires in which our friendship was riveted and welded were too hot for the bond ever to be broken."[13]

During the third week of August, Harrison was touched when a group of young girls dressed in red, white, and blue appeared at his home. The girls were escorted by a six-year-old boy on a pony. Candidate Harrison stepped onto the porch of his home and made some brief remarks, explaining, "Some of the best friends I have are under ten years of age, and after tonight I will have many more, for all your names will be added."[14]

Harrison's campaign gained momentum when two old icons publicly endorsed him—western explorer John C. Fremont and African-American orator Frederick Douglass. General Lew Wallace's biography of Harrison, published just weeks before Election Day, enjoyed a wide circulation (Wallace incidentally was the author of the best-selling novel *Ben Hur*).

Then, suddenly, bad news came. A letter, written by W. W. Dudley, treasurer of the Republican National Committee, was intercepted by Democrats. In the letter Dudley instructed GOP field workers to buy votes at prices ranging from two to fifteen dollars. The note instructed they "divide the floaters [repeat voters] into blocks of five," making certain they all vote for Harrison.[15] Republicans claimed the letter was a forgery, though Dudley remained silent on the subject. The practice of bribing voters was something commonly but cautiously done by both parties at that time. The letter, however, led to an open break between Dudley and Harrison and led to reform in the use of secret ballots.

Carrie had her supporters too. Carrie Harrison Clubs were formed in towns and cities, and when they came to visit, Benjamin talked to them from his front door. Another novelty, an idea borrowed from his grandfather's 1840 campaign, was the huge Harrison ball. Weighing over 1000 pounds, it was a steel-ribbed sphere, covered in red and white canvas with a pole through its middle where men pushed it through hundreds of communities. "Keep the ball rolling" was the expression back in 1840 and Harrison's supporters echoed the cry once again. Beginning in Cumberland, Maryland, the ball was covered in campaign slogans as it weaved its way to Indianapolis over more than 5000 miles through eight states. It arrived in Indianapolis on the eve of the election.

Cleveland, who adhered to the tradition that it was "un-presidential" for an incumbent to campaign, remained at his vacation retreat at Cape Cod and let other Democrats campaign for him. He even refused to let his Cabinet members campaign. On September 10, Cleveland issued a statement to the press, attacking high tariffs and accusing Republicans of offering "free tobacco and free whiskey" to bribe voters.[16]

More controversy followed. A California Republican, posing as an Englishman under the name of Charles Murchison, wrote a letter to Lionel Sackville-West, the British Minister in Washington. "Murchison" asked the ambassador which political party was favored by the British. Sackville-West answered that Murchison should vote for Cleveland. A week later the Minister's letter was published in newspapers. Irish-Americans, many of whom resented British rule in Ireland, now had another reason to reject Cleveland. President Cleveland was so upset at the controversy caused by the letter, he asked Great Britain to recall its Minister. Sackville-West was sacked and sent packing on October 30. Republicans seized the opportunity to remind voters that a vote for Cleveland was a vote for England.

Besides vetoing most of the veteran pension proposals sent to his desk, Cleveland further angered many northern voters when he promised to return captured Confederate battle flags taken by Union soldiers in the Civil War. This outraged veterans and their protests forced Cleveland to withdraw his promise, but the damage was done. Adding more fuel to the fire was when Cleveland went fishing on Decoration Day, refusing to give a speech at Gettysburg. He also announced he would not visit the GAR encampment in St. Louis, saying he feared for his safety after receiving threats of personal violence if he attended.

Harrison also faced public criticism. Because he was backed by wealthy individuals and business trusts, he was labeled as an enemy of the workingman by various labor groups. In several speeches he reassured labor leaders he was being falsely accused. He explained that the charges against him were lies "whose only purpose was to poison the minds of the workingmen."[17] The candidate's reply must have been convincing because many workers publicly announced their support for Harrison.

Some reporters described the 1888 presidential election as a contest between "Brains" Harrison and "Beef" Cleveland. Though Harrison lost the popular vote by one hundred thousand, he defeated Cleveland in the electoral college, the body of voters which officially meets to elect the president and vice president in December.

Harrison believed God played a major role in his win, announcing with tears in his eyes, "Providence has given us this victory!" Some Republican leaders who made deals without Harrison's consent disagreed. When the powerful Pennsylvania political boss Matthew Quay heard about Harrison's remark, attributing his victory to divine intervention, he responded, "Think of the man! He ought to know that Providence hadn't a damn thing to do with it," and added that Harrison would never know how many Republicans "were compelled to approach the gates of the penitentiary to make him President."[18] When Harrison later learned about the deals made in his behalf he complained, "When I came to power I found the party managers had taken it all themselves...I could not name my own Cabinet! They have sold out every place to pay the election expenses..."[19]

Irregularities in presidential campaigns are nothing new. Each political party has indulged in shenanigans and outright deceit in trying to get their candidate elected. The outcome of an election was sometimes decided on who out-cheated who. Democrats claimed Republicans stole the election. This was no more apparent than in the Midwest, where boxcars of paid Ohio, Kentucky, and Indiana voters were transported to other distant polling places to cast their ballots again. Labeled "floaters" or "repeaters" who voted early and often, these men were paid in advance. In Indiana alone, an estimated 20,000 floaters allegedly got $15 of gold apiece.

Harrison won his own state by just 2,348 votes. He carried New York by only thirteen thousand votes, after his Republican supporters made a deal with the fiercely Democratic Tammany Hall of New York City, which opposed Cleveland's ideas on reforming civil service. Cleveland was at least pleased he had made the tariff question a main target of discussion, and considered his failure to be reelected only "a temporary defeat."[20]

The Harrisons were happy the campaign was over. Hundreds of houseguests had broken their furniture, worn out the carpets, and created disturbances throughout their home. Carrie told the president-elect, "Well, it's the White House or the poor house with us now."[21] Upon leaving his beloved Indianapolis, Harrison realized his job as president would be a lonely one. Speaking briefly to a crowd assembled at the depot, he remarked, "The moment of decision is one of isolation."[22]

It may have been small compensation, but Harrison would be getting a significant pay increase. His presidential salary of $50,000 was more money than he had ever earned in a single year. But there would be times when even his pay didn't seem worth the pain he would face.

Chapter 7

Setting Sail

It rained for three days prior to the inauguration. With more rain in the forecast, rumors spread the outdoor activities would be cancelled. On Saturday, March 2 Harrison announced that if people were willing to stand in the rain for his inauguration, so was he. The wind and rain in Washington had torn down banners and decorations on the city's buildings. The steady downpour kept many people indoors, and many of them were inside saloons. On Saturday night scores of drunks staggered into the streets and one group of them marched to the White House demanding that President Cleveland provide them some rooms for the night. He did not.

Harrison arose at 7:30 a.m. and had breakfast with his family, then led them in a half-hour of prayer, Scripture reading and hymn-singing. That evening, in spite of the rain, Harrison left his room at the Arlington Hotel and took a long walk, by himself. His predecessor Grover Cleveland worked at his White House desk until 2:00 a.m., signing bills and finishing his correspondence.

Inauguration Day, March 4, began with confusion *and rain*. Harrison thought he would be picked up by President Cleveland at 10:00 a.m. at Willard's Hotel, so that is where he headed. On the other hand, Cleveland was under the impression that Harrison was to come to the White House by 11:00, and he was waiting. The management at Willard's was stunned to see Harrison drenched when he entered the lobby shortly before 10. After a speedy investigation President-elect Harrison got back in his open barouche for a quick trip to the White House.

That morning Cleveland and his young beautiful bride Frances made their final rounds in the White House to make certain everything was in order for the new occupants. As the couple was walking out the front door, they stopped as Mrs. Cleveland told the servants, "Now, I want you to take good care of everything, the furnishings, the china, the crystal, the silver. I want to see everything just as it is now when my husband and I move back in here precisely four years from today."[1]

Despite a steady downpour, Harrison rode to his inauguration with his carriage top down so the people could get a clear glimpse of him. When Harrison emerged from the Capitol Building where Vice President Morton was sworn in, he walked onto the East Portico to take his oath of office. Normally, fifteen hundred people would be expected in the stands behind him, but the wet weather kept the crowd to less than two hundred. Many watched the ceremony from the windows of the Capitol while others simply went home to get out of the rain. Among the many who stayed indoors rather than get soaked watching the proceedings was a young scholar and author. He was a history professor and football coach from Wesleyan University in Connecticut who one day would be inaugurated president; his name was Thomas Woodrow Wilson.

Using his family *Bible*, 55-year-old Benjamin Harrison placed his left hand on the Scriptures which had been open to Psalm 121, a prayer by King David which reads in part, "I will lift up my eyes into the hills from whence cometh my help." Raising his right hand, Harrison was sworn in by Chief Justice Melville Fuller as the Twenty-third President of the United States. First Lady Caroline Harrison and her daughter shared an umbrella then left before the new president began his address. As President Harrison began to speak, Grover Cleveland, in a gesture of courtesy, held an umbrella over Harrison's bare head as the new president looked out into a sea of soaked top hats and black umbrellas.

Harrison's inaugural speech had been published in newspapers, but those who came to hear it were disappointed. Only the first few rows of spectators, in an estimated crowd of 20,000, heard Harrison due to the pounding rain. Hundreds of people departed before he began to speak. Nevertheless, several of the president's remarks were memorable though his speech was too long considering the soggy circumstances. He began by saying, "The great masses of our people are better fed, clothed, and housed than their fathers were."[2] He spoke of limiting the growth of large corporations, which interfered with fair competition, and called for continued neutrality regarding European affairs. The president ended his brief speech by asking the American people to refrain from political bickering and to "exalt patriotism."[3]

Harrison and Morton headed back to the White House to change into some dry clothes before reviewing the parade. One reporter noted, "Pennsylvania Avenue looked like a mushroom field. All decorations were ruined, the bleachers were too wet to be sat on, and the parade was cut down to the District militia and the Seventieth Indiana, Harrison's old regiment."[4] The inaugural parade, which was shortened due to the weather, actually included several military units, some red-shirted firemen, two groups of black supporters, and William "Buffalo Bill" Cody, American scout, Indian fighter, and showman.

Afterward, the president went back to the White House to prepare for the inaugural ball, which was held in the Pension Building. Built in 1887 and used for Cleveland's inaugural festivities, the galleries and walls were lavishly decorated with flowers, flags, electric lights and red, white, and blue bunting. Carved eagles and coats of arms from all the states decorated the walls and garland embraced the pillars, including the eight huge Corinthian columns. From the center of each of the three courts hung a large figure symbolizing democracy: lights in the shape of a Liberty Bell, a ship of state, and a star with the word "Constitution" under it. At the east end of the Great Hall was an immense plate glass mirror sixteen feet high and ten feet wide set in a frame of six hundred pieces of colored cut glass. Rooms were also provided for the press, police and telegraph operators. The building, incidentally, still stands.

Twelve thousand people, including William Tecumseh Sherman and "Buffalo Bill," were waiting when the Harrisons and Mortons arrived at 10:30 p.m. Dancing was not scheduled until after the president and vice president arrived. After walking the length of the gallery, the Harrisons and Mortons shook hands with dignitaries then were taken to a three-room suite where they shook more hands for about half an hour. Each of the guests in the long reception line met the honored couples and were presented a red rose by an aide. Immediately following this ceremony, the party proceeded to the ballroom where the two honored couples danced one slow turn around the room. Two separate bands, including the Marine Band, played from inside a Japanese pagoda, accompanied by one hundred singers.

The rooms on the second floor were reserved for the different committees and the presidential party. The rooms between the Fourth Street and G Street entrances were set up as a dinner hall in which a sumptuous banquet was served by a Philadelphia caterer. The menu was composed of both hot and cold entrees. Boned Turkey a l'Americaine, Pate de Fois Gras a la Harrison and Republican Beehive Bon-bons were served. Notably absent were alcoholic beverages. Having met only a fraction of the thousands of attendees, before leaving the festivities the Harrisons mentioned to their Ohio and Indiana friends that they would be welcomed guests at the White House. It was a comment they later regretted.

That evening, just after midnight, Benjamin Harrison slept in the same bed his grandfather had used nearly a half century before. Perhaps the Harrisons wondered if their remarks to their disappointed supporters to come and visit them were only meant as passing comments.

For the next three days, amid clearing skies, thousands of Midwesterners flocked to the Executive Mansion. The crush of visitors was so great that the White House doors had to be bolted shut until guards could restore order. Harrison remarked that on his first full day as president he had "shaken the hands of eight thousand persons since daylight."[5] Executive business stood at a standstill as the reception line each day seemed never-ending. Carrie was exhausted. President Harrison observed that all the visitors and well-wishers of his first three days in office were not as bad as the hordes of office-seekers who later invaded his residence.

As many as twelve members of the Harrison family lived upstairs at the White House, including three grandchildren, the first lady's ninety-year-old father, and her young, attractive, widowed niece, Mary Dimmick, as well as Mary's mother Elizabeth Lord, who was Carrie's sister. This did not allow Benjamin and Carrie much privacy, and it put a strain on the five bedrooms and one bathroom which existed in the residence, though the addition of another bathroom would be soon coming.

One of the first decisions Harrison had to make was a personal and painful one. He asked his father-in-law to resign as a clerk in the mailroom division of the Pension Office, a position which Harrison had helped Scott obtain while he was serving in the Senate. Secretary of the Interior John Noble consulted with the president and first lady before approving the resignation. In his eighties, Scott had earned more money than he had as a minister, professor and college president. Scott explained to a friend that "my son-in-law has discharged me from my position…and I shall go to live at the White House now and do nothing. This is a very hard condition to be in."[6]

The First Family became a popular subject of the newspapers and, unlike the Clevelands before them, they did not try to hide from the public. It was reported that when Harrison's youngest granddaughter was baptized at the White House, water from the Jordan River was used. Afternoon teas, hosted by Carrie, Mamie, or Mary Dimmick, were held in the Red Room. Photographers and reporters were often invited and sometimes the president made a surprise appearance.

One incident which did not get reported until years later involved one of Carrie's friends. The first lady was giving a tour to a friend, Mrs. Findley, from Baltimore. Carrie had her four grandchildren with her as she guided the small group through several rooms. The children were making a lot of noise and interrupted the president. Harrison came out of his office, sneaked up behind his little granddaughter Mary McKee, and kissed her on the back of the neck. Mary wiped her hand across her neck and yelled, "Stop, Grandpa! That is cousin Marin's place to kiss!"[7] There was no laughter from anyone because Grandpa didn't think the comment was amusing.

Interruptions were nothing new to the president, but one such event took on a sinister tone. One evening in 1891 a mentally disturbed man entered the White House from South Portico window, climbing into the Red Room. Two doorkeepers struggled with the assailant and after the crash of some broken glass, Harrison came downstairs to investigate the commotion. He wrestled the man to the floor then cut a window cord to tie him up until more help arrived. After making sure none of his staff were seriously injured, he returned to work. Such incidents made the first lady cautious and nervous.

On April 30, 1889, President Harrison made a three-day visit to New York City in celebration of the one hundredth anniversary of the presidency. It was there, in the nation's first capital, that George Washington had been inaugurated as the first president. Huge crowds, lavish dinners, a parade, and fireworks greeted Harrison and the other dignitaries. A naval review of 600 vessels in New York harbor lasted two hours. The parade which followed consisted of more than 50,000 marchers and took six hours to pass the reviewing stand. After attending a special worship service at St. Paul's Church, the "Centennial President" spoke to a crowd of twelve thousand at Wall and Nassau Streets, the site of old Federal Hall where Washington had taken his oath. Thousands tried to shake Harrison's hand, almost ignoring the members of Congress, the Supreme Court, the Cabinet, and the thirty state governors who accompanied him. The president and first lady were guests at the Grand Ball, which was also attended by former First Ladies

Julia Grant, Frances Cleveland, and Mary McElroy (Chester Arthur's sister). As it turned out, Benjamin Harrison's popularity would never be greater than during this event.

Returning to the capital, the president soon fell into an organized routine back at the White House. Breakfast was served at 8:30, followed by lunch five hours later. Harrison worked diligently in the morning and afternoon, relying much on his private secretary Elijah Halford and two stenographers, Frank Tibbott and Alice B. Sanger.

Dinner for the Harrisons was served at 6:30 and prayers were spoken at every meal. State dinners held for diplomats and dignitaries were lavish, with music and dancing following the meals. For most occasions, the music was provided by the U.S. Marine Band, conducted by John Phillip Sousa. A gifted musician and eventually the best skeet shooter in the land, Sousa first played in the Marine Band as a fifer when he was 13 years old. Sousa's performances and original music proved so popular, people demanded he play more in public. Later, when Sousa asked President Harrison and his wife if he could leave the Marine Band and go on tour with his own musicians, Harrison said he would consider the request. Within a short time, he told Sousa, "I have thought it over, and I believe the country would rather hear you than see me, so you have my permission to go."[8] Sousa resigned on July 30, 1892, and formed his own band, which was hugely successful.

The Harrisons loved music. It was their passion for song and dance which crossed social and racial barriers. Both Carrie and daughter Mamie enjoyed playing on a Fisher upright piano, a Christmas gift from son Russell to his mother. Carrie particularly loved playing Louis Gootschalk's "The Last Hope." On Sundays the family gathered around the piano to sing hymns.

Harrison found time in his busy schedule to attend a reunion of his beloved 70th Indiana Regiment and in mid-September he arrived at Fort McHenry near Baltimore for the celebration of the 75th anniversary of the writing of the "Star Spangled Banner" by Francis Scott Key. He stayed only a day, but long enough to watch a four-hour parade of 1000 floats and 15,000 marchers.

One highlight took place on the evening of April 23, 1890 when Mamie McKee hosted a ball at the White House. Mamie had stated earlier she would like to have a dance in the East Room; it had been more than two decades since a formal ball had been held there. Serving as an assistant hostess to her mother, Mamie and her husband Robert invited 300 guests. The East Room was covered in canvas as couples danced for hours to waltzes and schottisches. Sousa's Marine Band played outside in the hallway while the president and first lady enjoyed "kicking up their heels."

Harrison was constantly on the move as president. In May he visited northeast Ohio, stopping in Euclid at Lake View Cemetery to dedicate the James A. Garfield Tomb. In October he embarked on a week long tour of the Midwest, giving 37 speeches in nine states. At one stop in Ottumwa, Iowa, he was met by his sister Sally Devin and their older brother John Scott Harrrison who had traveled from Kansas City, Missouri. Harrison was hailed everywhere, attending banquets and reviewing parades. His last two stops before returning to Washington were in Ohio at Canton and Alliance where he told the people, "...every wheel is running and every hand is busy. I believe the future is bright before us for increasingly better times for all...and that its beneficient help may come into every home."[9]

The First Family also sponsored outdoor concerts on the White House grounds, allowing the general public to attend. But it was Carrie's indoor musicales which drew rave reviews. These programs invited musicians and performers from the Washington area to play a variety of selections.

Musicians and singers became frequent guests at White House dinners. One such occasion featured the well-known European singer Madame Laura Schirmer-Mapleson. Another indoor presentation highlighted a black woman, Matilda Joyner, also known as Sissieretta Jones, who visited the Harrisons on separate occasions to sing. Nicknamed the "Black Patti," Joyner was a gifted vocalist, but her color prevented her from becoming a major opera star. Though she sang for two other presidents, she died in poverty years later while living in Rhode Island.

Nearly equal to their fondness for music, the First Family also loved animals. Indeed, neither the later collection of animals by the Theodore Roosevelts or the John F. Kennedys could compare to the menagerie found at the Harrison White House. Parrots, canaries, two rabbits, a large Siberian bloodhound, a mixed collie (Dash), a watchdog, four horses, two opossums (named Mr. Protection and Mr. Reciprocity), a burro, two ferrets, a goat and even a young alligator were part of the family unit. Separate housing was arranged for the goat in the horse stables. A small crisis arose when the White House stable hand threatened to resign if he was required to be responsible for the temperamental goat.

Benjamin Harrison was riding high on a wave of publicity. People named their children and pets for him, and even when the president limited his practice of kissing babies handed to him, the public still adored him. Published photographs—many of them taken by Frances Benjamin Johnston, whose fame as one of America's greatest photographers would not be realized until years after her death—showed the Harrisons and their grandchildren at play.

No greater happiness came to the Harrison than in the person of Benjamin Harrison McKee. Born to Harrison's daughter Mary (Mamie) in 1887, "Baby" McKee commanded center stage while spending three of his first five years living with his grandparents. Two years after his birth, the child was christened in the White House. He was baptized by his great grandfather, Reverend John Scott. As family members looked on, the baby was anointed with water from the Jordan River.

One unforgettable incident occurred when "Baby" McKee crawled upon his grandfather's desk and pushed all the buttons connected to office bells. In short order White House attendants came rushing in only to find the president concentrating on some paperwork while his grandson played on his lap. On another occasion an aide entered the president's office to find the child had scattered some official papers on the floor, a couple of which landed in the spittoon.

Folks soon developed a fascination for Harrison's grandson, who was often seen having his toy wagon pulled by a pony or goat. Once, the pet billy goat named "His Whiskers" took off through the gates down Pennsylvania Avenue with the child in the wagon and the president in hot pursuit, yelling and waving his cane.

During a formal ceremony Baby McKee picked up the conductor's baton and led the Marine Band. Several other times the boy was seen imitating the president's gestures. Indeed, all of his antics were recorded by the newspapers as the public was hungry for more news. But when the White House announced that the child's playtime was off limits, the photographers and reporters cried that it was unfair. The order was rescinded.

Harrison's pets and grandchildren had the run of the White House as their grandparents spoiled them. Toys of every sort arrived at the White House, but most of these were given to orphanages. Newspapers clamored for more stories about the grandchildren and the president and first lady had several bits of information released to reporters. This happy relationship between Harrison and the press, however, would not last.

First Lady Carrie Harrison was determined to find more room and seclusion for her large family in the White House. She confessed to a reporter,

"There are only five sleeping rooms and there is no feeling of privacy."[10] She converted several rooms which had been included as part of public tours into private quarters. Tourists were accustomed to walking through the White House and roaming at will, often unescorted because ushers were occupied with official callers. The Harrisons reduced visiting hours for the public and these restrictions angered more than a few.

Carrie Harrison drew more criticism when she made a change in protocol. In greeting her guests at formal functions, the first lady refused to shake hands. She had always detested this common ritual and its accompanying aches and pains. Instead, Carrie held a bouquet of roses while standing next to her husband in receiving lines, greeting her company with a simple nod.

The first lady took charge of her duties. She did her own shopping and personally set about making home improvements. The White House was dirty and dilapidated. The plumbing was in deplorable shape. Stairwells were rotting, and mildew and mold covered some of the walls. Rooms upstairs and down were infested with mice, cockroaches, and rats. More than once Carrie could be heard screaming as a staffer shot a rat in the musty attic. She even purchased two ferrets to keep the rodent population down. One problem she was not able to solve, however, was the infestation of mosquitoes each summer.

More than a good cleaning was needed. Internal improvements in the White House were necessary, and that meant spending money. For a start, the Harrisons appealed to Congressmen and other officials, pointing out the building's poor condition. The first lady campaigned for a comprehensive project that included major renovations and expansion. She enlisted the support of a wealthy widow, Harriet Lane Johnson of Baltimore, who had served as first lady in the 1850s when her bachelor uncle, James Buchanan, was president.

The first lady formed a White House Improvements Committee that included engineers, architects, and government officials. Studies were conducted, blueprints were made, and a budget request was sent to the Senate. Besides improvements, Carrie proposed expanding the White House by adding two wings, one of which included a museum. Secretary of State James Blaine warned Carrie she would not receive Congressional funds if she disturbed the basic integrity and history of the building.

The Senate overwhelmingly approved the plan and sent the bill to the House of Representatives. Most of the lawmakers there supported the project, except for Speaker of the House Thomas Reed. He was furious with President Harrison over a political appointment, and saw to it that any plan of expansion or improvement would have to wait. Eventually, Congress did appropriate $35,000—a mere fraction of what was requested.

In spite of being denied their full funds by Congress, the Harrisons made some modifications to the White House. Some of these changes were paid for out of the president's $50,000 annual salary. The first lady hired an interior decorator to remodel rooms, hang new curtains, upholster old furniture, and put up wallpaper. The president was quite pleased with the renovations. He noted the improved bathroom was "the greatest beauty of all," with new white tile and a porcelain-lined tub that he said "would tempt a duck to wash himself everyday."[11]

One project which had previously been approved was the installation of electric lights. Wires were buried in plaster or run through antiquated gas pipes. The electric generator to provide power was located next door in the War & Navy Building, with wires stretching over to the White House. Round switches were mounted on the walls, but the Harrisons never used them for fear of being shocked. Electricity was a relatively recent innovation, and many people were uncomfortable with it. On one occasion Harrison got jolted when he went to turn a light switch; this explains why the Harrisons often went to bed with the lights on. For quite some time, President Harrison even refused to push electric bells and buzzers, and used the newly installed telephone sparingly. Such duties were performed by White House staff.

During this time two highly publicized events briefly damaged the reputation of President Harrison. The first involved the head White House steward, Hugo Zieman. Initially, Zieman and the first lady got along well, but after a few months the two clashed over White House procedures and personnel. Zieman was fired. Then the White House's French cook, Madame Pelouard, was discharged. Pelouard and Carrie had been at odds, and Pelouard's weekly salary of fifty dollars was expensive. The Harrisons replaced her with Dolly Johnston, a black cook from Kentucky who had worked in the Harrison household in Indianapolis. Johnston was paid fifteen dollars a week and her simple recipes made the Harrisons happy. Madame Pelouard threatened to sue the Harrisons. Both she and Zieman went to the newspapers, where they were paid handsomely to provide stories about life inside the Harrison White House. Their accounts were uncomplimentary. One incident witnessed by Zieman told of the president falling asleep in a chair while holding a banana. According to Zieman, a rat scampered up

Harrison's lap and took it out of his hands. Political opponents relished such stories. As the newspapers became more critical of the Harrisons, the president and first lady in turn became more guarded, withdrawing somewhat from the press.

In a separate incident, an old Negro servant tossed a bucket of dirty water out of a second story White House window drenching a policeman standing below. The servant, Jerry Smith, had gotten a bit lax in his duties the past several years; his often sloppy appearance and untidy cleaning habits (like leaving dust balls or dirt piled in corners) became a small matter of concern. It was the soaking of the policeman, however, which led to his dismissal. Writing a note of apology and begging forgiveness, he personally gave the message to Harrison. The president hired him back.

Despite the negative publicity, the first lady continued to be gracious, optimistic, and friendly. Carrie Harrison was multi-talented—she was a fine artist (flowers being the main subjects of her canvases) and she conducted classes in painting ceramic dishes and cups. Many of her hand-painted pieces were sent to friends or organizations to raise money. Carrie also made high society and the diplomatic corps happy when she announced that ballroom dancing would be reinstated at the White House, a practice discontinued in 1845 by First Lady Sarah Polk.

Carrie also took measures to guarantee equal opportunities for women. In 1890, some citizens of Baltimore asked her help to raise funds for the newly found Johns Hopkins Medical School. The first lady agreed on one condition—that the school admit women students. With significant contributions from railroad heiress Mary Elizabeth Garret, Jane Stanford (wife of California railroad magnate Leland Stanford), Abigail Brown Brooks Adams (widow of Charles Francis Adams) and Julia Ward Howe, Carrie raised more than enough money. Thus, one of America's leading medical colleges became coeducational. The first lady's other valuable contribution was her creation of the Daughters of the American Revolution (DAR), an organization whose members could trace their ancestry back to the time of the American Revolution. The DAR met in the Blue Room at the White House and Carrie Harrison was chosen as its first president.

Carrie was fond of classical literature but it was her love of painting she enthusiastically pursued. This activity was in evidence throughout the Executive Mansion. In rooms, on china and on canvas her love of flowers gave testimony to her talent as well as her yen for decorating. Grandson Baby McKee recalled years later an incident where he standing in a small tub being bathed. He leaned out over the tub to touch the flowers grandma had painted on the side and fell out.

Carrie Harrison's domestic interests were further emphasized when she designed the cornstalk-and-flower border for the White House china. She then began a collection of Executive Mansion dinnerware patterns that had been chosen by preceding presidents and first ladies. Among her domestic chores was helping the servants prepare food and overseeing every detail of entertaining guests. The servants adored her and despite running a busy household, Carrie maintained an active social agenda when health permitted.

There was at least one major disappointment in mid-January of 1890 when Carrie had to postpone a White House Luncheon in honor of former First Lady Julia Grant. The lunch was cancelled due to the sudden death of Walker Blaine, son of James G. Blaine. Among the twenty-seven invited female guests were several wives of cabinet members, Jane Stanford and Edith Roosevelt, wife of a future president.

In the spring of 1891 the first lady arranged to have electricity installed, beginning a program to replace the open fireplaces and spits which had been used for cooking. Recognized by women's publications as a perfect example of heralding in new methods and adapting to change, Caroline Harrison may not have felt she was a trendsetter. In modernizing the White House, she was following, rather than setting, the national style.[12]

No less a subject of controversy was the personality of the president. Benjamin Harrison was a great orator and highly intelligent, but even his close associates felt he was often moody or sullen. These traits, which could be traced to his childhood, took on a greater dimension as he became an adult in public office. Harrison's dignified, often humorless approach to matters of politics, seemed to contradict his behavior toward those who knew him well. According to one Indianapolis friend, Harrison was a far different person away from the pressures of business and politics. He noted, "When he [Harrison] is on a fishing trip, Ben takes a drink of whiskey in the morning just like everyone else. He chews tobacco from a plug he carries in his hip pocket, spits on his worm for luck, and cusses when the fish gets away!"[13] This observation may have included a bit of embellishment.

Harrison's behavior toward his close associates and relatives, however, was not indicative of his attitude to others in social situations. His uneasiness and chilly demeanor was often described as distant or formal. Indeed, he could be quite stubborn and quiet at times, and to those who did not know him, he was looked upon as pious, reserved, and intensely private.

President Harrison was nicknamed "the Human Iceberg" by his critics. A Republican leader observed Harrison could "charm a crowd of 20,000—but he would make them all enemies with a personal handshake."[14] One U.S. Senator, frustrated with Harrison after meeting him in the White House, remarked, "It's like talking to a hitching post!"[15] And when Ohio Governor James Foraker arrived for an appointment, he found Harrison with a watch in his hand and a huge stack of papers on his desk. Harrison told the Governor, "I've got all these papers to look after, and I am going fishing at two o'clock."[16] He then opened his watch and waited for Foraker to finish his business.

It didn't take Harrison long to show frustration with his job. In preparing his 1890 State of the Union Message in mid-October of the previous year, Harrison focused his energies on writing the address. He declined to see any visitors in the afternoon for the last three months in 1889. He told Halford he was being driven crazy and longed for the days when he was just an Indianapolis lawyer.

The dispensing of patronage has been and continues to be a difficult task for presidents. A necessary evil of democracy and the spoils system, the practice of patronage has had an ill effect on every chief executive. The constant barrage of dealing with office hunters, or with party leaders wanting to hand out positions to campaign workers and friends, drained the life out of our presidents. Two casualties were Harrison's grandfather, President William Henry Harrison, who died after 31 days in 1841 (he caught a bad cold on inauguration day but found no rest from office seekers), and James A. Garfield. Presidents Jackson, Lincoln and Grant complained bitterly about the hordes of officeseekers descending on the White House like an endless plague of locust.

Each president has been able to appoint hundreds and even thousands of loyal supporters who helped elect him. These appointments are to go to individuals who are well qualified and honest, but that is not always the case. Besides handing out positions to those who are not capable or worthy, there is the problem of nepotism—giving jobs to relatives. As indicated previously, the Civil Service Act of 1882 established testing procedures and qualifications for hundreds of federal positions but hundreds of other civil service posts were not affected by the law.

After discussions with his Postmaster-General John Wanamaker, Harrison decided to give the unpleasant task of naming postmasters to Assistant Postmaster-General James Clarkson. About 70 per cent of the nation's postmasters, more than 33,000 of them, were replaced with Harrison supporters. And those who were replaced had received their reward through President Cleveland. This was customary with each new administration, but many of the appointments by Clarkson during the Harrison term were a disappointment to reformers and advocates of the merit system.

On the other hand, some critics seemed pleased when Harrison granted civil service classification to 626 teachers and administrators in Indian schools out West. He also approved other programs for their education and employment. Strides were also made when Harrison raised the number of classified positions from 27,000 to 38,000 meaning that more potential office-holders were now subject to competitive exams for their jobs.

When it came to appointing people to non-postal positions, Harrison did provide employment for three or four dozen relatives, though he had asked his elderly father-in-law to retire from the Pension Office. Providing positions for family members was a common practice among presidents and remains so to this day.

Many other kinfolk wanting employment, however, were turned away. Since Harrison's staff was small and overworked, and because Harrison did not delegate this responsibility wisely, the issue of patronage consumed much of his time and energy. During interviews with job applicants he even read other papers and documents while the perspective candidate was talking. In addition, Harrison appeared to be suspicious of office seekers and he no doubt appeared to be arrogant to some.

Harrison often showed little patience with job seekers and certain government officials. His cool attitude toward them did not endear him to politicians. In handling scheduled interviews with applicants, the president might leave them standing or waiting for hours. A one-armed veteran, A. H. Reed, came all the way from Minnesota to discuss appointments in his state, offering some suggestions. No sooner had Reed begun his talk when President Harrison said to him, "I know all about the political conditions up there much better than you do," then ended the meeting.[17] Captain Reed told a friend, "He's a doomed icicle" and agreed with others who believed that Harrison's handshake felt "like a wilted petunia."[18]

On another occasion, Harriet Blaine, wife of Harrison's Secretary of State James Blaine, dashed into the White House demanding to see Harrison.

When told she would have to wait, Harriet brushed past a guard and stormed into the president's office. Mrs. Blaine's son, Walker, had been appointed Examiner of Claims in the State Department and had unexpectedly died. The president, concerned about the young man's condition, had stopped to see Walker Blaine at his home only fifteen minutes before he died. Mrs. Blaine blamed Harrison for her son's death, claiming he was overworked. But she also demanded that her son-in-law be appointed a brigadier-general. Harrison listened politely and after Mrs. Blaine calmed down, said to her, "Madam, it is unbecoming [to] my high office and your sex for this conversation to continue longer."[19] Harrison then got up and left his office, leaving a stunned Mrs. Blaine all alone.

Harrison's relationship with the Blaines had been strained from the start of the administration. Harrison had rejected James Blaine's request to make his son Walker the first assistant secretary of state. Perhaps he felt the young man simply lacked experience, but whatever the reason, the relations between the two families cooled. Carrie wrote her daughter concerning the Blaines, "They are a strange family. You never know whether they are true or not. There is an air of mystery about them that gives an impression of cunning."[20]

While visiting New York in 1884, Harrison had met Theodore Roosevelt. Harrison admired Roosevelt's energy and honesty and when he was president, appointed the young man to the Civil Service Commission. Roosevelt vigorously pressed for stricter enforcement of laws and reforms within the commission. This angered many party officials, especially when Roosevelt's investigations turned up several instances of impropriety. Roosevelt complained to Harrison and was unhappy when he felt the president had done little to correct these abuses. Commissioner Roosevelt claimed Harrison was "the little gray man in the White House" who treated him "with cold and hesitating disapproval."[21] It was after another disagreement with Harrison over patronage that Roosevelt described him as a "cold-blooded, narrow-minded, prejudiced, obstinate, timid old psalm-singing Indianapolis politician...a genial little runt."[22] In fairness to Harrison, however, it should be noted that Roosevelt eagerly sought an appointment as assistant secretary of state but Blaine was concerned about the youthful New Yorker's impulsive and combative nature. Harrison had said the impetuous Roosevelt "wanted to put an end to all evil in the world between sunrise and sunset."[23]

Roosevelt was not the only major politician Harrison offended. Congressman William McKinley campaigned hard for Harrison's election and his efforts did not go unnoticed. As a reward for his valuable help, McKinley was promised by Harrison that he could name an appointment for a federal judgeship. McKinley waited patiently while Harrison sorted through thousands of applications from office seekers for civil service positions. In late 1890 McKinley called on Harrison at the White House and reminded him of his promise of patronage. The president listened attentively to McKinley's suggestion then politely refused his selection. In a rare show of anger, McKinley rose to leave, but turned to Harrison and remarked, "Mr. President, if you were in my place and I in yours, and you had made the sacrifice for me that I have made for you, you wouldn't leave this room without an appointment. Good-day."[24]

Senator Shelby M. Collum of Illinois submitted a long list of positions he wanted filled. Harrison didn't grant him all of the appointments he demanded. Collum observed, "I suppose he [Harrison] treated me about as well in the way of patronage as he did any other Senators; but whenever he did anything for me it was done so ungraciously that the concession tended to anger rather than please."[25]

Collum's observation was upheld by Harrison's own Solicitor-General, William Howard Taft who wrote his father in 1890, "The President is not very popular with the members of either house. His manner of treating them is not all that fortunate, and when they have an interview with him they generally come away mad…I think this is exceedingly unfortunate, because I am sure we never had a man in the White House who was more conscientiously seeking to do his duty."[26]

Patience was another virtue Harrison sometimes found in short supply. He rarely offered guests a chair as he sat behind his office desk, tapping his fingers waiting for them to leave. Close friends and aides warned White House visitors not to be offended by Harrison's actions, explaining, "It is only the president's way."[27] All of the people who met Harrison on a business level were universal in their description. One politician called him "a purely intellectual being with no bowels," while another declared that Harrison's re-election would mean "four more years in a dripping cave."[28]

An incident in 1890 further proved embarrassing to the Harrisons. A group of wealthy friends led by John Wanamaker presented them with the gift of a twenty-room "cottage" at Cape May Point, New Jersey. This action created a furor in the papers, until it was learned that Harrison had already repaid the $10,000 price tag of the house. Meanwhile the personal attacks against him continued in the newspapers and he became a favorite target of cartoonists and editorials. Once, while walking past the White House with his private secretary, the president pointed to the building and said, "*There is my prison!*"[29]

The press had only a little to complain about Harrison's choices of men to lead his administration. The Cabinet proved overall distinguished, even though its achievements have been largely overlooked by scholars and historians. Desiring to name the best able men for positions, Harrison chose James Blaine as secretary of state, a post he held under Presidents Garfield and Arthur. Blaine was one of the nation's great secretaries of state, and his accomplishments as a problem solver and promoter of relations with South and Central American nations solidified his reputation. When Blaine resigned after more than three years due to ill health, Harrison replaced him with John W. Foster of Indiana. Foster, like Blaine, brought experience, intelligence and insight to the post (his grandson, John Foster Dulles, later served as secretary of state under Eisenhower). Redfield Proctor of Vermont got the nod for secretary of war but resigned in 1891 to take a Senate seat; he was replaced by Stephen B. Elkins of West Virginia, a wealthy manufacturer who later became a U.S. senator after Harrison's term.

William Henry Harrison Miller of Indiana was Harrison's friend and former law partner, and Harrison chose him as attorney-general. Miller earned a reputation as a non-partisan, no nonsense man of the law. John Noble, a strong Missouri conservationist, became secretary of the interior. He was instrumental in working with Harrison to preserve millions of acres of timberlands and thus preventing their destruction. In addition, he organized the Oklahoma Territory for settlement. William Windom of Minnesota was selected as secretary of the treasury. He too had served the same position with Garfield and Arthur. Windom had been a close advisor to Harrison but died in 1891 and was replaced by Charles Foster of Ohio, a well qualified expert on finances and a longtime friend.

John Wannamaker, a reform-minded department store magnate from Philadelphia, became postmaster-general and instituted several reforms in postal service. He improved delivery systems and, together with Harrison, put a stop to lotteries using the postal service to promote their scams. Gambling by mail resulted in a heavy fine and prison time. The aggressive action by Wannamaker ended the business of state lotteries in the country for the next eleven decades. In addition, he promoted the idea of rural free delivery which was adopted a few years later.

The postmaster-general, however, had some difficulty. He ordered a change in uniforms for mail carriers but when the newspapers learned he was part owner of the company making the new uniforms, the public cried foul. He also banned a book by Tolstoy to be mailed on grounds of obscenity and took an active role in firing tens of thousands of postal workers who had worked under President Cleveland. A few reformers, including Theodore Roosevelt, criticized such moves, even though most Republican Party officials found no fault with these actions.

Jeremiah Rusk of Wisconsin was named secretary of agriculture (a recently created post) and established federal inspection of meat exports. Harrison's confidant and close friend Benjamin Tracy of New York became secretary of the Navy. This man made great strides in promoting an ambitious shipbuilding program and modernization of the navy which had been started by Grover Cleveland. Also, another appointment which proved wise was naming William Howard Taft as solicitor-general in the Justice Department.

The Harrison administration witnessed a number of milestones and achievements. Harrison was the first president with a billion dollar budget appropriated by Congress. Funds were increased to construct new steel battleships and strengthen coastal defenses. Business grew, even though the Sherman Anti-Trust Act of 1890 was passed to curb abuses of monopolies, though neither Harrison or his successor Grover Cleveland showed much interest in enforcing it. The McKinley Tariff was adopted, raising taxes on imports and generating revenues (its ill effects had not surfaced until towards the end of 1890). A Pan-American Conference was created to promote goodwill between the United States and Latin America. A land rush in the Oklahoma Territory opened up two million acres for homesteaders. Land in the Montana Territory was annexed when Indian tribes were moved onto reservations after mines began to yield their precious ore.

The ship of state under Harrison's command began its voyage with faith and optimism. Its crew, in navigating some rough waters, was well qualified as department heads, appointees and staff met adversity with confidence and assurance. Despite a few setbacks, the administration was earning a reputation for honesty and efficiency, enjoying a good relationship with the newspapers and receiving wide support from the public. But there were signs in the national and international communities which signaled potential danger and conflict. Nor could anyone foresee the personal and political problems which threatened to sink the Harrison administration into an abyss of self-doubt, sadness and blunder.

CHAPTER 8

Stormy Seas

Tragedy followed the 23rd President during much of his term. It first struck in December of 1889 when both Carrie's sister Elizabeth Lord (whose daughter would someday marry Harrison), and the president's twenty-five-year-old nephew, William Harrison, died. Then, in February of 1890, a fire destroyed the home of Naval Secretary Benjamin Tracy. Mrs. Tracy, an invalid, Tracy's daughter, and their French maid were all killed in the blaze. When President Harrison learned of the fire, he hurried to the Tracy home just two blocks from the White House. Tracy was unconscious and barely had a pulse. Harrison was among those who applied artificial respiration to revive him.

Funeral services were held in the East Room, with the caskets of Mrs. Tracy and her daughter covered with lilies. When Harrison discovered the French maid had no money or relatives, he paid for her burial. Then, in the spring of 1891, the wife of Elijah Halford, Harrison's secretary, died just days after Harrison started his Western tour. Other catastrophes would follow and the president's strength would be tested. It was the Christian faith of the Harrisons which sustained them during these trying times.

After years of isolation the United States found itself increasingly involved in international questions. For two decades, from 1850 to 1870, the nation was still ensnared with the problems which led to Civil War. Reconstruction, Manifest Destiny, racism, and imperialism, controversies which stirred passions in years past and waited to make their appearance again.

During the first two months of his administration, in a brilliant stroke of diplomacy, Harrison acquired Samoa (later called American Samoa). Located in the South Pacific, its islands are approximately 2300 miles from Hawaii. In 1872 the Samoans agreed to let the U.S. use Pago, its capital, as a naval refueling station. Germany and England were also given permission for a base there, but a confrontation with Germany nearly resulted in conflict.

For obvious advantages in trade and commerce, Germany wanted exclusive control of the islands. When some Germans were killed during an unsuccessful coup against the native government, Germany threatened war and dispatched some battleships there. President Cleveland sent three naval vessels to protect Samoans and American interests, making a show of force against Germany's Kaiser Wilhelm II. On March 16, 1889 two German and three U.S. ships were sunk or badly damaged during a hurricane. Fifty American sailors were killed and tensions remained high among Great Britain, Germany and the U.S.

The three countries involved agreed to a conference in Berlin to settle the dispute. Harrison and Secretary of State Blaine selected three experienced diplomats to attend. Blaine was too ill with lumbago to make the trip, so he supervised the conference through letters and telegrams. The first of nine sessions began on April 29, 1889, and ended on June 14.

Germany demanded too much, but American negotiators refuse to give in. England seemed content with just keeping her coal refueling base there and wanted little else. Our representatives, following the instructions of Blaine, made some minor concessions. Germany retained some authority of the western islands while the U.S. assumed control of the remaining islands. Years later Samoa was annexed to the U.S.

Four months after the Berlin triumph Harrison held a Pan-American Conference in Washington. A ten-man delegation of American business leaders and politicians met with sixteen Latin American countries. Harrison sought to expand American commerce and influence, and he asked Blaine to preside over the meetings. The American delegation was led by Andrew Carnegie. A shrewd millionaire steel manufacturer, Carnegie was a bit naïve and idealistic on the workings of government, but he proved to be an excellent choice to head the delegation. The participants met from October 2, 1889 to April 19 of the following year. After a 42-day tour of industrial centers throughout the country (with Carnegie serving as the tour guide), the conference resumed its discussions of communication, international law, tariffs, improved custom regulations, copyright laws and extradition policy. The various representatives also agreed to collect and share information. Except for the hostility from the Argentine delegates, business went smoothly. But after 70 meetings, 44 of them attended by Blaine, little was accomplished.

Carnegie had done an excellent job. He spent much of his own money entertaining the foreign delegates. One unforgettable evening came when he held a lavish dinner for them at the Arlington Hotel in Pittsburgh. A short time later, after his second book was published, Carnegie sent Harrison a keg of "the best Scotch Whisky in the world," and received a personal thank you letter from Harrison: "It was very kind of you to think of me as likely to need a 'brace' this winter in dealing with the new Congress."[1] In this response Harrison was exaggerating his fondness for drinking alcohol.

As it turned out, Blaine didn't have much left. His own ill health was compounded by a series of personal setbacks. About halfway through the conference period, Blaine's brother Melville died. In mid-January of 1890 his son Walker died suddenly, followed three weeks later by the death of his daughter Alice Blaine Coppinger, who ironically got sick while attending her brother's funeral. Blaine tried to overcome his sorrow by immersing himself in extra work, but eventually his health deteriorated. When he collapsed in 1891, he still remained in the Cabinet for another year. His top assistant, John Foster, assumed the duties of the office.

President Harrison, a staunch environmentalist, set aside a million acres of Western land by establishing more than a dozen national parks and forest reserves. There had been petitions signed by hundreds of citizens, including John Muir and members of the Sierra Club, to preserve forested regions. The Land Revision Act of 1891 gave Harrison the powers to reserve public lands in any state or territory.

Six new states entered the Union: North Dakota, South Dakota, Montana, Washington, Idaho and Wyoming. At one signing ceremony the president showed he was not beyond a bit of political chicanery. On November 2, 1889, South and North Dakota were officially admitted to the Union. Harrison, aware that one state might claim priority over the other, shuffled the admission papers so that no one knew which was signed first. By mutual agreement years later, North Dakota became the 39th state and South Dakota the 40th.

Harrison was also responsible for marked improvements in meteorology. In 1891 he put the U.S. Weather Bureau under civilian control when he transferred the agency to the department of agriculture. Established by President Cleveland in his first administration, the bureau had been run by the military. Harrison had its functions expanded; forecasts were sent by telegraph to weather stations, railroads and the press. This was a major help to farmers especially, despite inaccuracies in forecasting.

All of the Senators and Representatives from the new western states were Republicans, a total of 18 men. What looked like a political advantage in numbers for Harrison and the GOP was not so. Various members of Congress from the West opposed Harrison, especially on the issues of tariffs and gold versus silver for currency. In the 1892 Congressional elections, for the first time since the Civil War, the Democrats gained control of both the House and Senate.

One does not usually think of the Bering Sea as a hot spot, but that's what it became during Harrison's term. After years of overhunting, the U.S. Navy stopped Canadian ships and arrested their crews of poachers who slaughtered millions of fur seals in Alaskan waters. Since the U.S. purchase of Alaska from the Russians in 1867, there had been an agreement on hunting rights by Great Britain and her Canadian ally. Many of the seals were killed while looking for food in the open waters miles from the Pribilof Islands where the animals had their rookeries. Harrison argued that the U.S. had a legal right to ban seal hunting in international waters. The sticking point was how far out.

Congress passed a new law directing Harrison to issue a warning to both England and Canada, but enforcement was at times lax. Harrison's real intent was to preserve the seal herds, and using his legal expertise along with Blaine's input, left the matter to be arbitrated in Paris. Despite pressure from the American Commercial Company which had a monopoly on hunting seals, Harrison moved to make things more favorable to the U.S. but negotiations stalled.

The British and Americans both sought to limit the number of seals killed but Great Britain, upon the insistence by the Canadians, refused to agree to the demands. Blaine wanted a limitation of 30,000 seals taken from the Pribilof Islands. The British wanted hunting rights well beyond the 30 miles from the rookeries. When the two nations came to an impasse Harrison responded that his country would defend the property rights with force if necessary.

Blaine was sick once again and Harrison visited him, urging the ailing statesman to remain firm on the issue. The President was gambling that the British were not willing to go to war over hunting rights in the Bering Sea. He had in fact learned this through reliable diplomatic channels. Although the British ambassador Julian Pauncefote referred to Harrison as "that obstinate and pugnacious little President," he followed Prime Minister Lord Salisbury's orders and backed down.[2] Harrison, not Blaine, handled most of the particulars, though the press gave Blaine the credit. A new treaty was signed which ironically was almost identical to the original agreement. The herds, however, were preserved.

President Harrison's four U.S. Supreme Court appointments were not spectacular but balanced and solid. The first appointee was David Brewer of Kansas, a judicial conservative and a progressive thinker who served for 20 years until his death in 1910. Harrison's second selection was Henry Brown of Michigan. An expert on admiralty law and tax matters, Brown retired in 1906 after 16 years on the bench. Next came George Shiras of Pittsburgh. A top corporate lawyer, Shiras served on the Supreme Court for 11 years until he stepped down in 1903. Harrison's last appointment went to Howell Jackson of Tennessee, a Democrat who died of tuberculosis in 1895, just two years after serving as an associate justice.

To meet the ever increasing correspondence and the unending demands of visitors, Harrison made a move to expand his staff. The president's secretary was Elijah Halford, a personal friend who had resigned his job as editor-in-chief of the *Indianapolis Journal*. If any outside family member was close to Harrison, it was Elijah Halford, or "Lige" as Harrison called him. They spent a lot of time with each other, playing billiards on rainy days, taking carriage rides or walking three or four miles together if time permitted. Harrison's stenographers, Frank Tibbott, whom he had brought with him from Indianapolis, and Miss Alice B. Sanger, provided suitable efficiency. Miss Sanger became the first female secretary officially assigned to a president. All three individuals were kept extremely busy, occasionally complaining about their long hours and being overworked. In early October of 1889, Halford had collapsed from exhaustion and missed three weeks of work.

Halfway through his four-year term President Harrison realized he might have difficulty getting reelected. He had found a four-leaf clover in mid-July of 1889, but as time would show, he would need to find more. In the off-year election of 1890, the GOP lost seats in both Houses of Congress, with the Democrats gaining control of the House. There were also troubling economic signs.

The issue over tariffs was a complex one. During the first half of the 19th century, the federal government imposed a tax on imported goods, thus maintaining a healthy revenue. A major stumbling block of course was the duty on imported clothing made from southern cotton. This angered the wealthy cotton growers in Dixie, who insisted the duties were not only unfair but even unconstitutional. Claiming they had a legal right *not* to collect this duty, the issue over tariffs was perhaps the leading cause which led to the Civil War.

The McKinley Tariff of 1890 was signed into law by President Harrison and went into effect immediately. This measure was meant to strengthen the economy, but it turned out to be one of the main reasons for Harrison's defeat in 1892. Hundreds of imported products were taxed, forcing American consumers to buy American-made goods because foreign-made products cost more. Initially, during the early part of 1890, the McKinley Tariff appeared beneficial.

The higher tariffs soon showed some negative side effects. These duties on imports angered foreign neighbors trying to sell their goods in America. There was a sharp decline in trade while American businessmen reaped huge profits, often at the expense of the blood, sweat and misery of American workers. Former President Cleveland accused the Republicans and the McKinley Tariff of protecting big business and special interests, claiming that it "invited corruption in political affairs" and that the "net result was a program favorable to private-selfish gains."[3] McKinley lost his seat in Congress while Cleveland campaigned for a reduction of duties, reminding voters that he opposed absolute free trade. Harrison's views on the tariff and foreign trade began to soften a bit as he leaned more and more toward a policy of reciprocity, a mutual interchange or exchange of favors with each particular country.

Angry farmers throughout the South and West abandoned the GOP. When Harrison began his term there were nearly 23,000,000 wage earners in the nation, but farmers weren't sharing in the prosperity of the manufacturers. Their hostility was due to falling prices on crops and livestock, as well as increased costs of machinery and the tariffs.

The tariff hurt farmers more than it helped, because it raised prices on some imported products they needed, namely tools, raw sugar (this tariff was later removed by Harrison), woolen goods and certain seeds. Many had to take out loans just to buy equipment. By 1891 in just the state of

Kansas 11,000 mortgages were foreclosed, nearly all of them on farmers. There also had been a devastating blizzard which destroyed livestock. At the same time there were more than 1300 abandoned farms in Maine. Nationwide, farm foreclosures totaled more than $1 billion. The fact was *nobody knew what to do.*

Adding problems to the agricultural conditions was a severe drought in 1889 and 1890. Farmers in the Great Plains and Midwest saw a significant decrease in corn production. Where Kansas and Nebraska had produced a combined 287,000,000 bushels in 1885, in 1889 their amount of corn decreased to 111,500,000 bushels. The cost of both corn and wheat fluctuated greatly, sometimes dropping so low in prices that farmers could not make enough profit to offset their losses.

Millions of farmers not only joined granges, they also left the Republican Party. Many found the Democrats indifferent too and joined the Populist Party, another name for the Peoples' Party. The Populists attracted many followers because of their liberal views. Party leaders advocated an eight-hour work day, an income tax to shift the burden of taxation from property to income, the direct election of U.S. senators (a task which lay with state legislatures), lower tariffs, abolishing all national banks, free coinage of silver, and government ownership of all telegraph companies and railroads to guarantee fairness and uniformity.

Their candidate for president in 1892 was General James B. Weaver, a former Civil War officer who was born in Ohio and made his home in Iowa. He had served three terms as a U.S. Congressman and had run for president in 1880 on the Greenback ticket. An author and fine orator, Weaver traveled all throughout the country, attacking the Harrison administration where "the corporation has been placed above the individual and on armed body of cruel mercenaries permitted in times of public peril to destroy police duties which closely belong to the state."[4] Founded in 1891, the Populists saw their views accepted as many candidates won offices on the local and state level.

Labor and management were still at odds. Discontented laborers and factory workers, many of whom had their wages slashed, were further enraged by the show of force from federal and state governments during labor disputes. Strikes at Andrew Carnegie's steel mill in Homestead, Pennsylvania, and at silver mines near Couer d' Alene, Idaho, resulted in numerous deaths after clashes with Pinkerton police, strike breakers and

U.S. soldiers. There were miners' strikes in Tennessee, Ohio and other states as well. Hungry, unemployed workers and their families expected more sympathy from the White House.

Adding to the economic woes, there was a monetary crisis in the making. The nation's gold reserves became depleted because silver was purchased with U.S. treasury notes redeemable in both gold and silver. Many holders of these notes promptly redeemed them for gold. The result was a drain on the government's gold supply. Westerners basically wanted to see paper currency totally backed by silver, since it was more plentiful than gold as a result of productive mines in the West.

Paper money during the Harrison administration was devalued when more dollars were printed and backed by silver. Though the federal government maintained an official gold standard, it was also required by law to purchase up to $4 million worth of silver bullion each month for the purpose of coinage. Harrison was not a gold standard man, as Cleveland and McKinley both were, and allowed the expansion of paper currency backed by silver. But neither did he favor the unlimited coinage of silver. He essentially favored bimetallism, with limitations on how both silver and gold should be used.

When Harrison took office the nation's money supply had grown to about $600 million, half of which consisted of coins or coin certificates. This money dilemma was compounded when, in 1890, London's largest bank failed. The shock waves were soon felt across the Atlantic when Wall Street fell victim, plunging the country into a brief monetary crisis. The ill effects continued and just months after Harrison left office, a full-fledged financial panic gripped the nation.

All was not well in the Hawaiian Islands either. Trouble occurred in Hawaii when sugar exports to the U.S. were deeply affected by the tariff during the 1880s. King Kalakaua had died and his sister Queen Liliuokalani took over control of the islands. She opposed the attempts by American businessmen to annex the islands to the United States. The queen irked the American sugar cane and pineapple growers when she announced that the native majority, not the white minority, should control the islands.

An unstable political situation led to revolution when nine Americans, two Germans and two Englishmen led a bloodless revolt, helped by 150 U.S. Marines and sailors who landed to keep the peace. Our ambassador in Hawaii, John L. Stevens, had kept a U.S. warship stationed in Honolulu Harbor, and along with the Marines, there happened to be a couple artillery pieces on board. The takeover was done with tacit approval by Harrison and Secretary of State John Foster (Blaine had resigned in 1892). A treaty of annexation was hastily negotiated with the new Hawaiian government. In his message to the Senate on February 14, 1893, Harrison urged ratification of the treaty, explaining in a written letter, "The overthrow of the monarchy was not in any way promoted by this government, but had its origins in what seems to have been a reactionary and revolutionary policy on the part of Queen Liliuokalani, which put in peril not only the large prepondering interests of the United States in the islands, but to all foreign interests....⁵ In the same message he told the Senators "I do not deem it necessary to discuss at any length the conditions which have resulted in this decisive action...Prompt action upon this treaty is very desirable."⁶

Not willing to compromise or debate the issue, Harrison met opposition. Democrats and a handful of Republicans also felt that Americans in Hawaii had not acted honorably in aiding the overthrow of the islands. The treaty was still in committee and the center of much controversy when President Cleveland withdrew it in March. Though the Hawaiian Islands were not officially annexed, the country did keep Pearl Harbor as a naval and refueling base, much to the frustration of the Japanese.

Relations with Japan and China suffered not just over trade issues, but also when Harrison signed a new Oriental Exclusion Act into law, extending the original act an extra ten years. Illegal Chinese immigrants who entered the U.S. through British Columbia were prosecuted and sent back to their native land. Harrison had voted against the original law in 1882, but the new bill was less objectionable and better phrased legally. The policy of limiting Chinese found much favor among the white segment of the population living in the West Coast region.

Race riots and lynchings occurred, the most publicized one coming in New Orleans. In October of 1890 Police Chief David Hennessy was walking home when he was ambushed by a group of men hiding in a shanty. A respected, aggressive crime fighter, Hennessy revealed he had been attacked by some Italian and Sicilian immigrants. He died the next day. Many citizens believed the Black Hand, or Mafia, was behind the attack since it was believed the group had been responsible for a hundred unsolved murders in the New Orleans.

After Hennessey's funeral dozens of Italians were arrested. Nineteen of them were indicted for murder and jailed. Their defense lawyer was a high-profile attorney who had been an opponent of Hennessey. Several key witnesses failed to appear at the trial and there were widespread reports that some jurors had been intimidated or bribed. On March 13 six of the defendants were found innocent and a mistrial was declared for the three others. Because there were still some outstanding warrants, all of the accused were returned to Parish Prison.

An angry mob, led by a vigilante committee, stormed the jail. Police barred some of the crowd but the leaders gained entrance through a back door. With city police greatly outnumbered, the jailers were forced to hand the defendants over to the mob. Eleven of the nineteen Italians, none of whom were found guilty, were lynched and shot in front of a crowd of 7000 citizens. Since some of the prisoners killed were Italian citizens, the murders brought forth protests from the Italian government.

When Italy expressed shock and outrage to Harrison, he explained that the matter had to be resolved by the state of Louisiana, and that the federal government had no jurisdiction. Harrison was correct in assuming the murders were a state matter. Nevertheless he telegraphed the governor of Louisiana to prevent further violence. Pressure mounted from Rome as well as the Vatican. The Italian government, not satisfied with action from Harrison, withdrew her ambassador from the U.S. Harrison responded in kind by having Blaine recall our minister from Italy and for several months the dilemma remained unresolved. The United States, after an investigation, paid $75,000 to Italy in damages as well as compensation directly to the affected families. Intimidation of Italian-Americans continued for decades and despite this, Sicilian and Italian immigrants continued to settle in New Orleans. As a somber sign of the times many newspapers across the country approved the mob's actions. Even though President Harrison had done the right thing legally, he incurred the mistrust and frustration of many Catholics.

One catastrophe beyond the control of the president had taken place on May 31, 1889. The Johnstown Flood in Pennsylvania killed more than twenty four hundred people when the South Fork Dam collapsed under pressure from the rain-swollen Lake Conemaugh. Years earlier the dam had been constructed by the state to create a reservoir for the canal system. It was later purchased by the Pennsylvania Railroad, then sold to private owners to provide wealthy industrialists who vacationed there a fishing and hunting haven on higher ground. Members of the South Fork Hunting and Fishing Club included Andrew Carnegie, Henry Frick and Andrew Mellon. But the dam was poorly maintained and its defective state drew concerns as leaks in the dam continually sprang up. For three decades seeping gaps were repaired by packing them with dirt, straw and manure. More than a week of constant heavy rain in late May created more breeches in the dam. Citizens in the valley were constantly warned of leaks.

When the dam broke in mid-afternoon on May 31, an enormous wall of water 90 feet high, traveling over 100 miles per hour, let loose. The wave of death caused flooding and death for nearly 130 miles. Many people simply had no chance to escape the deluge. The entire three-mile long lake emptied in less than an hour. Hundreds who were fortunate enough ran up the hillsides, but others were not so lucky. One pregnant woman, Anna Fenn, lost her husband and all seven children (she lost her eighth child just a few weeks after its birth). Fourteen miles away at the Johnstown Stone Railroad Bridge, accumulated debris including houses, barns, equipment, carcasses of animals, outhouses, telegraph poles, furniture and humans had created a huge logjam. The rubble was piled 50 feet high and covered 40 acres; then it caught fire. More than 80 people who were trapped and still alive drowned or burned in the wreckage as onlookers were helpless to provide aid. Two large whirlpools formed nearby where the swollen Stone Creek merged with the Conemaugh River, taking even more lives.

Property damage was mammoth and a total of 99 entire families perished. Three villages had been obliterated. A total of 777 unidentified bodies were buried in unmarked graves. Clara Barton and the Red Cross spent five months in the disaster area. Though rebuilding took place immediately, the aftereffects lasted years. Bodies were still being recovered as late as 1911 when one flood victim's remains were discovered hundreds of miles away in Cincinnati, not far from Harrison's boyhood home. President Harrison made a generous contribution while his wife helped organize relief efforts, but even by the end of his single term four years later, Johnstown and the surrounding communities had not recovered.

Other calamities were entirely man-made, such as the one in South Dakota. The events leading up to the tragic result at Wounded Knee in December of 1890 began when settlers discovered gold in South Dakota in the 1870s. The U.S. broke its treaty with the Lakota Sioux and ordered them to move to reservations. Their land apportionment was reduced and the distressed Lakota found it difficult to farm on such barren soil. Many Indians complained of this and other injustices. By the time Harrison had become president, the Sioux also had had their government rations cut in half.

One who complained the loudest and challenged the authorities was the great medicine man Sitting Bull. By 1889 he had popularized the Ghost Dance, a religious practice where the Indians danced in a circle and chanted prayers. Introduced to Sitting Bull by another Indian, the Ghost Dance was performed to ward off evil spirits, promise the return of the bison, and bring death to Indian enemies. The Lakota were also convinced that the ritual made them immune to soldiers' bullets by providing an invisible shield.

The white Indian agent at the Pine Ridge agency in South Dakota was inexperienced and nervous. He saw the Ghost Dance as an act of aggression and sent telegrams to Washington asking for help from the cavalry. Harrison sent orders to General Nelson Miles to guard against an attack. Indian police were ordered to Standing Rock Reservation to arrest Sitting Bull, since he refused to stop encouraging his men to perform the Ghost Dance. As the Seventh Cavalry approached the camp the Indians sensed danger. When Sitting Bull refused to leave his people gunshots rang out, resulting in the death of Sitting Bull, his son, and eleven other Sioux. The remaining Indians on the reservation moved to Wounded Knee but more than 500 soldiers pursued them. Harrison ordered the Interior Department to conduct a full investigation of the incident.

The troops took four Hotchkiss guns with them. This weapon, similar to the Gatling Gun, was a repeating rifle-type of artillery. The guns were positioned at four sections around the reservation at Wounded Knee. A detachment of soldiers under Colonel James Forsyth asked the Sioux to hand over their weapons as a sign of friendship. A deaf tribesman refused to give up his rifle unless he was paid for it. This set off a chain reaction of shouting and confusion. Reportedly, one Indian shot his rifle into the air and the soldiers returned fire with their machine guns and rifles.

Though accounts of casualties vary, the end result was a tragedy. When the firing ceased, 25 soldiers lay dead in the snow; another 40 were wounded. More than 250 Indians were slaughtered, with another 50 wounded. Most of the Indian dead were older men, women and children. Several Indian babies were found wrapped in blankets by their mothers to protect them from the soldiers' bullets. These children were collected and taken to an orphanage. Another 150 Indians escaped into the cold where many no doubt froze to death.

Ironically, Harrison learned of the incident at Wounded Knee while he was reading the report from the Interior Department. The account exonerated the Indians. Harrison ordered General Miles to hold a hearing to determine exactly what happened and why. The Indian agent was fired and Colonel Forsyth was demoted (though he later retained his rank). President Harrison met with a delegation of Sioux leaders in Washington, urging them to return to the reservations, take up farming and send their children to mission schools. With no other choice, they agreed. To add more fuel to the fire, the U.S. Army recommended that several members of the Seventh Cavalry be awarded the Congressional Medal of Honor.

Reaction to the massacre at Wounded Knee was mixed. Depending on which article one read, there was more than one variation of what happened. Most Americans seemed to support the cavalry and its actions, while others were simply outraged. Other events, however, were taking place on distant shores and requiring much of Harrison's time and attention.

In Chile on October 16, 1891, two U.S. sailors were killed and 17 wounded during an uproar in Valparaiso. What began as a brawl between unarmed sailors and enraged Chileans turned into a full scale riot. Several Chileans were injured and three dozen Americans never made it back to their ship; they were arrested and jailed.

Part of the dispute may have been over the issue of Americans in the past trying (and failing) to ship weapons to revolutionaries in Chile. A private steamer, the *Itata*, loaded arms and munitions in San Diego for Chilean insurgents. On May 6, 1891, the ship was seized by the *USS Charleston* and forced to unload its war provisions. Efforts to ship weapons to Chile, however, continued.

Harrison and Blaine made it very clear that the U.S. was willing to go to war if the Americans weren't released and other problems remedied. The president called a cabinet meeting to discuss the matter and formulate a response.

The ill feeling between the two nations actually went back a decade earlier when Blaine was secretary of state under James Garfield and Chester Arthur. At that time Chile and Peru were at war and Blaine had announced that the U.S. would support Peru. This angered the British who had a foothold in Chile and were on good terms with their people. A similar predicament still existed when Harrison became president, even though the Chilean government had changed hands. Sympathetic Americans continued to raise funds and tried to ship arms to anti-British rebels.

To make matters worse, Harrison, almost certainly in a move to intentionally agitate the British, named Patrick Egan as our ambassador to Chile. Egan was a wanted man in Great Britain for crimes committed in the service of Irish independence. He had fled to the U.S., becoming an American citizen in 1884 and rising up through the ranks of Republican politics.

As unrest and uncertainty mounted in Chile, Harrison ordered the *USS Baltimore* to anchor off shore at Valparaiso as fighting again broke out between pro-British and pro-American forces for control of the government. The situation was further complicated when Egan provided sanctuary inside the American embassy for some rebel leaders, and refused to hand them over to the pro-British faction which ruled. When the captain of the *Baltimore* gave shore leave to 117 sailors, many Chileans interpreted the move as an act of aggression. The Americans, suspecting a planned assault upon reaching Valparaiso, went bar hopping intent on having a good time. After a heated exchange of words between the Americans and Chileans inside the True Blue Saloon, a fight ensued outside in the street and quickly spread. Even days after the riot tempers flared and Blaine, in particular was outraged. But the secretary of state was quite ill and the burden of handling the situation fell on Harrison personally.

In January of 1892 yet another Chilean government came into power, one which was more sympathetic to the Americans. Blaine, through Harrison, made several demands and threatened war if the imprisoned American sailors weren't released. When Chile didn't respond, Harrison consigned the matter to Congress which had the power to declare war. And when he mentioned the possibility of a war to his cabinet, they voted in favor of it.

Finally, a Chilean court, realizing that the U.S. would take action, ruled that its government release all prisoners, pay the U.S. $75,000 in reparations for damages and issue a formal apology. The entire affair, though muddled with old prejudices and sword waving, proved a diplomatic triumph for the Harrison administration. And despite protests from the Chileans, Egan remained as ambassador until he was removed by President Cleveland in 1893.

In other areas of foreign policy, there was trouble brewing. Talk of a canal in Central America led to a bill in Congress to help finance a private construction company to built it. Harrison supported the idea to have the U.S. government guarantee the company's bonds but the bill failed to reach a vote before Harrison's term expired.

The president also wanted a naval base in Haiti. He instructed our ambassador there, Frederick Douglass (the former slave and abolitionist), to proceed in negotiations with the Haitians. When Douglass was rebuffed by the Haitian government, Harrison ordered nine U.S. warships there to "assist" him. The political conditions in Haiti, however, were unstable. The U.S. then approached her neighbor, the Dominican Republic, which was bankrupt and in no mood to accommodate our desire. Both nations rejected our proposals, as did Portugal when Harrison tried to establish a base in the Azores.

Although Harrison had good intentions, the concern of pensions to Union veterans proved to be an enigma, if not an altogether utter fiasco. President Cleveland had vetoed hundreds of bills to award pensions to former Civil War soldiers and this was one of the reasons there was a healthy surplus in the U.S. Treasury Department. Harrison saw to it that needy members of the Grand Army of the Republic and other impoverished Civil War veterans were going to be compensated for illnesses or injuries they suffered during their time of service. For the important post of Commissioner of Pensions, Harrison selected James R. Tanner of New York. As commander of the state's GAR, Tanner was a genuine hero, having lost both legs at the Second Battle of Bull Run.

He promised to be generous with federal pension money and he kept his word. In doling out funds, Tanner announced in a speech in Tennessee, "I am thankful that at these finger tips there rests some real power...God help the surplus."[7] It was Tanner's loose tongue, his bragging and outspoken criticism of high-ranking government officials which attracted attention. He continually ignored directives from his boss, Secretary of Interior Noble, to use discretion in giving out large payments and reducing requirements to prove applicants' disability.

Harrison finally asked for Tanner's resignation on September 11, 1889, only after six months as commissioner. After several weeks of inaction, Harrison appointed Green B. Raum, an Illinois veteran, as Tanner's replacement. Raum assumed his position with only a bit more intelligence and discretion. Rumors circulated that he had accepted bribes from lawyers to expedite their pension claims. The House investigated the charges twice but Raum avoided conviction because the investigating committee was split along party lines. Democrats in the House and Senate concluded that Raum "prostituted his office for the purposes of private gain."[8] Despite considerable but circumstantial evidence of wrong-doing placed under his nose, President Harrison kept Raum on the job while the doling out of pensions continued.

While former Confederates understandably received no benefits or public assistance from the U.S. government, Union veterans received so much money that the treasury was soon depleted. Most of the pension money given out was deserved and needed, but hundreds of claims were frivolous and illegitimate. It was reported that some ex-soldiers were even compensated for injuries incurred in the act of desertion (indeed some of those receiving money had been deserters), while other disabled veterans received benefits for injuries that occurred *after* the war. In addition, some veterans received pensions who had not even applied for one! In 1890 Harrison signed the Dependent and Disability Act, providing generous pensions for widows and even dependent parents of veterans. Annual expenditures for these programs increased from $81 million to $135 million.

During Harrison's term in office the number of pension applicants rose from 489,725 in 1889 to 966,012 in 1893, with a corresponding cost increase of $89 million to $157 million. In four years the national budget surplus was reduced by $68 million just to pay pensioners. The citizenry soon grew weary of such excesses, and a handful of journalists and gifted cartoonists lambasted Harrison for such extravagance. Nor did Democrats forget to remind the public in 1892 of Harrison's lavish appropriations, though it should be noted that the Democratic Party controlled both the House and Senate by then. Thus, the surplus evaporated and along with it, prosperity.

If troubles weren't enough, there was a sore which had been festering for two decades within the American economy—the growth of monopolies. Huge business trusts developed in steel, oil, railroads, sugar production and various types of manufacturing. Unfair business practices were used by large companies to eliminate smaller ones. Some of these big corporations, along with their owners, created conditions which made some Americans blush with shame, and angry to the point of demanding action. No president had been successful in dealing with this problem and until 1890, Congress would not give any attention to the matter. Many reform minded public officials believed that regulation of big business should come from state or local powers. (More on this topic will be mentioned in the next chapter.)

The president found rest by taking a few vacations amid the watchful eye of a critical press. He often cruised the Potomac River on the Navy's *Despatch* or visited his Deer Park retreat in Maryland. One incident proved he was not the able bodied hunter he used to be. If Harrison entertained any thoughts he was a keen-eyed marksman, he must have been humbled on a hunting trip where he shot and killed a pig, thinking it was a raccoon. He also liked to bowl and play billiards, but was not very skilled at these activities. While Harrison went fishing or duck hunting, the first lady spent time with her easel, pallet, and brushes, dabbling in her watercolor sketches.

His favorite spectator sport was the national pastime—baseball. Though several presidents had invited teams to the White House or had watched amateur matches, none had gone to a major league contest. On June 2, 1892, Harrison became the first incumbent chief executive to attend a major league baseball game, watching Cincinnati defeat the Washington Nationals 7–4 in eleven innings (ex-President Grant had attended a game in New York City ten years before). The game was held at Swampoodle Grounds, a ballpark long since torn down to accommodate Washington's Union Station. Harrison proved not to be a good luck charm when he showed up a second time on June 25 to watch Philadelphia defeat Washington 9-2.

For extra leisure, Harrison often enjoyed rides into the country in his dark green Studebaker carriage, pulled by his prized Kentucky thoroughbreds. Albert Hawkins, a Negro coachman for Harrison, was also in charge of the White House stables, taking good care of the president's four white horses Abdullah, Billy, Lexington and John. The president's hunting dog proved a companion as well, as did the family mixed breed collie Dash. To relax, Harrison relied on his small cigars, supplied to him by an Indianapolis tobacco dealer, though he rarely passed up an opportunity to smoke larger Havana cigars. On rare occasions Harrison took a few sips of wine or whisky.

In the spring of 1891 the president embarked on an extended tour of the South and West, traveling more than 10,000 miles in five weeks. Going along were his family, the Cabinet, newsmen, and the White House staff. Tumultuous crowds, parades and banquets, along with lavish floral presentations and triumphant arches awaited him. The First Family was showered with momentos, gifts, honors, souvenirs and special commendations.

The entourage didn't just travel in style, it did so in splendor. For months the Pullman Company had been busy designing several railroad cars for presidential travel. Sparing no expense in providing the latest conveniences and elaborate fixings, Pullman's skilled craftsmen created five railroad cars in Delaware which were fit for a king. One car, located behind the locomotive engine and the coal car, carried a large generator, a library, a barbershop, a well-stocked liquor cabinet and the water supply. This vehicle was dubbed *Aztlan*. This was followed by four other cars: *The Ideal* (with six compartments and a drawing room), *The New Zealand* (a sleeper and plush private quarters upholstered in blue used exclusively by the Harrisons), *The Coronado* (dining car) and the end car with a small library and an observation platform, called *The Vacuna*. Service was provided by employees from the Pennsylvania Railroad. Future presidents and their families, even two generations later, would find these train accommodations elegant as the same vehicles were used later.

The first official stop was in Atlanta, rebuilt after Sherman's destruction of it in 1864. As the train pulled into Atlanta a military salute was fired from a cannon mounted on a flatcar on an adjacent track. The concussion from the cannon blast shattered the thick plate glass in *The Coronado*, knocking down a Negro steward. Luckily for the Harrisons, they were in another car and escaped any injury. Following a procession down Peachtree Street, the carriages drove ten miles north to the battleground of Peach Tree Creek where Harrison and his men had fought a quarter of a century before. The president was touched at the site where so many from both sides had died. Indeed, Harrison's old feelings of resentment and rancor had disappeared the day he took his oath to be president of *all* the people. Throughout the South his visits soothed the old scars of war. At Birmingham he was welcomed by the largest crowd ever gathered in Alabama. The city of Memphis was decked out in U.S. flags and flowers for his parade.

Large throngs greeted him in cities such as Knoxville, Omaha, El Paso, Galveston, Los Angeles and San Diego. He stopped in Seattle, Tacoma, Pocatello, Salt Lake City and Denver. At each stop Harrison promoted the ideals of unity, honesty, patriotism, and self-reliance, giving a different speech to each audience. No one would deny this trip was for political reasons though the president considered it a goodwill excursion. His humor even got some big laughs, especially when he told a Nebraska crowd, "I don't know whether it is prejudice or not, but I always have a very high opinion of a state whose chief production is corn."[9]

Harrison's visit to El Paso was significant, as he was the first sitting chief executive to visit Texas. Harrison was to meet with Mexican President Porforio Diaz, a first for diplomatic relations between the two countries. The train arrived in El Paso on Tuesday, April 21 (Texas Independence Day) at 9:00 in the morning where a big crowd greeted the First Family, including a large contingency of Mexican citizens. But President Diaz was not there— the Mexican Constitution prohibited its president from leaving the country while in office without the permission of the congress. And besides, it would not have looked good for Diaz to be in El Paso on the anniversary of its struggle for freedom from Mexico. The city was adorned in patriotic bunting with large cheering crowds along the streets.

The elite 11th Mexican Battalion Band struck up "Hail to the Chief" as Harrison emerged. The U.S. Army Band from nearby Fort Bliss was also there, despite a slight disagreement. The commander of the fort had demanded $50 for expenses from the city of El Paso, but he was overruled by General David S. Stanley who was traveling with the Harrison party. The procession, consisting of ten carriages for the Harrison guests, made its way through the city to the courthouse where a group of schoolgirls dressed in white lined the walkway. Meanwhile, Caroline Harrison, already showing signs of fatigue due to her undiagnosed bout of tuberculosis (though several days later her doctors would discover the source of her condition), gathered enough energy to cross the Rio Grande and do a little shopping in Juarez. Among the articles she bought was a hat for herself. Perhaps without realizing it, she established a new precedent, for Carrie Harrison became the first incumbent first lady to step on foreign soil.

Harrison's address may have surprised many of his listeners. He apologized for the United States being an aggressive and unpleasant neighbor (the controversial Mexican-American War had ended less than fifty years before). He then spoke of friendship and trade while praising the efforts of both Mexicans and Americans in promoting peaceful relations. The president announced that he hoped the two nations had passed the time when bitterness towards one another existed. Some of the hostility which still endured between the two nations seemed to melt away in the Texas sun. Harrison was interrupted a dozen times with applause and cheering. Following his speech, the president was presented a bouquet of flowers by six-year-old Carrie Fewell, who proclaimed herself a Democratic girl. Admist laughter from the crowd, Harrison thanked her and gave her a pat on the head. The Harrisons and their guests returned to the depot and, after a brief reception to host several Mexican officials, left El Paso at 11:10.

The visit to El Paso, a Democratic stronghold of 11,000 citizens at the time, was inspiring and festive, yet it failed to yield any political dividends. The city's hospitality and patriotism touched Harrison, but the residents, as well as most of the male population of Texas, were overwhelmingly opposed to any Republican in the White House. In the 1892 election Grover Cleveland defeated Harrison by a three to one margin in Texas. Even the Populist candidate James Weaver received 18,000 more votes than Harrison.

On April 23 he began a triumphant week in California. In San Francisco the first lady christened the *USS Monterey,* an armored coastal defensive ship, while her husband gave nine speeches in one day. In one of them, he told an audience, "I believe that we have come to a new epoch as a nation. There are opening portals before us inviting us to enter, opening portals to trade and influence and prestige such as we have never seen before."[10] By the time the party made stops in Washington, Oregon, and Utah Carrie was exhausted and near collapse. Attending the Harrisons in their private railroad car *The New Zealand*, doctors feared she might have tuberculosis.

The tour was the longest ever undertaken by a president in office. Altogether, Harrison gave 142 speeches and visited 21 states and two territories. The Harrisons received more than 400 gifts. When they arrived in Washington on May 15, they were met by their grandchildren. The gifts were later exhibited at the White House before many of them were donated to charity. What some supporters believed was a masterful stroke in promoting the popularity of his administration, realized months later this was not the case. The tremendous outpouring Harrison witnessed all along his journey through the South and West was more out of respect for the presidency than the president himself.

During the summer of 1891 the Harrisons vacationed in Cresson, Pennsylvania (near Altoona), and Cape May Point. They were gone until the electrical wiring was completed at the White House, a period of four months.

There were no guarantees Harrison would be renominated in 1892. He discovered small groups of Republicans conspiring against him and told his wife, "No Harrison has ever run from a fight, Caroline, and *there is going to be a fight!*"[11] Senators Matthew Quay and Tom Platt, along with House Speaker Tom Reed, opposed him.

The wealthy Quay was also influential among millions of Civil War veterans. The Pennsylvanian had been a Medal of Honor recipient for gallantry at Fredericksburg and commanded respect among nearly all party leaders. Quay and Harrison had a heated argument at the White House. After being reminded that loyal Republicans were responsible for his election, Harrison told Quay that God had put him where he was. The powerful boss snapped at Harrison, "Let God reelect you then!"[12] Weeks later, when Reed was urged to join the Harrison bandwagon, the Speaker of the House spoke for many dissenters when he said he would never hop on the Harrison *Ice Wagon.*[13]

Despite the bickering among GOP leaders, Harrison was renominated on the first ballot. Vice President Morton, who did nothing to promote his candidacy, was replaced by Whitelaw Reid, a native of Cincinnati, Civil War veteran, Minister to France, and a New York newspaper publisher. Reid was also a graduate of Miami University, and this marked the first time in history that running mates were graduates of the same college. Reid's request to Harrison for an ambassadorship to Great Britain had been denied four years earlier but he was now willing to do anything to win the election. Upon being congratulated on his renomination, Harrison received the news at the White House. In a jovial mood, the president told one of his Negro servants from Virginia, "Now Jerry, you must be sure to find a possum for me as soon as the frost falls."[14]

The Democrats nominated Grover Cleveland for the third consecutive time. Congressman Adlai E. Stevenson of Illinois was nominated for vice president. Though Cleveland disliked speaking and campaigning, he made several speeches to large crowds at New York City rallies. Suffering from attacks of gout, he found walking difficult, adding to his distress. Many Republicans condemned his attacks on Harrison as unpatriotic or inappropriate.

The Democrats weren't the only political party on the offensive. After meeting in St. Louis and selecting Weaver, the Populists chose an ex-Confederate from Virginia, James Field, as Weaver's running mate. Together, they drew large crowds, traveling by rail all through the South and West and denouncing "Little Ben." At two stops in Georgia, Weaver was pelted with tomatoes and other assorted vegetables but his campaign by and large attracted big receptive crowds.

Benjamin Harrison's greatest concern during this time was not his reelection—it was his wife. In the spring of 1892 Carrie began suffering from terrible coughing spells, followed by a bout of pneumonia. When she began spitting up blood, doctors were quickly summoned. In the spring of 1892 she was diagnosed with tuberculosis. No doubt the death of two servants and a White House staffer added to her melancholy.

Carrie was taken to Loon Lake in northern New York where doctors hoped she would recover. Her health seemed to improve and the president returned to Washington in July. Carrie later contracted pleurisy and her spirits sunk rapidly. Her deeply depressed husband wrote his daughter, "Politics and business have been annoying me day and night, and this, with the anxiety of your mother, makes life just now a burden, and ambition an illusion."[15] Before the end came, Carrie, barely audible, told her husband, "I will soon be gone. Make me a promise. Find somebody to take care of you. You can't make it by yourself. Don't wait too long. You'll be helpless."[16]

Just the day before she died, the first lady's vital signs seem to stabilize. Doctors applied a hot, flaxweed poultice to her side which gave her some relief. She died in the Garfield Room in the southwest corner of the White House, two weeks before the election. Grover Cleveland announced he would not campaign out of respect for Harrison and the family.

A funeral service was held in the White House. Among the mourners standing at Carrie's casket, adorned with orchids and roses, was her ninety-two-year-old father, Dr. Reverend John Scott. A second service was held in Indianapolis where she was buried.

Caroline Harrison had taken an interest in every detail of activities in her husband's presidency, and her staff adored her. The first lady also shared the president's inclination to wax philosophically when it came to observations concerning patriotism, success and the American spirit. She once noted, "We have within ourselves the only element of destruction; our foes are from within, not from without. Our hope is in unity and self-sacrifice."[17] As a woman of grace, style, beauty, and charm she proved an essential asset to both her family her country.

In the meantime, the GOP campaign team was in shambles. Several key campaign organizers resigned, and when Republican Walter Gresham bolted the GOP convention and joined the Democrats (Gresham in fact was later named by Grover Cleveland as secretary of state). Another blow came to Harrison when financier Andrew Carnegie, a generous contributor to Republican causes, announced he was backing Cleveland. In addition, Matthew Quay and Tom Platt (who was still upset with the president for rejecting several appointments he submitted) worked behind the scenes to defeat Harrison. The aging Platt also felt Harrison still disapproved of him because of a minor sex scandal in which he had been involved a decade earlier. Harrison tried to convince Platt that he held no personal animosity and asked for his support. Ultimately, Platt did campaign for Harrison but it was too late.

Another former loyal supporter, president Charles W. Eliot of Harvard, defected over to the Democrats as well. One more blow came when Tammany Hall of New York City, which had been partly responsible for Cleveland's defeat four years earlier, declared it would not actively oppose the Democratic candidate from Buffalo. Thus, Harrison had little hope for reelection but still remained hopeful he could set about the difficult task of political fence mending.

Noted newspaper editor and historian Henry Adams remarked about Harrison and Cleveland: "The two candidates were singular persons, of whom it was the common saying that one of them had no friends; the other only enemies."[18] Cleveland enjoyed a big victory, winning both the popular vote and the electoral college. In 1888 Cleveland had beaten Harrison in the popular vote by more than 100,000, even though he lost the election. He now bested Harrison by more than 400,000 despite the turnout of support for the Populist James Weaver. The Populists, incidentally, won ten seats in the House.

Weaver won several Western states and captured 22 electoral votes. He became the only third-party candidate between 1860 and 1912 to carry a single state. Even if Harrison had received all of the electoral votes won by Weaver, it would not have been enough. Interestingly, large numbers of blacks in the South voted for Weaver, but eventually many Populists jumped on the Democratic bandwagon to back William Jennings Bryan in 1896.

There were other reasons for Harrison's defeat. Some Republicans cited the loss as a failure by Harrison to fulfill his commitments on civil rights, pointing to the results of the 1890 off-year elections. They felt that Harrison, as president, seemed to lose his vigor in his fight for racial justice. Catholics were also angered when Harrison appointed two bigoted anti-Catholics, General Thomas J. Morgan and Dr. Daniel Dorchester, to high offices in handling Indian affairs. Though many Catholics voted Democrat anyway, many in the Midwest who had supported Harrison in 1888 jumped on Cleveland's bandwagon.

It seemed as if Harrison could do nothing right, even when he made a right decision. In the late summer of 1892 a cholera epidemic threatened to break out in New York City. Its roots were traced back to some newly arrived immigrants. Overriding state authorities, Harrison issued an executive order extending the mandatory quarantine of ships to 20 days. Steamship companies were also ordered not to bring immigrants from infected areas of Europe. An epidemic was averted but critics of Harrison renewed charges of discrimination. The publicity resulting from anti-immigrant propaganda efforts, however, overshadowed the news of his nomination.

Like most presidents before and after him, Harrison felt he had been mistreated by the press. Perhaps in an attempt to make amends and practice some damage control, the president told a group of reporters after the convention, "While I am very averse to interviews, my door has always been open to a friendly call from any of you, and any information about public business has been at your disposal."[19] There may have been some stretching of the truth in this statement.

President Harrison told a friend his defeat brought him "no personal disappointments or grief...Indeed after the heavy blow that the death of my wife dealt me, I do not think I could stand the strain a reelection would have brought."[20]

Benjamin Harrison was understandably disappointed in his failure for reelection. But he was very tired and only a couple years later came to realize how much he would miss a second term, despite the interruptions and personal problems. The ex-president described the White House as "an office and a home combined—an evil combination. There is no break in the day, no change of atmosphere. There is only one door—one that is never locked—between the president's office and what are not very accurately called his private apartments."[21]

Harrison's last four months in office proved difficult. The Executive Mansion became a place of loneliness and grief. In December his 93-year-old father-in-law died. Then, in January a scarlet fever epidemic struck the nation's capital causing widespread panic. Both the president's son and four-year-old granddaughter Marthena were diagnosed with the illness while staying at the White House. Russell and Marthena were quarantined in the Arlington Hotel.

Harrison sent his son a letter, demonstrating his sadness and faith. In it he wrote, "It seems very hard to be shut of[f] from you all so long—while you are so near. But God has been very good to us & we should be grateful. Things are very quiet in our end of the house—no one calls, except at the office & not many there. I have not gone anywhere not even to church for while there is I suppose no danger—some might think so & be made uncomfortable. You must not fail to take the utmost care that Marthena does not get any cold—there is need of the utmost & continued care to avoid exposure." Harrison went on to admit he longed for Cleveland's inauguration and wrote, "I can get along I think until I am released on March 4—though the strain has been very hard—& I do long to get out of the House." The president concluded his letter by offering his son some help: "I have thought you might need a little money as you have been interrupted somewhat in your affairs & send you a small check."[22]

After a close call, Marthena survived, as did Russell. More bad news came while his son and granddaughter were recuperating when, on January 27, former Secretary of State Blaine who was suffering from gout, Bright's disease and lumbago, died. Even after returning to Indianapolis Harrison continued to sink into despair when Marthena contracted a debilitating case of the measles. The child was once again quarantined, but survived.

Others close to him passed on, including former President Hayes, who had died on January 17. Secretary of the Treasury Windom, two senators, Supreme Court Justice Lamar, and the wife of Harrison's private secretary E. W. Halford also died. This was almost too much for Harrison to bear. He lamented to Reid, "My period in the Executive Mansion has been full of care and labor, and I am very much worn out and full of longing for rest."[23]

Republican Senator William B. Allison of Iowa, once a supporter of Harrison, reflected on the outcome of the election a few years later when he stated, "It was God's mercy to this country that Grover Cleveland, and not Harrison, was elected President."[24]

This is the only known daguerreotype of William Henry Harrison, grandfather of Benjamin Harrison. This photograph was probably taken in 1841, just before he was sworn in as the ninth president.

Library of Congress

The Big House, home of William Henry Harrison, where his grandson Benjamin Harrison was born. The Ohio River and the Cincinnati and Whitewater Canal are in the foreground. The home was destroyed by fire on July 25, 1858.

From an engraving by W. Woodruff for *The Ladies Repository*.

Benjamin Harrison's family crest and coat of arms. The blue shield depicts three gold demi lions symbolizing justice, honor and generosity. Above the shield is a helmet topped with a lion, signifying a knight in battle. The Latin motto *In omnia paratus* means "Ready for All Things."

Author's Collection

Benjamin's mother, Elizabeth Irwin Harrison. From Mercersburg, Pennsylvania, she was the second wife of Benjamin's father, John Scott Harrison.

The President Benjamin Harrison Home, Indianapolis, Indiana.

This photograph of Benjamin Harrison was taken while he was a student at Miami University in Oxford, Ohio.

Stark County (Ohio) Historical Society

MIAMI UNIVERSITY.

PROGRAMME OF THE
Exercises on Commencement Day.

JUNE 24, 1852.

MUSIC.
PRAYER.
MUSIC.

Latin Salutatory,	David Swing,	Williamsburgh.
Poetry of Religion,	Harmer Denny,	Pittsburgh, Pa.
Poor of England,	Benjamin Harrison,	North-Bend,

MUSIC.

	James A. Hughes,	Somerville.
Public Opinion,	John P. Craighead,	Dayton.

MUSIC.

Free Thought and Free Action,	Isaac S. Lane,	Middletown,
The Federal Constitution,	Lewis W. Ross,	Butler County.

MUSIC.

Harmony of Contrasts,	Samuel Lowrie,	Pittsburgh, Pa.
He is the Freeman whom the Truth makes Free,	James H. Childs,	Pittsburgh, Pa.

MUSIC.

Science and Art as Aids of Christianity,	Wm. H. Prestley,	Pittsburgh, Pa.
The Useful,	A. C. Junkin,	Xenia.

MUSIC.

Mystery,	David Moorow,	Cambridge. (Excused.)
Oration,	John Knox Boude,	Oxford. (Excused.)
Oration,	John S. Baker,	Cincinnati. (Excused.)
Death of Socrates,	Joseph Walker,	New Concord.

MUSIC.

Valedictory,	Milton Saylor,	Lewisburgh.

BENEDICTION.

Intelligencer Print, Hamilton.

Harrison's name was misspelled on the commencement program. A pen was used to correct it.

Author's Collection

Harrison's first home in Indianapolis.

Edgewood Publishing Company

Carrie and Benjamin Harrison. These photographs, taken in 1863, show Harrison in his colonel's uniform and Carrie looking quite serious.

Stark County Historical Society

Colonel Benjamin Harrison during the Civil War.

National Archives

From an engraving, a scene of the Battle of Peachtree Creek, Georgia.

Library of Congress

Frank Opper published this cartoon just before the 1888 election. It depicts James G. Blaine as the power behind the presidency, holding control of "Little Ben." Harrison later named Blaine as Secretary of State.

Library of Congress

Illustrator Frank Opper shows a disappointed Uncle Sam examining President Harrison under a microscope. Captioned "The Smallest Specimen Yet," the cartoon appeared in *Puck*.

National Archives

The Twenty-third President of the United States.

Library of Congress

First Lady Caroline (Carrie) Harrison.

National First Ladies Library

In this Joseph Kepler cartoon, President Harrison wears his grandfather's hat and seems a bit overwhelmed. Originally in color, this cartoon appeared in 1890 editions of *Puck* and *Judge* magazines.

Stark County Historical Society

Harrison's Vice President, Levi Morton.

Edgewood Publishing Company

Harrison's friend and former college classmate, Whitelaw Reid. A newspaperman with outstanding credentials, Reid was Harrison's Vice Presidential nominee in the 1892 election.

Stark County Historical Society

James G. Blaine, Senator from Maine, served as secretary of state under three presidents, including Benjamin Harrison. The powerful Republican leader lost the presidency to Grover Cleveland in 1884.

Library of Congress

Newspapers attacked Harrison for freely spending the government's surplus of money. This cartoon was published by W. Bencough of the Democratic National Committee in 1892.

National Archives

Frederick Douglass, an escaped slave who later bought his freedom, became editor and publisher of *The North Star*, an abolitionist newspaper. Harrison was an admirer of Douglass and later appointed him as the U.S. minister to Haiti.

Library of Congress

Matilda Joyner, called "Black Patti," sang for the Harrisons at the White House. She also performed for Presidents McKinley and Theodore Roosevelt.

National Archives

The President and his grandson, Benjamin Harrison McKee.

Library of Congress

This giant wood and steel ball was rolled hundreds of miles in Harrison's 1888 presidential campaign. It was similar to the one used to generate excitement in his grandfather's 1840 race. "Keep the ball rollin'" became a popular phrase.

The Benjamin Harrison Home, Indianapolis, Indiana

From left to right: Harrison's son Russell, daughter Mamie (Mary), and father John Scott.

The Benjamin Harrison Home, Indianapolis, Indiana

Many Republican leaders were unhappy with Harrison's presidency in 1892 and tried to "unseat" him in the White House. In this unflattering cartoon, Grover Cleveland peers through the window at Harrison on the pot while other hopeful candidates anxiously wait their turn.

Library of Congress

Life in America during Harrison's presidency was changing, particularly in technology.

The pennyfarthing, or high wheeler, was popular at the beginning of Harrison's term. This vehicle, however, was giving way to the safer and more convenient two wheeled bicycle where both tires were the same smaller size.

Author's Collection

America's first automobile was built by Gottfried Schloemer of Milwaukee in 1889. It had an internal combustion engine with one cylinder.

Author's Collection

Two young ladies having fun on the New Jersey shore. Their swimming apparel was typical of the early 1890s.

Library of Congress

This telephone model was in use during the 1890s. It had hand-cranked magnets that generated a current to signal an operator.

Stark County Historical Society

The Duryea brothers of Springfield, Massachusetts, were also working on a "horseless carriage" soon after Schloemer's vehicle.

Author's Collection

A woman's work was never done. This photo by Frances Benjamin Johnston was taken in Lynn, Massachusetts.

National Archives

"Buffalo Bill" Cody (1847–1917) was a former pony express rider, Indian fighter and scout who formed his popular Wild West Show. Cody was a personal friend to Harrison and one of the world's greatest showmen.

Library of Congress

The mass destruction and near extinction of the buffalo, evidenced by the bison skulls seen here, marked the closing of the American frontier.

National Archives

EXECUTIVE MANSION,

WASHINGTON

Nov 8, 1892

My dear Genl.,

I have your most kind letter of the 8th inst, and the second volume of the History of New York where do you have done me the favor to dedicate to me. For all this I am your grateful debtor.

Very Sincerely Yours

Benj Harrison

Copy of a thank you letter from President Harrison to author James Wilson.

Stark County Historical Society

Lillian Russell (1861–1922) was the ideal of feminine beauty during the late 1800s. The singer/actress combined her charm, stature and talent to reign as the undisputed queen of the American stage.

Stark County Historical Society

John Phillip Sousa, the "March King." At the age of 26 he became conductor of the White House Marine Band, called "The President's Own." Sousa served from 1880 under Rutherford B. Hayes until 1892 when Harrison was president. After years of highly successful tours around the country and the world, Sousa became conductor of the U.S. Navy Band. Few composers have had a greater impact on American music. Of all the chief executives he served under, Sousa's closest relationship was with Harrison.

National Archives

Mr. Benjamin Harrison
and
Mrs. Mary Scott Dimmick

announce their marriage

on Monday, April the sixth,

eighteen hundred and ninety-six, at

Saint Thomas's Church,

New York.

A Harrison-Dimmick wedding invitation. Harrison's adult children did not approve of their father marrying the much younger niece of his deceased wife.

From the collection of Ben Benson of Hartford, New York

The former president with his youngest daughter Elizabeth. She was born in 1897.

The Benjamin Harrison Home in Indianapolis

Benjamin Harrison's final resting place at Crown Hill Cemetery in Indianapolis.

Author's Collection

Mary Lord Dimmick, Carrie's niece and Benjamin Harrison's second wife.

Library of Congress

Mary Dimmick in her later years. She published a book about her husband years after his death.

Library of Congress

CHAPTER 9

The President's America

Benjamin Harrison, dignified, refined and aloof, represented the Victorian Age in America. This era, named for England's queen who was still mourning her husband's death in 1861, has been partly viewed as one of snobbery and repression. Queen Victoria's influence set the standard in the Western World in terms of dress, style, manners, art, morality and even speaking. Americans, in their admiration for their English brethren, adopted and promoted most of these ostentatious values which were based on upper-class European traditions.

However, the Victorian Era took on a different dimension in the United States. The American psyche, born and bred in Puritan ethic, nurtured in independence and schooled in a homespun philosophy embraced by moral values advocated in children's textbooks like the *McGuffey's Readers*, manifested itself in stark contrast to the British. In every facet of American society the country was flexing its muscle and the world began to take notice, but it had taken a generation or two before America came into her own.

What's been also referred to as The Gilded Age (a term coined by Mark Twain), the post-Civil War period of industrialization continuing to the Spanish-American War, a new wealthy class emerged. Lacking tradition, these elite rich built enormous mansions and spent their time engaged in activities they believed were signs of refinement. Though many other

Americans had a far different view of culture, the disparity between the top and lower classes grew. Government was marked by widespread corruption and along with other wrongs, spurned a reform movement to reduce poverty and regulate big business.

Dress codes were strictly enforced and middle class decorum was maintained at public events, restaurants, and museums. Sex, as both a topic and a *word*, was not mentioned in public by proper ladies and gentlemen. Women had their bodies clothed from neck to foot while swimming at the beach and men were not permitted to swim unless their chests were covered. Even piano legs were draped with skirts because bare legs were unseemly. But views and mores on sex were slowly changing in the United States as American travelers and writers returned to their country with differing attitudes toward sex. After his first view of the high-kicking cancan dancers in Paris (who, incidentally wore *nothing* under their skirts), Mark Twain, quipped, "I placed my hands before my face in shame, but I looked through my fingers."[1]

The Victorian Age in America was marked by some unique features and characteristics during the four years in which Harrison was president. One of these cultural attributes from 1889 to 1893 was a rapid transformation in transportation. This metamorphosis was accelerated by a tremendous growth spurt in population and industry. Another feature was that many Americans were working slightly fewer hours and accumulating more free time. At least one astute official, Congressman James A. Garfield, noticed a decade before that Americans were slowly acquiring more spare time for recreation and relaxation when he posed the question, "What shall we do with our leisure once we have it?"

In the four decades following Zachary Taylor's presidency in 1850, there were some significant shifts in demographics and the types of jobs held by Americans. In 1890 there were more than 65,000,000 people in the United States. About 88 percent of the population was white and 68 percent lived on farms or in very small villages. More than 8,000,000 out of a workforce of 22,700,000 were engaged in agriculture (nearly 40 percent). The work on the farm required great labor with little time left for rest and relaxation. The farmer's plight was further burdened by two other major factors: they were always at the mercy of mother nature, and they had little control over the price of their products.

One important technological change began with the government itself when the Census Bureau modified the way it tallied its information. Collected data was transferred to punch cards and fed into a machine which allowed an electrical current to pass through holes. This method of tabulating, devised by Dr. Herman Hollerith, saved much time and effort and proved to be the precursor of the modern computer industry.

Unlike the previous forty years, many jobs in 1890 revolved around the railroad, where there was danger to workers and passengers alike. There were approximately 463,000 railroad employees when Harrison took office. Improvements had been made after the Civil War, but in 1875 alone, despite the use of the telegraph and other safety measures, there were 104 recorded head-on collisions. The loss in human life was still appalling. By 1891 train wrecks were minimal, resulting in fewer passenger deaths, but more than 2400 railroad *workers* were killed and 22,000 maimed or seriously injured. Many of the injuries and fatalities occurred while men were coupling cars. Harrison demanded action. Congress mandated improved changes in the coupling devices, but little else was accomplished. It would take ten more years before better life-saving measures would be adopted.

This growth, however, brought with it additional problems, including the displacement of both farmers and American Indians. In fact, the 400,000 Native-Americans in 1850 had been reduced to 250,000. This dramatic decrease was due of course to several non-railroad events, but the "iron horse" played a major role in the demise of Indian culture.

There were 200,000 miles of railroad tracks which had a direct effect on other types of occupations, namely mining, lumbering, raising livestock (especially sheep and cattle), commercial fishing, steel making and scores of other types of manufacturing. Refrigeration made it possible to ship meat in Chicago by rail to New York City without it spoiling. Railroads commerce also played a vital role when both Cleveland and Harrison strengthened the navy with new steel ships and expanded trade markets. This growth, however, brought with it additional problems.

Another phenomenon was taking place, one not so readily noticed. A new middle class was emerging. It was characterized by a growing per capita income, new forms of corporate organization, an expansion of public education, faster communication, and more free time. These traits provided Americans of moderate means with a set of common interests which distinguished themselves from the wealthy elite and common laborers.

More and more women were entering the workplace and by 1890 there were more than 4,000,000, giving rise to a new sense of independence. The woman's separate sphere of domesticity, child rearing, mundane housework and moral education was being challenged by a younger generation of females. They began bicycling, playing croquet and pursuing intellectual activities and social reform. The so-called New Age woman replaced her plump, matronly mother who was garbed in richly adorned dresses, and evolved into a slightly taller, thinner, more athletic female with more practical styles of attire and wearing a simple skirt below a shirtwaist fashioned after men's clothing. Women were also pursuing formal education at an accelerated rate. In the three decades following the end of the Civil War, the number of female college graduates quadrupled. Old urban institutions such as restaurants, museums, and department stores adapted to meet women's new needs for public space for rest and amusement.

Other changes had taken place in the employment numbers as well. There were more than 1,000,000 bookkeepers, clerks and salesmen, 500,000 dressmakers, milliners and seamstresses, another half million employed in lumbering and other related mill production, 148,000 iron and steel workers, 120,000 carpenters, 90,000 lawyers, 46,000 involved in the grist milling of grains, 44,000 in the leather and tanning industry, 42,000 painters, 35,000 plumbers and gas pipe fitters, 13,000 chemical workers making gunpowder, paint and fertilizers, and 2100 clock and pocket watch makers. Life insurance, real estate, the stock market, oil, and the tobacco industry became big business. Electricity was replacing steam and animals as a source of power.

Even in the African-American community there were small gains as progress was made in establishing middle class status. Several black intellectuals, poets, and writers lifted up their own race out of the poverty and ignorance which had plagued them since slavery was first introduced in Jamestown, Virginia, in 1619. Among some of the better known and more successful blacks during the early 1890s were educator Booker T. Washington, banker/humanitarian Maggie Walker, poet Paul Laurence Dunbar, novelist Francis Harper, author Charles Chestnutt, inventor Granville T. Woods and scientist George Washington Carver (W. E. B. DuBois was still preparing for his Ph.D. at Harvard). Though recognition for many black Americans would not come until generations later, these citizens and many others made significant advances in their respective fields.

There were transformations in other facets of society. Land values increased as real estate prices skyrocketed. One example was in Los Angeles where one 25-acre tract, worth an estimated $11,000 in 1886, found no buyers. The following year it sold for $80,000 as the city's population doubled in four years, necessitating the mayor to hire a man to collect and haul garbage for five dollars a week. Property values in New York City, Chicago and Cleveland rose at a dizzying pace.

In their everyday life, people took notice of modern conveniences. Change occurred at a fast pace while many inventions and discoveries ushered in a sense of pride and accomplishment. This feeling was proudly showcased at expositions and exhibits. In fact, the U.S. Patent Office was inundated with so many applications for patents, it was unable to keep up with the paperwork. Between the Civil War and 1890, more than a half million patents were issued. The old was giving way to the new. Even the practice of cutting and collecting blocks of ice from frozen lakes and storing it for the summer was becoming a thing of the past. By 1892 there were 200 factories in the nation either making ice, or supplying ice boxes in kitchens to preserve food.

Two devices in particular had a profound effect on the growth of business. James Ritty of Dayton, Ohio, along with his brother, invented the cash register, dubbed "the incorruptable cashier." James Burroughs, a bank clerk from upstate New York, developed an adding machine, used initially in banks. Both labor-saving machines were endlessly improved and by the 1890s a distinctive system of merchandising and accounting expanded private enterprise.

The exception to this rapid change in technology did not apply to labor-saving devices in the home. For the average housewife life consisted of child bearing, child rearing, and never-ending hours and days of monotonous housework. Work in the kitchen never stopped. Except for meat, there were few processed foods and nearly everything had to be made from scratch. This condition was slowly changing, however, as A & P markets and a dozen Frank W. Woolworth "five and dime" stores sold new kinds of merchandise at low prices. For the most part though, few married women worked outside the home and a housewife's duties were assigned to a constant struggle of managing a family, preparing meals, doing laundry, cleaning and other household chores. Life was not only sheer drudgery for women, it was often short.

On the other hand, fashion conscious ladies spent $14 million a year just on corsets. Women also began discarding the traditional bonnets, so common in the first half of the 1800s, for fancier and more expensive hats. Their newer hats were so elaborate that the feathers used to decorate them resulted in the endangered species of some birds. But styles were changing for all women, faster than the styles of clothing for men. Crinolines, bustles and long, cumbersome dresses began to give way to looser, lightweight garments as the mass production of clothing allowed women of all social classes to wear different types of apparel at lesser cost.

Indoor plumbing, central heating, and electricity began appearing in newly constructed homes and businesses. Tooth powder, sold in tin containers and used to mix with water, gave way to toothpaste which in 1892 was being offered in flexible tubes, thanks to an enterprising dentist in Connecticut. Toothbrushes still consisted of animal bristles imbedded into slender sticks made of animal bone.

Skyscrapers were being built with elevators inside. Trolleycars (streetcars) on rails, both electric and horse drawn, carried people for considerable distances. If one did not care to ride the train, he or she could take a trolley. For instance, by simply changing streetcars, a man might go the distance of approximately 60 miles from downtown Canton, Ohio, to Cleveland to watch the Spiders play baseball against the Baltimore Orioles. Such an activity would take up most of the day.

Much of America's genius and creativity had been demonstrated at fairs and expositions. On April 25, 1890 Harrison signed the Exposition Bill which created a national commission for the 1893 World's Fair in Chicago. Privately built outside the city, 600 acres of swampland were transfixed into an awe-inspiring city along Lake Michigan. The entire world was invited to send exhibits but the biggest attractions were those displays and programs provided by the United States. Though no federal funds were provided the Columbian Exposition proved a huge success.

Travel by railroads, streetcars, horses, and canals were all being challenged as a mode of transportation. At least eight pioneers—the Duryea brothers of Massachusetts, with their one-cylinder four horsepower vehicle, along with William Morrison of Iowa, John Lambert of Ohio and Henry Ford and Ransom Olds, both from Michigan—were all tinkering (independently of one another) with a new device they called the horseless carriage or automobile. A lawyer and inventor from Rochester, New York, George B. Seldon, had been working on a cumbersome "road locomotive" which showed promise, and an industrious mechanic from Milwaukee, Gottfried Schloemer, made much progress on his horseless buggy. Their methods of construction and design differed, as did their power sources, namely steam, electricity or a gasoline combustion engine. Despite the technological advances in creating automobiles, there were a quarter of a million blacksmiths in 1890, but their numbers were diminishing as travel by horse was becoming outdated.

Other new marvels appeared as well. Typewriters were not yet commonplace, but becoming more acceptable. Copying machines emerged when Alfred B. Dick manufactured his mimeograph, which used a rotary drum to quickly reproduce copies (this machine was an improvement upon an Edison invention). After a letter was typed or written on an ink-backed master copy, it was attached to a cylinder then hand cranked. The process could be messy but it proved efficient.

In New Jersey, Edison was perfecting his kinetescope to create motion pictures and George Eastman's hand held camera, with enough rolled film for 100 exposures, became the rage. One could buy Eastman's Kodak camera for $25, and that included the film. After you were done taking the pictures, you sent the entire camera to the factory. After a couple weeks you got your photos and a new roll of film installed for $10.

Several inventions had not yet been available to the public, but would soon appear. These included the ballpoint pen, color film, the zipper (called the slide fastener), a much improved telescopic gunsight, a hand-pushed rotary lawn mower and the drinking straw. *Popular Science* magazine, first published in 1872, carried stories about John Holland and his practical submarine. Even more fascinating were the articles about bold adventurers in Europe and America who flew gliders and experimented with powered flight. This dizzying rate of innovation was so prolific that a couple government officials in Washington felt we had peaked in our creativity and development of gadgetry, and that nothing more could be invented. It was suggested the patent office be closed.

Advertising became a big business; mail order catalogues from Montgomery Ward or Sears and Roebuck could be found in almost any home, if not to order products then to use the thin pages as a substitute for toilet paper. Traveling hucksters of medical quackery, with wild claims of bottled elixirs which produced miracle cures for everything from baldness to cancer, peddled their remedies to every hamlet.

Reforms began in education, as kindergartens emerged and high schools introduced vocational education to boys. School teachers earned about $500 a year while some states and local communities made a push for compulsory education. But even in 1890 the dropout rate was very high. The public high school "touched only a tiny minority of the American people; of the nation's children aged 17 years, the number of enrolled in all high schools and private secondary schools amounted to less than seven percent. Of that number, only an insignificant percentage went on to college."[2] The number of female graduates in high school and college began to increase in 1890, as did the number of women in the work force. Still other changes took place when written tests were being designed for accountants, lawyers and college-bound students.

Those who could read, which totaled about 80 percent of the population, demonstrated a voracious appetite for literature. Andrew Carnegie began donating his first of thousands of libraries throughout the nation. The biggest selling book of the early 1890s next to the *Bible*, was Edward Bellamy's *Looking Backward*, a novel about a Utopian time traveler who attacks capitalism. This book had an astounding success, with more than 1,000,000 copies eventually sold. Other popular titles were *How The Other Half Lives* by Jacob Riis, *Black Beauty* by Anna Sewell, *The Adventures of Sherlock Holmes* by Arthur Conan Doyle, *The Gospel of Wealth* by Andrew Carnegie, *The Origin of Species* by Charles Darwin, and books by William Dean Howells, Rudyard Kipling and Theodore Roosevelt. Dime novels thrilled millions of readers while James Whitcomb Riley, close friend of Benjamin Harrison, became a renowned speaker and poet, writing popular prose in the expression of his Indiana dialect. Scores of magazines, including *Puck* and *Harper's Weekly*, not only lampooned public officials and wealthy businessmen, they also carried articles which focused on a romantic figure, the American cowboy. One author, however, stood above the rest as far as popularity—Mark Twain. Perhaps Twain's greatest admirer was the president himself, evidenced when Twain was the special guest at a White House dinner and Harrison asked him to autograph a menu insert.

While telephones were still a novelty in the 1890s, except in affluent neighborhoods and in the White House where Harrison used the device sparingly, most Americans could afford certain other luxuries. Many homes had pianos and folks listened to hymns by Fanny Crosby (though blinded as a child, she wrote more than 9000 of them), tunes by the prolific Ohio songster Will K. Thompson, ballads by the ever-popular Stephen Foster (even though he had been dead for a quarter of a century) and marches by John Phillip Sousa. Probably the most popular song in the 1890s was Charles K. Harris' *After The Ball*, which sold more than five million copies of sheet music. Edison phonographs were being purchased but were not commonplace in parlors until the second half of the decade when they were mass produced and more affordable.

A major change in music was taking place in the early 1890s. A new sound could be heard coming from Negro bands in New Orleans which eventually made its way north—ragtime or early jazz. These tunes were a unique mixture of rhythms out of West Africa, strains from minstrel shows, and harmony from European classical music and spirituals dating back to slavery days. Ragtime and jazz were strummed on banjos and guitars, accompanied by horns, drums, clarinets and an energetic style of piano playing, creating a strong and syncopated melody. Initially this music was heard during black funerals, then in saloons and gambling houses of New Orleans. Eventually the fresh tunes spread to Chicago and other major northern cities when blacks migrated there. Considered the "granddaddy" of rock and roll, ragtime was slowly gaining respectability among whites.

Another invention also appeared on the scene—the player piano, which many musicians looked upon with disgust. An enterprising Civil War veteran in Canton, Ohio, John McTammany, suffered a serious hand injury in the war. He had been a musician and made a living repairing musical instruments. After he returned home he began working on a voting machine and a player piano. McTammany was also a composer, writing two books on the player piano, a device which could be found in hundreds of saloons, hotels and businesses all over the nation.

Americans who weren't singing or listening to folk tunes, ragtime, classical music, hymns or minstrel melodies seemed captivated by operettas and martial music, especially those songs by the "March King," John Phillip Sousa. Son of a trombone player in the White House U.S. Marine Band, Sousa became the band's conductor in 1880 at the age of 26. Almost at once the music at the White House took on a different tone.

After President Harrison granted Sousa permission to take the band on a five week tour, Sousa returned to the White House almost completely exhausted. He was ordered by his doctor to rest and take a long vacation. Returning from Europe, Sousa made a decision to strike out on his own. His $1500 annual salary was soon supplanted by $6000 and 20% of receipts from his concerts. His compositions, which previously commanded $35 a piece by a Philadelphia publisher, eventually made him a wealthy man. Marching bands throughout the Western World played his music while phonographs blared his marches and operetta tunes. Hundreds of imitators in the U.S. copied his personal style and rhythmic vitality. Sousa's plethora of marches such as "Semper Fidelis," "The Washington Post," and "Stars and Stripes Forever" have endured the test of time. A man of many talents, Sousa also wrote five novels and a best-selling autobiography.

Sports and recreation took on new looks. Bicycling became immensely popular, as did bicycle races. High-wheelers, or pennyfarthings, proved dangerous and not very maneuverable. Then, in the late 1880s, the high-wheelers were replaced by the safety bicycle, which had two smaller wheels of the same size. By 1890 a coaster brake, adjustable handlebars and air-filled rubber tires became standard. In 1885 there were approximately 50,000 cyclists (many of them women) peddling around the country; just ten years later the number of bicycle sales reached 10,000,000.

In 1891 James Naismith of Springfield, Massachusetts, invented basketball, which later spawned volleyball. Basketball spread quite rapidly, evidenced by the first game held west of the Alleghenies in 1892 when Mount Union College in northeastern Ohio played an official game. Within a short time amateur and collegiate teams sprung up across the country. And in bare-fisted boxing, John L. Sullivan of Boston remained the undisputed world heavyweight champion, beating Jake Kilrain in 75 rounds in Richburg, Mississippi, in front of 5000 fans. Sullivan was beaten in 1892 by James Corbett in the first match where boxing gloves and three-minute rounds were used according to the Marquis of Queensbury rules. Efforts were also being made to legalize boxing in several states.

Horse racing, once looked upon as undignified by some people, was gaining acceptability. By 1890 there were 314 racetracks in the country. But there were problems with the sport. Gambling led to corruption, and African-American jockeys were being forced out. Also, standards needed to be set in breeding practices and new rules were instituted to regulate the "Sport of Kings."

Nearly every sizeable town could be identified by two tangibles—a community band and a baseball team. Bragging rights often depended on the success of one or the other. Some cities of 5000 or more had two orchestras, made up of different ethnic groups or organizations like the GAR, the Swiss or Germans. A few larger cities were fortunate enough to have a professional baseball team with the best skilled players available. There were two top major divisions on the professional level, the National League and the American Association, consisting of eight teams in each league. And golf, tennis and college football had devotees and enthusiasts as well, mostly from the well-to-do younger set who lived in the East. The gridiron got a boost in 1889 when Walter Camp named his first All-American football team. As for golf, it was more of a social event played for relaxation by wealthy men dressed in their Sunday bests.

For sportsmen and pet owners alike, in 1890 the American Kennel Club, organized six years earlier, recognized the introduction of three new breeds of foreign dogs. From China came the Chow Chow; the Standard Schnauzer was brought over from Germany and the Borzoi or Russian Wolfhound also made its appearance in the states. The Victorian passion for breeding small dogs, however, continued well into the nineteenth century among the upper class of the urban East.

There were other forms of entertainment too. Millions of Americans flocked to the theater to see minstrel shows, vaudeville acts, opera and musical comedy. Actor Joe Jefferson delighted audiences with his portrayal of Rip Van Winkle.

The greatest beauty of the age was singer and stage star Lillian Russell. Perhaps no woman other than Queen Victoria had such an impact on style and fashion. Born Helen Louise Leonard in Clinton, Iowa, in 1861, Russell's reputation as the ideal of feminine elegance and charm extended beyond the boundaries of America, and she knew every president from Chester Arthur to Warren Harding. Her adoring fans didn't seem to mind that she had been married four times. Lillian Russell appeared in one silent film (in 1915) and died after returning from a fact-finding tour in Europe for President Harding.

For a half dollar or less one could attend other outstanding shows. B. F. Keith and E. F. Albee, who both had circus backgrounds, toured with their "freak shows" of human oddities before combining to create their variety show, also known as vaudeville. William F. "Buffalo Bill" Cody's Wild West Show attracted millions in America and Europe. Beginning in 1883, the long running spectacle had a cast of hundreds, including sharpshooter Annie Oakley. For others there was the Ringling Brothers' Two-Ring Circus or Barnum and Bailey's extravaganza. In New York City, Charles Hoyt's urban musical "A Trip to Chinatown" began its run of 650 consecutive performances, setting the record for any production during the twentieth century.

In the world of art, several Americans gained distinction as being original and enticing. Thomas Eakins, a sculptor and realist painter, was influential with his oil landscapes and depiction of the human athletic form in paintings such as *Between Rounds*. Two of Eakins' students, Eastman Johnson and Henry O. Tanner, went on to notoriety. Johnson painted portraits, including that of President Harrison, while Tanner, a black, gained recognition for his depiction of plantation life in works like *The Banjo Lesson*.

Winslow Homer, with his seascapes and nostalgic images of Americana like *Snap The Whip*, attracted worldwide attention in reaching the most powerful heights of realism. Thomas Moran, who enjoyed capturing the beauty of Western landscapes, was Harrison's favorite artist. At the same time, two gifted illustrators, Charles Dana Gibson and Howard Chandler Christy, found their talents much admired and profitable. Another celebrated painter and author, Frederic Remington, captured the vitality and spirit of the West with his unique sculptures. John Singer Sargent's works, many painted in Europe, also became very popular, resulting in Sargent receiving many awards and honors. His paintings were elegant and often fashionable and flattering, but always realistic. The French impressionists on the other hand made only a small impression on the tastes of the American public in 1890, with the notable exception of artist Mary Cassatt. Several great American artists' works, however, weren't showcased until after their death.

Americans have always loved parades and exhibits. Church socials, going to the beach, county fairs, the circus, zoos, museums and amusement parks attracted millions. People also took up ice skating in the winter, hiking, camping, canoeing, and a relatively new activity—roller-skating. Skeet shooting became popular with sportsmen (among the greatest marksman at shooting clay pigeons was musician John Phillip Sousa), and bowling became more credible when it was learned that Harrison enjoyed the sport.

A paradox of sorts was also in the making. As society overflowed with moralists, denominations such as Methodists, Baptists and Presbyterians sent spiritual and medical missionaries to distant corners of the globe, a practice which began in earnest during the antebellum period. Itinerant preachers and Biblical scholars converted thousands of Americans to "take up the cross." At the same time, some of the great thinkers of the day were praising science and questioning human creation, existence and the purpose of life. Among these better known scholars were Robert Ingersoll, Carl Shurz and Darwin (though he had died in 1882 his book on evolution was still controversial and greatly discussed). Through their articles, books and lectures these men, along with a handful of noted skeptics, challenged Christian fundamentalists and the beliefs of common folk alike. Through their introspection of science and philosophy these men raised more questions than answers, generating a storm of controversy and criticism as they challenged the status quo.

This same period of skepticism, unlimited opportunity, unparalleled growth, affluence and mechanical marvels also had its darker side, leading Mark Twain to describe the era The Gilded Age, for beneath the apparent veneer of opulence lay some very unpleasant and irksome conditions. The latter half of the 19th century was also marked by excesses and eccentricities which could be described as profane, exorbitant, vulgar and stuffy, and many people saw disturbing signs in all the so-called progress.

America in the early 1890s was at the mercy of the trusts and monopolies. For two decades following the Civil War, many of the big corporations and "robber barons" extended their tentacles of greed and ruthless domination. Though big business had generated vast fortunes, it had also spawned extreme poverty. The monopolies eliminated competition, engaged in price-fixing, outlawed unions, imposed starvation wages and 14-hour days, exploited women factory workers and child labor, produced shoddy goods, ignored horrible working conditions and raped the environment. In the late 1880s several states passed anti-trust laws but they were unable to deal with interstate commerce. Aware of this predicament, Harrison in his inaugural address announced his opposition to the trusts, describing these conditions as "an abominable and un-American system that is going too far."[3] Even some of the members of society's upper crust recognized that these conditions posed a threat to democracy itself. Reformers, whose energetic indignation alerted their fellow Americans, gained a growing audience.

William Dean Howells observed that the institution of slavery had aspects preferable to these evils with "commercialism...the poison at the heart of our national life...stolen insidiously upon us...the infernal impulse of competition [embroiling] us in a perpetual warfare of interests, developing the worst passions of our nature, and teaching us to trick and betray and destroy one another in the strife for money, till now that impulse had exhausted itself and we found competition gone and the whole economic problem in the hands of the monopolies..."[4]

Harrison certainly realized that some of his wealthy contributors were business owners who, in turn, created monopolies. In attacking them, he would be "biting the hand that fed him," so it is understandable that he proceeded with caution. He signed the 1890 Sherman Anti-Trust Act into law. But a major factor why he was not successful in dealing with the trusts lay with the legislature, where some of the more influential Representatives and Senators were puppets of big business. The U.S. Senate in fact was labeled by some as "The Millionaires Club."

The law itself proved inadequate. It did not define "trusts" or provide for a practical means of "restraint." No department was created to investigate complaints (like the Federal Trade Commission or the Security Exchange Commission which came later). Some Republicans wanted to see the law applied to labor unions. Congress failed to appropriate funds to investigate the monopolies. Also, Attorney-General Miller, understaffed and overworked, failed to involve his district attorneys on the complexities of the Sherman Anti-Trust Law. Its vagueness proved its ineffectiveness. Only three cases were tried and only one was won by the federal government. It would be another decade or so when Presidents Theodore Roosevelt, William Howard Taft and Woodrow Wilson applied anti-trust laws with vigor and success.

The gap between the rich and poor widened and the contrast between them was profound. Much of the nation's wealth was concentrated in the pockets of affluent industrialists. In 1890 there were 4000 millionaires in the country while, at the same time, millions lived in squalor in crowded, disease-ridden tenement houses grouped together in ghettos. Most of these neighborhoods were made up of immigrants who settled in the large cities in the East. Crime, gang activity and pestilence became rampant throughout the slums while the prosperous, perhaps living only a mile away, resided in luxury and extravagance. In New York City for example, members of high society's "400" such as the Vanderbilts, Astors, or Carnegies might hold a masquerade ball where a single costume would cost $5000 and the host might spend $400,000 just for the party. Several New York millionaires gave banquets in honor of their dogs, horses, monkeys and even dolls. One plutocrat, Henry Lehr, sent out a hundred invitations to dogs and their wealthy masters to attend his "bow-wow banquet." All the while tens of thousands of his fellow New Yorkers lived in abject poverty and filth. Whereas there was a lack of equal opportunity, few lower class Americans overcame the odds of ignorance, despair and hopelessness.

No doubt Harrison was referring to the privileged when in his inaugural address he chided "the educated and influential classes" for their selective compliance with the law.[5] Money was power and there were many examples of aristocracy and arrogance. William K. Vanderbilt called his marble house in Newport, Rhode Island, a "cottage," even though it cost $11,000,000 to build and maintain. His horse stables were palaces compared to the shanties of the poor. Financier John Pierpont Morgan remarked, "You can do business with anybody, but you can only sail with a gentleman."[6] Morgan rarely sailed with more than three companions, not counting the 85-man crew on his yacht.

But some of the same men who were ruthless in making their millions were also generous. Either out of shame, pity or a real concern for their downtrodden fellow man, some industrialists were benevolent. In fact, a few of them like Carnegie and John D. Rockefeller, tried to outdo each other in seeing who could give away the most money.

Although Americans have always been considered a benevolent people, the government policy of foreign and domestic aid was almost non-existent. When famine struck Russia in 1891 and the Russians appealed for help, Congress refused aid. It had done the same regarding the victims of the Johnstown flood, and when drought-stricken folks in Nebraska were denied assistance on constitutional grounds, the burden of relief fell on the states and private donations from churches, organizations and a generous public.

The Woman's Home Missionary Society with its 40,000 members assumed an active role in helping others. Beginning in 1881, former First Lady Lucy Hayes served as president and during her eight-year term the WHMS established mission schools to educate Indians and Spanish-Americans in the West and built schools for Negro children in the South. With the help of newspaper publisher Whitelaw Reid, the group also aided immigrant children and women in an effort to assimilate them into American society.

Carrie Harrison was active with the WHMS also. As a leading member she recruited missionaries and conducted fundraisers to provide them money. Her generosity was felt by Christians working in Persia, Lebanon, Syria, Italy and the West coast of Africa. These responsibilities were coupled with her teaching young children in Sunday school.

One scourge which was enthusiastically addressed by millions of respectable ladies was the consumption, or over consumption, of alcoholic beverages. Temperance groups, warning of the evils of "Demon Rum" and "John Barleycorn," existed in every sizeable community. The Women's Temperance Christian Union carried the fight of drinking to every corner of the country. Theirs was a real challenge; in 1890 there were more than 2500 breweries distilling liquor for 100,000 saloons in the United States. Some members of the WTCU, including a growing number of male supporters, were passionate enough to lead crusades to physically destroy taverns and other drinking establishments. Perhaps the best known of these zealots was a tall, 175-pound wife of a Kansas minister, Carrie Nation. Beginning in 1889 in an attack on the evils of alcohol and other vices, she described herself as a bulldog running and barking at the feet of Jesus. Wielding a hatchet while leading groups of women into saloons, Nation was arrested more than 30 times for trespassing and destruction of property. Her efforts and the national impact of the temperance movement would not be fully felt until 1919 when prohibition forbid the sale and distribution of liquor.

Thousands of WTCU members played a dual role in their push to exert change. They wanted suffrage, a protest movement which had begun five decades earlier when Zachary Taylor was president. Led by Susan B. Anthony, Elizabeth Cady Stanton, Lucy Stone, Harriet Ross Tubman and others (including a few men), women demanded the right to vote.

Some states had already granted women's suffrage, namely Wyoming and Colorado, while a handful of others, including Ohio, allowed women to vote in local elections. In the West, where women were generally more self-reliant and self-sufficient, their nurturing nature tamed and civilized the men on the frontier. The ladies there argued that their experience as mothers and household managers would enable them to improve standards and clean up some of the corruption in the political process.

Beginning in the 1890s, the new suffragettes argued that women were *not* equal to men, that they possessed a moral sense and maturing quality which men lacked. Earlier generations of women had insisted that they were fundamentally equal to male counterparts. Their complaints, protests, and demonstrations challenged existing conditions where universal voting applied only to men.

But not all women of the 19th century agreed on the issue of suffrage. Many wives of Boston bluebloods believed voting was undignified, and that politics was a man's business. Even some of the more ardent supporters of suffrage opposed extending the right to black women. After a major split over race, the progress of the women's rights movement lost some of its momentum.

Though Benjamin and Carrie Harrison were sympathetic to women's rights, they both declined from giving suffrage their full endorsement. The same may be said of Harrison's predecessors and the next four chief executives which followed him (President Wilson endorsed the cause only after he realized the 19th Amendment would be adopted). It would take two more decades, when Tennessee approved women's suffrage by a single vote, before the ladies won their battle for the ballot box.

Few blights on society in 1890 generated more misery than child labor. Almost two million boys and girls between ages ten and fifteen, were employed. This figure represented about 17 percent of the nation's children. A typical boy worked for two cents an hour, fifteen hours a day, six days a week. There was no such thing as workmen's compensation or insurance. If a child got injured or became ill in the loom factory or coal mine, he or she was simply discarded and replaced. Children, like beasts of burden, were expendable. In fact, it was cheaper for companies to hire three or four children than one man.

The issue of child labor was not a federal problem, that is, not until the early 1900s. The various states had laws against it. Though the minimum age for employment in most states was fourteen, no proof was required, and no person or organization bothered to check. This practice surfaced in the latter half of the 19th century, creating thousands of children in bondage. Child labor "turned those who reached adulthood into maimed, stunted slaves with no reserves of bodily strength or sense of responsibility to the community which exploited them...If they were not rescued, they turned into the souless drudges of vicious exploiters..."[7]

In addition to children, people of color and creed became victims. Racial discrimination was alive and well, and not confined just to the South. Ethnic and cultural barriers existed in every corner of America. In the West one could find the hatred towards Orientals and Native Americans at a fever pitch. As thousands of Japanese settled on the West Coast, anxiety sprouted among the white population. In the Southwest white Americans basically looked with disdain upon Latinos. In the East, particularly in cities, immigrants were considered by many as dregs of society.

Discrimination wasn't just confined to skin color, but to religion and one's heritage. Even in the Midwest and North where people tended to be more tolerant, individuals and neighborhoods, along with classrooms in some public schools, were distinctly racially or culturally separated (in some Northern schools where blacks could attend, they were seated outside the classroom). There wasn't much tension because racial and ethnic groups didn't mix much. But numerous groups and organizations sprang up to play on the fears and prejudices of white, non-Catholic Americans and embrace policies of mistrust, hatred and isolation.

Nowhere was racial tension so prevalent, however, as in the South. The violence Harrison learned about in New Orleans was only a small sample of racial incidents and injustice. Though Catholics, Jews and other minorities experienced countless indignities and infliction, it was the Negro who suffered the most. Little did Harrison or the rest of the country know that an incident in 1892 would reinforce the black codes of the Southern states. In that year a Louisiana man, Homer A. Plessy, challenged the legality of segregation laws for railway passengers. Plessy, who was only one-eighth Negro and could easily pass for white, sat in the white section and let it be known that he was partially black. He was arrested and tried.

John Ferguson, a criminal district court judge, overruled Plessy's plea that the law was unconstitutional. Within four years the case had worked its way up through the court system and in 1896, the U.S. Supreme Court ruled in its landmark decision of *Plessy v. Ferguson* that "separate but equal accommodations" were legal. Thus, segregation continued wherever it was practiced, though facilities and conditions for African-Americans were never equal. It would take three generations of protest, blood, sacrifice and soul-searching to right such wrongs.

Efforts to strengthen civil rights for blacks failed during the Harrison administration. When the legislation he pushed wasn't accepted by Congress, Harrison called Southern leaders to the White House, urging them to guarantee existing rights. But Congress had changed after the 1880s. To many Republicans in the House and Senate civil rights were no longer a major priority. Harrison convinced himself that racial problems in the South would be resolved by good faith and a sense of fair play. This naïve assumption on his part proved a disappointment to minorities. Some black Republicans sensed they were being sold out. In addition, the president's powers of persuasion and communication skills, did not lend themselves to convincing others.

One such piece of civil rights legislation was introduced by Senator Henry Cabot Lodge. The bill provided for federal supervision of all Congressional races. It was aimed primarily at the South and though it passed the House along party lines, it was defeated in the Senate. Several Republicans felt the price tag of $77 million over a five-year span was excessive. Another bill, one dealing with education, was designed to aid Negroes in their schooling.

It failed to pass out of committee because Democrats and a handful of Republicans were convinced the measure was an effort by the federal government to control schools.

Another somber milestone of sorts took place in Harrison's first year as president. After the 1890 Census Bureau had released its information, its superintendent announced that the frontier was closed. There were few places in the nation left to explore. The Westward Movement as we knew it had stopped, and future developments would have to take a different form. These views were confirmed when the works of noted historian and University of Wisconsin professor Frederick Jackson Turner declared it so. Though several scholars questioned some of Turner's conclusions, no one doubted his insight and brilliance.

One certainty Turner nor anyone else could deny was the disappearance of the vast numbers of buffalo which once grazed the plains. From an estimated population of 33,000,000 in the 1860s, the animal was close to extinction, with less than a thousand left in 1890. This situation was realized in early 1891 when the first bison were purchased for the Golden Gate Park in San Francisco. A pair of buffalo, named Benjamin Harrison and Sarah Bernhardt, in honor of the famous French actress, were delivered.

Diversity existed on every level of society. Whatever one called it, the Victorian Age or the Gilded Age, throughout the last quarter of the 19th century farmers remained the backbone of the country. New waves of immigrants continued to come to America. Southerners, particularly blacks, moved to the urban areas of the North and Midwest. There was a growing tension between employers and employees and an intense rivalry for subsistence-level jobs. With the changes in demographics came a technological revolution. Americans, however, could not imagine the scope of changes about to take place. Without even realizing it, their country was in transition. The social, economic and political problems shocked many Americans into realizing that they had taken their liberties for granted. Progressive reformers, later called muckrakers, would be needed to cure the ills of a growing urban/industrial society.

Within a dozen years after Harrison left the White House came new developments in motion pictures, automobiles, powered flight, and radio, as well as great changes in fashion, morals and lifestyles. Discoveries in science and medicine, as well as reforms in practically every avenue of human existence, ushered in a different era.

The passing of both Queen Victoria and Benjamin Harrison only two months apart in early 1901 marked the end of the Victorian Age. It was McKinley's death from an assassin in September of the same year which ushered in a new age, with Theodore Roosevelt at the helm.

Chapter 10

Private Citizen and Elder Statesman

After attending the inauguration of Grover Cleveland, Harrison returned to Indianapolis where he was met by a large crowd. Settling in at home, the former president spent weeks unpacking boxes and assessing the needs of his house. He painted and remodeled the interior and had a front porch and new stables built. Harrison's daughter and her children moved in, filling the void of loneliness created by Carrie's death.

The ex-president turned down many job offers and made it clear he would only accept high profiles cases which commanded a hefty legal fee. When he was not riding his bicycle along the streets of Indianapolis, Harrison could be found arguing important cases in court. His yearly income during the mid-1890s averaged about one hundred and sixty thousand dollars, three times what he earned as president.

In the spring of 1894 Harrison gave a series of lectures at Stanford University, earning $25,000 for his labors. Teaching International and Constitutional Law, Harrison took his family with him. His time at Stanford was not without incident. Harrison attended a baseball game and entered the ballpark without paying the 35-cent admission fee. The ticket taker, too embarrassed to ask the former president to pay, approached the baseball team's student manager and explained the situation. The young man went to Harrison and asked for the money. Harrison apologized and cheerfully gave him a dollar, refusing to accept any change. The student manager insisted that Harrison take his change, and when Harrison again refused, was handed some tickets to future games. That student manager was Herbert Hoover, the future Thirty-first President. Years later, Hoover reflected, "Justice must occasionally be done even to ex-Presidents."[1]

That summer Harrison vacationed in New Jersey and saw some old friends, including John Phillip Sousa and Benjamin Tracy. Harrison saw a revival in his reputation when he gave a rousing speech at Carnegie Hall to help Levi Morton win his bid for governor of New York. He was also offered a professorship at the University of Chicago but turned it down. In the fall of 1894 he wrote nine magazine articles for *The Ladies Home Journal*, receiving a total of $9000. This effort became the basis for his book *This Country of Ours*, which became a bestseller two years later.

In March of 1895 Harrison contracted influenza just after he had begun arguing a lengthy probate case. Both Mary McKee and Mary Dimmick (Harrison called her Mame) left New York by train and arrived at the house to help him recover. Daughter Mary was well aware of the feelings her father had for Mame and the two women did not get along. Mary wrote her husband, "I freely confess I so thoroughly despise the woman that I cannot form an unbiased opinion nor a wise one."[2]

After two weeks of recovering from the flu Harrison resumed his four-month-long probate case in Richmond, Indiana, collecting a fee of $25,000. He then traveled to New York to have his official White House portrait painted. The former president stayed active in his Presbyterian church, where he held a national office, raising money for missionaries, orphanages, and black schools in the South. Harrison accepted a position as trustee of Purdue University and later that summer, built a modest cottage in the Adirondacks, naming it *Berkeley Lodge* after the Harrison ancestral home in Virginia.

During Christmas of 1895 Harrison made a surprise announcement—he was getting married. His bride-to-be was no stranger to the family: Mary Lord "Mame" Dimmick, the widowed daughter of Carrie's sister (not to be confused with daughter Mamie). Mame's first husband, Walter Dimmick, had died in 1882 not long after their marriage. In announcing his engagement to Mame, Harrison realized that his children disliked her. He invited his son and daughter and their families to join him at his cabin in the Adirondacks he dubbed "Camp Reconciliation." He urged them to be cordial to his future bride, but any hope of reconciling differences vanished when they refused to come.

In March of 1896 Russell and his wife May returned to the house in Indianapolis to remove all of their possessions. Harrison's daughter Mary and her husband Robert McKee were in town the same week but would not enter the house while the ex-president was there. Harrison was deeply distressed over the split in the family and was moved to tears when his grandson Benjamin promised "that he would always love me…It broke me up very much."[3]

Russell and Mamie did not approve of the match for two reasons: Mary was their cousin and considerably younger than their father. Nevertheless, 62-year-old Benjamin Harrison and 37-year-old Mary Dimmick were married in New York City on April 6, 1896. This made Harrison the oldest president ever to marry. Former Cabinet member Benjamin Tracy was the best man. Among the other guests were Harrison's vice president, Levi Morton. Russell and Mamie declined to attend. Harrison wrote his son a letter, remarking, "A home life is essential to me…I am sure [my children] will not wish me to live the years that remain to me in solitude."[4] But that is exactly what Russell and Mamie expected from their father.

The bridegroom had legal work waiting for him in Indianapolis so the honeymoon was postponed. The happy couple followed an active social agenda, attending church functions, parties, and concerts. Harrison explained, "I am not devoted to music, but Mrs. Harrison is. And I am devoted to her."[5] Unfortunately, Russell and Mamie distanced themselves from their father and Harrison left them out of his will, though he did leave some money for the education of his grandchildren.

Rumors circulated that Harrison would be the Republican candidate in 1896. Some close friends took him for his word when he said, "There has never been an hour since I left the White House that I have felt a wish to return to it."[6] In comparing himself to the frontrunner William McKinley, Harrison told a reporter, "Few of the newspaper writers seem to get on to the fact that a poor ass, that is carrying three loads, cannot expect to be as frisky as a led colt."[7] He added further, "I am altogether pleased to be out of the political struggle ... It is a great comfort to have newspapers turn their attention to somebody else."[8]

McKinley was nominated. Harrison received a visit in the Adirondacks from Mark Hanna, McKinley's campaign manager. Hanna was worried that Democrat William Jennings Bryan might win the election, and he asked

Harrison to campaign for McKinley. Reluctantly, Harrison agreed and gave nearly fifty speeches in numerous cities in the Midwest. After McKinley won the 1896 election, Harrison announced he was retiring from politics.

On February 21, 1897, Mary Dimmick Harrison gave birth to a baby girl. The proud parents named her Elizabeth, after Benjamin Harrison's mother. The ex-president now had a daughter younger than his four grandchildren. Elizabeth Harrison graduated from New York University law school in 1919 and later married James Walker Blaine, the grandnephew of her father's secretary of state. She was the founder and publisher of *Cues on the News*, an investment newsletter for women. Elizabeth died in 1955, surviving her mother by seven years.

If Harrison was feeling he was a bit unappreciated, or out of touch with people and politics, he got a boost from President McKinley who showed him the nation still valued his services. McKinley hosted a White House dinner party for Harrison and Mame, with corsages and boutonnieres made of orchids placed at each setting.

Harrison continued to argue important cases. In 1898 he appeared before the U.S. Supreme Court, convincing the Justices that an Illinois state inheritance tax was unconstitutional. And when the Spanish-American War broke out in April, Harrison gave a patriotic speech to the Indiana National Guard, though he privately voiced concerns about America's expanding role in world affairs. Son Russell Harrison was president of a streetcar company in Terre Haute, Indiana, and joined the Army to serve in the war. Later, Benjamin Harrison would say that America had "no commission from God to police the world."[9] This comment appeared to be a direct criticism of McKinley's foreign policy.

Harrison disapproved of McKinley's imperialism, especially what was happening in the Philippines where thousands of American soldiers had perished against a firm, entrenched native population. The former president feared the nation's conscience and love of liberty had been diminished. Americans, he believed would "break through this crust of sordidness and realize that those only keep their liberties who accord liberty to others."[10]

Harrison had agreed to serve as legal counsel for Venezuela in that country's boundary dispute with England, which claimed ownership of Guyana. Both Great Britain and Venezuela agreed to have the matter settled by an international panel of judges in Paris. In agreeing to argue the case before the Paris tribunal, Harrison insisted on hiring his own team of lawyers and demanded an initial fee of $20,000. Harrison also requested an additional fifty thousand dollars for the legal services of his friend Benjamin Tracy. For two years Harrison studied letters, maps, and documents, some dating back four hundred years and written in Spanish. He set up offices in New York City and Indianapolis, and even converted his cottage into a study. In early 1899 he and his family, their servants, and secretary Frank Tibbott set sail for England and France.

Harrison had prepared an eight hundred page report for the judges, and readied himself to make an oral presentation as well. He spent five days arguing the cause of the Venezuelan government. His testimony was so convincing that England's attorney sent a message of defeat to the English Prime Minister. On October 3, 1899, the tribunal announced its decision— the judges unanimously agreed with the claims made by Great Britain, and 90 percent of the disputed territory remained in British hands.

American newspapers criticized the ruling, hinting that England may have bribed the judges. Even the Vatican in Rome sided with Harrison and the Venezuelans. Harrison was furious.[11] In commenting about the English judge on the tribunal, Harrison wrote his friend and former attorney-general William Henry Harrison Miller, "Law is nothing to a British judge...when it is a matter of extending British dominion."[12]

Harrison failed, but had done his best. He and his entourage visited France, Germany, and Belgium before returning home. Resuming his law practice, he began spending less time with work and more time with his wife and daughter. In the spring of 1900 the Harrisons went on a lengthy trip to Yellowstone National Park and the Northwest. In doing so, the elder statesman missed attending the GOP convention which renominated McKinley. Harrison then spent the rest of the summer at their Berkeley retreat.

President McKinley appointed Harrison to serve on the International Court, beginning in 1901. But in early March of that year he caught a chill and developed a fever. Mame summoned the doctors who discovered that the former president had pneumonia. Harrison lapsed into a coma. The physicians, which included Drs. Jameson and Dorsey, administered medicine with hypodermic needles as well as oxygen, but it proved useless. Harrison's sister, Sarah "Sallie" Devin of Iowa, was ill and not able to attend her brother's bedside. His daughter Mary McKee was also sick and she and her husband James did not arrive in Indianapolis until after Harrison's death. In fact, none of the children born to his first wife were present at Harrison's death.

Drifting in and out of consciousness, Harrison's last discernable words were, "Doctor, my lungs..." On the afternoon of March 13, 1901, at 4:45, the Twenty-third President of the United States died peacefully in his wife's arms. Besides his wife, youngest daughter and the doctors, several others were at Harrison's bedside. Among them were his two sisters, Anna and Jennie, an aunt, two nurses, Reverend M. L. Haines, William H. H. Miller and a couple of friends.

Dash, the collie mixed breed which had been a family pet since 1885, outlived its master by four months.

On Friday, March 16, the president's body lay in state in Rotunda of the State Capitol and was viewed by thousands. This was followed the next day with a private service at the Harrison home, after which funeral services were conducted at the First Presbyterian Church in Indianapolis. Mourners there stood outside for more than two hours, and once inside occupied every foot of space, including the aisles. The altar overflowed with violets, roses and lilies. The church choir sang "Rock of Ages," one of Harrison's favorite hymns.

Hoosier poet James Whitcomb Riley, a neighbor and friend, delivered the eulogy. Riley observed, "One of the characteristics of General Harrison always commanded my profound respect—his fearless independence and stand for what he believed to be right and just...A fearless man inwardly commands respect, and above everything else Harrison was fearless and just."[13] Harrison's children and other family members did attend the graveside services as several of the pallbearers included former cabinet members. Three white carnations were placed on top of his walnut casket. Enclosed in a granite tomb, the casket was lowered into the ground to the sound of cannon fire. Benjamin Harrison was laid to rest at Crown Hill Cemetery next to his beloved Carrie.

His earthly possessions were appraised at approximately $400,000. In February of 1901 it was announced that the bulk of Harrison's estate would go to his second wife and their four-year-old daughter Elizabeth. A few assorted close friends were also left small sums, including Frank Tibbott who served as Harrison's private secretary after the White House years.

Because Harrison became estranged from his two other children following his remarriage, he left only a small amount to his daughter Mamie and son Russell.

Chapter 11

Reflection and Assessment

PRESIDENT MCKINLEY, SPEAKING AT THE FUNERAL OF HARRISON SAID, "THE COUNTRY has been deprived of one of its greatest citizens. A brilliant soldier in his manhood…a leader of the bar, an orator and legislator…he displayed extraordinary gifts as administrator and statesman. In public and private life he set a shining example for his countrymen."[1] Famed journalist William Allen White later noted that, "Harrison…brought to leadership in American politics the incarnate nobility of what his party would have been, were it not for its partisans."[2] Former President Grover Cleveland, not one to generously hand out compliments, told the *New York Times*, "In public office he was guided by patriotism and devotion to duty, often at the sacrifice of temporary popularity, and in private station his influence and example were always in the direction of good citizenship…"[3] Close friend General Lew Wallace, former soldier, diplomat and author, noted that Harrison "had every quality of greatness…a courage that was dauntless, foresight almost to prophecy, a mind clear, strong and of breadth of nature…"[4]

In his private life, Harrison loved his family deeply and enjoyed playing with his grandchildren and their friends. Neighborhood children in Indianapolis adored him and he always had a kind or playful word for them.

He was also a man of devout faith. His Christian values and convictions remained an important part of his daily life.

While serving in the army during the Civil War he learned about war and how men behave. He had personally witnessed the conduct of black troops in battle and expressed his admiration for their service. Benjamin Harrison was fearless in battle and devoted to his fellow soldiers and their causes. Just as importantly, he played a critical role in Sherman's victory in the South, one of history's most renowned and loathsome military campaigns. And as a United States Senator, Harrison got to know his country better than most of his colleagues. He chaired two important committees, dealing with transportation and new territories. This, combined with his wide travels, gave him a first-hand look and understanding of different people and places. And nicknamed the "Soldier's Senator," he endeared himself to millions of veterans and their families in helping them.

Benjamin Harrison was only one of two presidents in the nineteenth century—Lincoln being the other—to give serious attention to the preservation of land and natural resources. Through his vision and love of the outdoors, Harrison set aside large areas out West, more than 22 million acres, for the benefit of future generations. The Land Revision Act of 1891 for instance secured several sources of water supply, insuring irrigation for farmers and water for livestock while preserving the beauty of natural scenery.

He also strengthened the Navy, avoided war with Germany and England over Samoa, and other islands. He convinced Congress to make appropriations to construct battleships and cruisers, forming the Squadron of Evolution which sailed along the Atlantic Coast. As the American fleet grew under Harrison's tenure a more determined foreign policy was forged.

The claim that Benjamin Harrison was a passive, caretaker president content to let Congress run the country certainly has an element of truth, for he would do nothing to misuse or exceed his constitutional powers as Chief Executive. Some scholars would put it in stronger terms that Harrison enthusiastically embraced the principle of legislative supremacy and that his administration "marked a retreat in the struggle to revive the status of the presidency."[5] But this is only partially true.

Harrison himself believed that a president "should have no policy distinct from that of his party and that is better represented in Congress than in the executive."[6] But there are those who challenge this view, for Harrison *did* communicate with Congress, initially holding informal lunches and receptions to convince legislative leaders to support his programs.

Standing firm once his mind was made up, he threatened the power of the veto if he didn't get his way. In his four years in office, Harrison used the veto 44 times, and only once did the Senate override one. It may be said that Harrison's power and influence over the Senate was sufficient enough to forestall the repeal of legislation passed during the first half of his administration.

Harrison was conscious of the new forces at work to change the American life, particularly a new sense of nationalism. He sought to heal the wounds of the Civil War. The nation saw a revival in patriotism during Harrison's term, due in no small measure to his efforts. President Harrison ordered the U.S. flag flown at all federal buildings, and encouraged schools and businesses to do the same. His speeches constantly reminded his fellow Americans about the virtues of good citizenship. In his inaugural message, the Twenty-third President observed that there were "marvelous and, in great part, happy contrasts between the country's past and present,"[7] and further suggested the establishment of a strong federal government (though not necessarily a strong executive). One achievement by the Harrison administration, however, has gone largely unrecognized. A milestone in American law occurred on March 3, 1891 when Harrison signed a historic measure creating nine Circuit Courts of Appeal. These new courts were established to relieve many of the judicial demands on the U.S. Supreme Court.

On the issue of civil rights, Harrison's actions may seem disappointing. His failure to push through legislation to guarantee liberties for blacks was not entirely his fault. Certainly he could have taken a stronger stand and forced the Senate to comply, but doing so would have alienated many of his white constituents. Though he did appoint a few Negroes to minor posts, he was certainly no Lincoln or Garfield when it came to civil rights.

There is consensus that Harrison lacked understanding, personal passion and magnetism. Yet, despite his courtly manners and bearing, he still managed to convey an atmosphere of informality at White House functions compared to several of his predecessors. In regard to his political insight, Harrison may be faulted for failing to recognize the existing depth of economic hardships which led to the industrial and financial crises of 1893, though President Cleveland received the same criticism. But as is the case with all chief executives, none of them have the privilege of using a crystal ball to read into the future.

Harrison lived what he preached. His sense of justice, industry, courage, faith, and sound statesmanship set a high standard. One of President

Harrison's greatest personal satisfactions came in 1892 when he signed the *Pledge of Allegiance* into law. He made no apologies for his patriotism. He wrote, "I rejoice in nothing more than…of placing a starry banner above every schoolhouse. I have been charged with too sentimental appreciation of the flag. I will not enter upon any defense. God pity the American citizen who does not love it, who does not see in it the story of our great free institutions, and the hope of the home as well as the nation."[8]

The 23rd Chief Executive traveled extensively away from the White House, more so than any president before him. He visited every state, many of them several times. He took the presidency to the people and his trips enhanced his political image. Ultimately, however, he could not overcome the circumstances which led to his unpopularity. The heartache and tragedy he faced soon after assuming office left him even more distant and aloof.

To some, Benjamin Harrison was not an inspiring leader, and critics claimed he "did not wear his grandfather's hat well." In looking back at Harrison's career in public office, particularly his presidency, one has to remember and consider the circumstances of American democracy during his adult life. Three weak presidents in the decade prior to the Civil War (Fillmore, Pierce and Buchanan) opened the way for the United States Senate to assume a dominant position in the federal government for years to come, with Harrison as a part of that august body in the 1880s. Though the presidency of Lincoln reversed this trend, the post war controversies and crises resulted in the re-emergence of congressional dominance until the McKinley administration, though it may be argued that Garfield (briefly) and Cleveland in his first term provided strong leadership.

Harrison's association with the press had begun cordially. However, just a few months into his administration this relationship began to sour. The two conflicting forces of the White House and the fourth estate co-existed on antagonistic terms, particularly after 1890. The Gridiron Club, founded in 1885 in Washington, was happy and somewhat surprised when Harrison accepted an invitation to their annual dinner. President Cleveland had refused to attend.

Harrison thus became the first chief executive to banter with the press in their satirical musical skits and listen to remarks by noted public figures. To this day, speeches by officials from both political parties are expected to be self-deprecating or otherwise distinctly amusing. Dispelling the perception that he was humorless, Harrison told the assembled newspapermen at the Gridiron Dinner in 1889, "This is the second time this week I have been called upon to open a congress of inventors."[9] The assembled journalists gave out a hearty laugh and applause. The tradition of "roasting" presidents and having them respond in like manner, continues to the present.

It has been noted by some presidential scholars that Harrison was not effective as a party leader. He could, they believe, analyze problems but not manage them very well. Some of this inefficiency may be traced to his attitude toward patronage. Congressional leaders, upset that Harrison rejected many of their suggestions and demands for appointments, made certain any proposals sent to Capitol Hill for legislation would receive a close scrutiny, if not outright opposition. House Speaker Thomas Reed's "dislike was cordial and undisguised" toward Harrison. "Czar" Reed incidentally banned speeches when he saw fit, took liberties in recognizing quorums when the House was in session, and killed several pieces of legislation advocated by Harrison. Public business was held hostage by faction and filibuster.[10]

Harrison came from a long line of distinguished Americans. And there were times during his career when he struggled to escape from his grandfather's specter. Most of his adult life, be it in the military or in public office, Harrison was constantly subjected to comparisons. What is truly remarkable is that he never possessed a sense of entitlement.

Harrison's independent streak was never more evident than in his criticism of his fellow Republicans. His differences with Presidents Grant and McKinley were honest disagreements based on principle. He opposed the signing of the 1898 Treaty of Paris which ended the Spanish-American War on grounds that it embraced colonial imperialism. He looked at our international role in terms of commerce, not possession. Harrison also saw a need for social and political reform.

President Benjamin Harrison's life and service was one of dignity, integrity and high ideals—qualities which will never be "old fashion." He was a figure who earned the peoples' trust and respect, if not their affection. And he attacked injustice, though at times without much fervor, when he saw it. Within a couple years after leaving the White House, Harrison earned the title of "distinguished elder statesman."

The results of Harrison's contributions and his service can be found in many places, and there are still reminders of his presence. Besides a handful of statues, there is an actual recording of his voice, taken in 1889 when he reread a portion of his inaugural address (Rutherford B. Hayes had his voice recorded at the White House decade earlier by Edison but the recording is lost). During World War II the *S.S. Benjamin Harrison VI*, a Liberty ship, was launched. It was torpedoed in the North Atlantic in 1942 and had to be scuttled. Harrison has also been depicted on a commemorative U.S. coin and four times on postage stamps, beginning in 1903. A handful of schools in three different states bear his name.

Benjamin Harrison's devotion to his country leaves behind a legacy which is not only to be admired, but difficult to emulate. His high standards of virtue, loyalty and candor set him apart from his peers. Few of his predecessors or successors in the White House could match his conduct and sincerity. And though it can be argued that he was not a great president, there can be no question he was a great American.

One prominent historian has noted that Harrison "hoped others would recognize his morality, his energy, his bravery and his patriotism. He wished they would accept his partisan stances in the way a jury accepts the arguments of a good trial attorney. He did not emphasize personal style and resisted public interest in his family and private life. He helped shape the politics of the Progressive Era...he is simultaneously our first modern president."[11]

Benjamin Harrison may have announced his own eulogy with the words found at the base of his memorial in Indianapolis. The words are his own: "Great lives never go out. They go on."

Benjamin Harrison Chronology

1833   Born August 20 in North Bend, Ohio

1847   Attended Farmer's College in Cincinnati

1852   Graduated from Miami University in Ohio

1853   Married Caroline (Carrie) Lavinia Scott on October 20

1854   Admitted to the Ohio Bar; moves to Indiana; son Russell is born

1856   Joined the Republican Party

1858   Daughter Mary (Mamie) is born

1860   Elected Reporter of the Indiana Supreme Court

1862–65   Formed the 70th Indiana Regiment; fought in several battles of the Civil War; commissioned brigadier general

1876   Defeated as Republican candidate for governor of Indiana

1881–87   Served as U.S. Senator from Indiana

1889–93   Served as 23rd President of the United States

1892   Wife Carrie died; defeated by Grover Cleveland in his attempt for reelection

1893   Returned to private practice

1896   Married his second wife, Mary Lord Dimmick, on April 6

1897   A daughter, Elizabeth, is born

1899   Counsel for Venezuela in boundary dispute with Great Britain

1901   Died on March 13 in Indianapolis at age sixty-seven

A Timeline During Benjamin Harrison's Term of Office (March 4, 1889 to March 4, 1893)

1889

March 31   Eiffel Tower in Paris is completed

April 6   George Eastman's Kodak camera goes on sale

April 22   Indian Territory (Oklahoma) opens to homesteaders (50,000 people claim 2 million acres)

May 31   Johnstown flood occurs when the South Fork Dam collapses; more than 2200 killed

June 8   *Wall Street Journal* first published

July 10   Former First Lady Julia Gardiner Tyler dies at age 69

July 30   Boxing champ John L. Sullivan defends his crown by defeating Jake Kilrain in 75 rounds (this was the last bare knuckle match)

Oct. 6   Edison demonstrates the first motion picture

Nov. 2   North Dakota and South Dakota become the 39th and 40th states

Nov. 8   Montana becomes the 41st state

Nov. 11   Washington becomes the 42nd state

Nov. 14   Nellie Bly (Elizabeth Cochran) of the *New York World* begins her round-the-world trip, completed in 72 days

Nov. 15   Brazil ends its monarchy and becomes a republic when Emperor Dom Pedro is deposed

Nov. 23   The first coin operated juke box debuts in a San Francisco saloon; invented by Edison one has to use a listening tube to hear the music

Dec. 6   Jefferson Davis, ex-Confederate president, dies in New Orleans at the age of 81

1890

Jan. 25   The United Mine Workers is founded

Jan. 31   James Duke creates the American Tobacco Company and revolutionizes the cigarette industry

Feb. 10   Montana is opened for settlement when the U.S. buys 11 million acres of land from the Indians

July 3   Idaho becomes the 43rd state

July 10   Wyoming becomes the 44th state

Aug. 6   Pitcher Cy Young of the Cleveland Spiders wins his first of 511 games; William Kemmler becomes first person executed in the electric chair (Auburn State Prison in New York)

Sept. 25   President Harrison signs a bill creating Sequoia National Park; the army is assigned to patrol it

Oct. 1   The McKinley Tariff is passed; Yosemite National Park is created and the U.S. Weather Bureau is restructured and made part of the Department of Agriculture; Harrison signs all three measures

Oct. 11   The Daughters of the American Revolution is founded; Caroline Harrison is the first president

Nov. 29   First Army-Navy football game (Navy wins 24-0 at West Point)

Dec. 15   Sitting Bull and 11 other tribesmen are killed in South Dakota

Dec. 29   At Wounded Knee, South Dakota, U.S. soldiers kill 150 Indian men, women and children

1891

Jan. 20   Princess Liliuokalani becomes queen of Hawaii at age 52

Feb. 14   General William Tecumseh Sherman dies at age 71

Feb. 26   The first buffalo is purchased for Golden Gate State Park in San Francisco

March 14   Race riots occur in New Orleans when Italian immigrants are arrested for the murder of the police chief

April 1   Wrigley Company founded in Chicago

April 7   Showman and circus promoter P. T. Barnum dies at age 81

May 5   Carnegie Hall opens in New York City with Tchaikovsky as guest conductor

Aug. 5	The first travelers checks are issued by the American Express Company
Aug. 12	Author James Russell Lowell dies at age 72
Aug. 14	Former First Lady Sarah Polk dies at age 88
Sept. 28	Author Herman Melville dies at age 72
Nov. 6	Comanche, the only Seventh Cavalry horse to survive Custer's Last Stand in 1876, dies at age 28 (Comanche was a very popular and pampered celebrity)
Nov. 10	The first meeting of the Women's Temperance Christian Union is held in Boston
Dec. 1	Basketball in invented by James Naismith in Springfield, Massachusetts (peach baskets are used)

1892

Jan. 1	Ellis Island in New York harbor opens as a reception center for new immigrants
Jan. 8	Coal mine explosion near McAlister, Oklahoma, kills 100
Feb. 8	The bottle cap with a cork seal is patented by William Painter of Baltimore
Feb. 29	Britain and the U.S. sign a treaty on seal hunting in the Bering Sea
March 26	Poet Walt Whitman dies in Camden, New Jersey, at age 73
April 15	General Electric Company is founded
April 19	Frank and Charles Duryea of Springfield, Massachusetts finish building the first gas-powered car
May 28	The Sierra Club is founded by naturalist John Muir
Aug. 4	Lizzie Borden's parents are axed to death in Fall River, Massachusetts (Lizzie is found innocent)
Aug. 5	Harriet Tubman, Negro abolitionist, scout and Union spy, receives a pension from Congress
Sept. 7	First heavyweight boxing match with gloves is held as "Gentleman" Jim Corbett defeats John L. Sullivan in the 21st round; author John Greenleaf Whittier dies at age 85

Sept. 8   *The Pledge of Allegiance*, written by Francis Bellamy and James Upham, is published and recited in public schools the next month on Columbus Day

Sept. 26   Former Marine Band leader John Phillips Sousa conducts the first performance of Sousa's band; book matches are patented by the Diamond Match Company

Oct. 15   Crow Indians sell 1.8 million acres of Montana land to the U.S. for 50 cents an acre

Oct. 18   First long distance phone call from New York to Chicago (only one call at a time)

Oct. 21   Vice President Morton dedicates the opening of the Columbian Exposition in Chicago where Buffalo Bill's Wild West Show, Little Egypt and the new Ferris Wheel become the main attractions the following year)

Nov. 8   Grover Cleveland defeats Benjamin Harrison in the presidential election

1893

Jan. 2   The U.S. commemorates the first stamp depicting a woman

Jan. 4   President-elect Cleveland announces he will grant amnesty to Mormons who practiced polygamy

Jan. 17   Intervention by U.S. Marines in Hawaii set up a U.S.-backed government; former president Rutherford B. Hayes dies at age 71

Feb. 1   Edison finishes construction of the first movie studio in West Orange, New Jersey

March 4   Grover Cleveland is sworn in as the 24th President

Quotes by Benjamin Harrison

Great lives never go out; they go on.

It is a good thing in the interest of peace and commerce to show the flag of our navy in the ports where the flag of commerce is unfurled.

The bud of victory is always in the truth.

We Americans have no commission from God to police the world.

I will protect the interests of the United States by every means in my power.

Unlike many other people less happy, we give our devotion to government, to its Constitution, to its flag, and not to men.

It is quite as illogical to despise a man because he is rich as because he is poor. Not what a man has, but what he is, settles his class.

I pity the man who wants a coat so cheap that a man or woman who produces the cloth will starve in the process.

We cannot afford in America to have any discontented classes, and if fair wages are paid for fair work we will have none.

Perhaps no emotion cools sooner than that of gratitude.

It seems to me that the work that is unfinished is to make that constitutional grant of citizenship, the franchise to the colored men of the South, a practical and living reality.

I have only a vague memory of my grandfather as I was only a child when he died, but I will show all that my family's famous name is safe in my keeping.

I have often thought that the life of the President is like that of the policeman in an opera, not a happy one.

The system of universal education is in our age the most prominent and salutary feature of the spirit of enlightenment.

Will it not be wise to allow the friendship between nations to rest upon deep and permanent things? Irritations of the cuticle must not be confounded with heart failure.

My life is about as devoid of anything funny as the great desert of grass.

We cannot right matters by taking from one what he has honestly acquired to bestow upon another what he has not earned.

Don't let us be afraid of the people.

There is no better school for the cure of modesty than Washington, D.C.

The law, the will of the majority…is the only king to which we bow.

Let the national flag float over every schoolhouse in the country, and the exercises be such as shall impress upon our youth the patriotic duties of American citizenship.

There is not a square foot of ground [at the White House], not a bench or shade tree that the President or his family can use in privacy.

Power has some compensations but no joy in itself.

Public opinion is the most potent monarch the world knows.

A high sense of duty and an ambition to improve the service should characterize all public officials.

We should not cease to be hospitable to immigration, but we should cease to be careless as to the character of it.

Chapter Notes

Chapter 1. Following in Grandpa's Footsteps

1. James Grant Wilson, *The Presidents of the United States 1789–1914* (New York: Charles Scribner's Sons, 1914), p. 3.

2. Richard L. McElroy, *American Presidents*, *Vol. II* (Canton, Ohio: Daring Books, 1992), p. 48.

3. Henry J. Sievers, *Benjamin Harrison: Hoosier Warrior* (Chicago: Henry Regney Company, 1952), p. 22.

Chapter 2. Ancestry and Youth

1. James A. Green, *William Henry Harrison: His Times* (Cincinnati, Ohio: Garrett Publishing Company, 1941), p. 429.

2. Henry J. Sievers, *Benjamin Harrison: Hoosier Warrior* (Chicago: Henry Regnery Company, 1952), p. 25.

3. Sievers, p. 23.

4. James B. Cash, *Unsung Heroes* (Wilmington, Ohio: Orange Frazer Press, 1998), p. 92.

5. Nathan Miller, *Star-Spangled Men* (New York: A Touchstone Book, 1998), p. 74.

6. Walter Havinghurst, *Men of Old Miami 1809–1873* (New York: G. P. Putnam's Sons, 1974), p. 115.

7. Jeff Young, *The Fathers of American Presidents* (Jefferson, North Carolina: McFarland & Company, Inc., 1997), p. 109.

8. Sievers, p. 62.

9. Ibid., p. 63.

Chapter 3. Law Practice and Marriage

1. Bonnie Blogett and D.J. Tice, *At Home with the Presidents* (Woodstock, New York: The Overlook Press, 1988), p. 138.

2. Sievers, pp. 71–84.

3. Henry Davenport Northrup, *Lives of Harrison and Reid* (Chicago: 1892), p. 38.

4. Paul Boller Jr., *Presidential Wives: An Anecdotal History* (New York: Oxford University Press, 1988), p. 178.

5. Richard L. McElroy, *American Presidents, Vol. III* (Canton, Ohio: Daring Books, 1992), p. 105.

6. Charles W. Calhoun, *Benjamin Harrison* (New York: Henry Holt and Company, 2005), p. 16.

7. Sievers, p. 117.

8. James B. Cash, *Unsung Heroes: Ohioans in the White House* (Wilmington, Ohio: Orange Frazer Press, 1998), p. 91.

Chapter 4. Off to War

1. Rita Stevens, *Benjamin Harrison: 23rd President of the United States* (Ada, Oklahoma: Garrett Education Corporation, 1989), p. 53.

2. Lew Wallace and Murat Halstead, *Life and Public Services of Benjamin Harrison and Whitelaw Reid* (Chicago: Edgewood Publishing Co., 1892), p. 179.

3. Seivers, p. 179.

4. James M. Perry, *Touched with Fire: Five Presidents and the Civil War Battles That Made Them* (New York: PublicAffairs, 2003), p. 216.

5. James B. Cash, p. 95.

6. James M. Perry, p. 217.

7. Page Smith, *Trial by Fire* (New York: McGraw-Hill Book Company, 1982), p. 71.

8. Sievers, p. 199.

9. William A. DeGregorio, *The Complete Book of Presidents* (New York: Dembner Books, 1984), p. 334.

10. Sievers, p. 213.

11. Freeman Cleaves, *Old Tippecanoe* (New York: Scribners and Sons, 1939), p. 123.

12. Sievers, p. 246.

13. Wallace and Halstead, p. 197.

14. Sievers, p. 252.

15. Perry, p. 242.

16. Sievers, p. 254.

17. Ibid, p. 255.

18. Ibid, p. 256.

19. Wallace and Halstead, p. 240; Stevens, p. 8.

20. Cash, p. 97.

21. Henry L. Stoddard, *As I Knew Them: Presidents and Politics from Grant to Coolidge* (New York: Harper and Brothers Publishers,1927), p. 167.

22. Sievers, p. 264.

23. Wallace and Halstead, p. 230.

24. Jane and Burt McConnel, *Our First Ladies* (New York: Thomas Y. Crowell Company, 1969), p. 233.

25. Benjamin Harrison, *Views of an Ex-President* (Indianapolis: Bowen Merrill Publishers, 1900), p. 478.

26. Sievers, p. 294.

27. Stevens, p. 59.

28. Joslyn T. Pine, ed. *Wit and Wisdom of the American Presidents* (Missoula, New York: Dover Publications, Inc., 2001), p. 35.

29. James M. McPherson, *"To The Best of My Ability"—The American Presidents* (New York: A Dorling Kindersley Book), p. 168.

Chapter 5. Veteran and Politician

1. Roger Matuz, *The Presidents Fact Book* (New York: Black Dog and Levanthal Publishers, 2004), p. 369.

2. Sievers, p. 316.

3. Calhoun, p. 28.

4. Ralph D. Gray, editor, *Gentlemen from Indiana: National Party Candidates 1836–1940* (Indianapolis: Indiana Historical Bureau, 1977), p. 148.

5. James M. McPherson, p. 170.

6. Calhoun, p. 30.

7. Brian Lamb, *Who's Buried in Grant's Tomb?* (Washington, D.C.: National Satellite Cable Corporation, 2000), p. 101.

Chapter 6. Senator and Presidential Candidate

1. Harry Davenport Northrup, p. 115.

2. Ralph D. Gray, ed., p. 151.

3. Harry J. Sievers, *Benjamin Harrison: Hoosier Statesman* (New York: University Publishers Incorporated, 1959), p. 225.

4. Cash, p. 100.

5. Sievers (*Hoosier Statesman*), p. 325.

6. Ibid., p. 240.

7. Calhoun, p. 45.

8. William A. DeGregorio, *The Complete Book of Presidents* (New York: Dembner Books, 1984), p. 335.

9. Sievers (*Hoosier Statesman*), p. 331.

10. Stefan Lorant, *The Glorious Burden* (Lenox, Massachusetts: Author's Edition, Inc., 1976), p. 399.

11. Sievers (*Hoosier Statesman*), p. 373.

12. Charles Hedges, *Speeches of Benjamin Harrison* (New York: Lovell, Coryell and Co., 1892), p. 41.

13. Perry, p. 301.

14. Hedges, p. 107.

15. Allan Nevins, *Grover Cleveland: A Study in Courage* (New York: Didd, Mead and Co., 1932), p. 436.

16. Sievers (*Hoosier Statesman*), p. 388.

17. Ibid, p. 395.

18. Paul F. Boller, *Presidential Campaigns* (New York: Oxford University Press, 1996), p. 161.

19. Stefan Lorant, p. 408.

20. Robert McElroy, *Grover Cleveland: The Man and the Statesman* (New York: Harper & Brothers Publishers, 1923), pp. 299–300.

21. Lewis L. Gould, editor, *American First Ladies* (New York: Garland Publishing, Inc., 1966), p. 268.

22. Hedges, p. 191.

Chapter 7. Setting Sail

1. Kittler, Glenn D. *Hail to The Chief!* (Philadelphia: Chilton Book Company, 1965), p. 128.

2. Homer E. Socolofsky and Allan B. Spetter, *The Presidency of Benjamin Harrison* (Lawrence, Kansas: University of Kansas Press, 1987), p. 3.

3. Ibid., p. 3.

4. Kittler, p. 126.

5. McElroy, *American Presidents, Vol. III*, p. 80.

6. Socolofsky and Spetter, p. 212.

7. McElroy (*Vol. III*), p. 90.

8. Ibid, p. 48.

9. *New York Times* (Harrison Speeches), October 14, 1890, p. 286.

10. Paul Boller Jr., *Presidential Wives: An Anecdotal History* (New York: Oxford University Press, 1988), p. 176.

11. Ibid., p. 180.

12. Betty Boyd Caroli, *First Ladies*, Garden City, New York: Guild America Books, 1989), p. 142.

13. Edmund Morris, *The Rise of Theodore Roosevelt* (New York: Coward, McCann and Geoghegan, Inc., 1979), p. 399.

14. Bob Dole, *Great Presidential Wit* (New York: Scribner's, 2001), p. 225.

15. Ibid., p. 225.

16. Ibid., p. 227.

17. Arthur Wallace Dunn, *From Harrison to Harding, Vol. I.* (New York: G. P. Putnam's Son, 1992), p. 87; Morris, p. 413.

18. Dunn, p. 87; Morris, p. 413.

19. Harry J. Stoddard, *As I Knew Them* (New York: Harper & Brothers Publishers, 1927), p. 175; McElroy (*Vol. III*), p. 108.

20. Charles W. Calhoun, *Benjamin Harrison* (New York: Macmillan Company, 2005), p. 76.

21. Morris, pp. 426 and 441.

22. Dole, p. 226; Morris, p. 441.

23. Nathan Miller, p. 69.

24. H. Wayne Morgan, *William McKinley and His America* (Kent, Ohio: Kent State University Press, 2003), p. 106.

25. Socolofsky and Spetter, p. 33.

26. Cash, p. 104.

27. B. S. McReynolds, *Presidential Blips: Dips, Flips, Lip, Pips, Quips, Rips, Tips and Zips* (Universal City, California: B. S. Publishing, 1998), p. 145.

28. Robert C. Post, ed. *Every Four Years* (New York: Smithsonian Books-W. W. Norton, 1984), p. 128.

29. Asa E. Martin, *After the White House* (State College, Pennsylvania: Penns Valley Publications, Inc., 1851), p. 342; Socolofsky and Spetter, p. 162.

Chapter 8. Stormy Seas

1. David Nasaw, *Andrew Carnegie* (New York: The Penguin Press, 2006), p. 403.

2. Calhoun, p. 132.

3. Stefan Lorant, *The Glorious Burden—The American Presidency* (Lenox, Massachusetts: Author's Edition, Inc., 1976), p. 421.

4. Lorant, p. 423.

5. James D. Richardson, ed. *A Compilation of the Messages and Papers of the Presidents, 1789–1897, Vol. IX* (Washington, D.C.: U.S. Government Printing Office, 1900), pp. 348–349.

6. David C. Whitney, *The American Presidents* (Garden City, New York: Doubleday & Company, Inc., 1969), p. 204.

7. Socolofsky and Spetter, p. 35.

8. Thomas A. Bailey, *Presidential Saints and Sinners* (New York: The Free Press, 1981), p. 134.

9. B. S. McReynolds, p. 201.

10. Charles W. Calhoun, *Benjamin Harrison* (New York: Macmillan Company, 2005), p. 122.

11. Kathleen Prindville, *First Ladies* (New York: The MacMillan Company, 1964), p. 208.

12. Paul F. Boller, *Presidential Campaigns* (New York: Oxford University Press, 1996), p. 165.

13. Dole, p. 226.

14. Henry Davenport Northrup, p. 295.

15. Harry J. Sievers, *Benjamin Harrison: Hoosier President* (Indianapolis: Bobbs-Merrill Company, Inc., 1968), p. 242.

16. McElroy (*Vol. III*), p. 9.

17. Roger Matuz, p. 93.

18. William Seale, *The President's House—A History, Vol. I* (Washington, D.C.: White House Historical Society, 1986), p. 601.

19. Henry Davenport Northrup, p. 293.

20. Rita Stevens, p. 111.

21. Havinghurst, p. 126.

22. Letter from Harrison to Russell Harrison, February 5, 1893, now part of the collection of Harold "Skip" Hensel.

23. Sievers (*Hoosier President*), p. 25.

24. Horace Samuel Merrill, *Bourbon Leader: Grover Cleveland and the Democratic Party* (Boston: Little, Brown and Company, 1957), p. 168.

Chapter 9. The President's America

1. Daniel Boorstin, *The Americans: The Democratic Experience* (New York: Random House, 1993), p. 515.

2. Ibid, p. 490.

3. Lloyd Brice, ed. *The Life of Benjamin Harrison and Whitelaw Reid* (Washington, D.C.: Political Publishing Company, 1892), p. 52.

4. Cash, p. 102.

5. Jeffrey Simpson, *The Way Life Was* (New York: Praeger Publishers, 1974), pp. 71–72.

6. Martin W. Sandler, *This Was America* (Boston: Little, Brown & Company, 1980), p. 146.

7. J. C. Furnas, *The Americans: A Social History of the United States, 1587–1914* (New York: G. P. Putnam's Sons, 1969), pp. 731–732.

Chapter 10. Private Citizen and Elder Statesman

1. Eugene Lyons, *Herbert Hoover: A Biography* (Garden City, New York: Doubleday & Company, Inc., 1965), p. 29.

2. Calhoun, p. 159.

3. Ibid., p. 161.

4. Bonnie Blodgett and D. J. Tice, *At Home with The Presidents* (New York: The Overlook Press, 1988), p. 141.

5. Paul Boller, *Presidential Wives: An Anecdotal History* (New York: Oxford University Press, 1988), p. 178.

6. McElroy, p. 99.

7. Sievers (*Hoosier President*), p. 257.

8. Ibid, p. 261.

9. Benjamin Harrison, *Views of an Ex-President* (Indianapolis: Bowen-Merrill, 1901), p. 483; McElroy, *American Presidents, Vol. III*, p. 136.

10. Calhoun, p. 165.

11. Sievers (*Hoosier President*), p. 272.

12. Letter from Benjamin Harrison to W. H. H. Miller (author's collection), October 7, 1899.

13. DeGregorio, p. 341.

Chapter 11. Reflection and Assessment

1. David C. Whitney, *The American Presidents* (Pleasantville, New York: The Reader's Digest Association, Inc., 1993), p. 195.

2. William Allen White, *Autobiography* (Boston: Houghton-Mifflin, 1918), p. 358.

3. *New York Times*, March 14, 1901, p. 1.

4. Ibid.

5. Sidney M. Milkis and Michael Nelson, *The American Presidency: Origins and Development 1776–2002* (Washington, D.C.: C Q Press, 2002), p. 190.

6. Michael Nelson, ed. *The Presidency* (New York: A Salamander Book, 1996), p. 118.

7. Phillip G. Henderson, ed. *The Presidency Then and Now* (Lanham, Maryland: Bowman and Littlefield Publishers, Inc., 2000), p. 175.

8. McElroy (*Vol. III*), p. 107.

9. Ibid., p. 103.

10. Michael Nelson, ed. *The Presidency* (New York: Salamander Books, Ltd., 1996), p. 118.

11. Philip Weeks, ed. *Buckeye Presidents: Ohioans in The White House* (Kent, Ohio: Kent State University Press, 2003), pp. 168–169.

Other sources used in this work include:

James Truslow Adams, *The Epic of America* (New York: Triangle Books), 1931.

David A. Clary, *Eagles and Empire* (New York: Bantam Books), 2009.

Frank Freidel, *Our Country's Presidents* (Washington, D.C.: The National Geographic Society), 1981.

Ernest V. Heyn, *A Century of Wonders: 100 Years of Popular Science* (Garden City, New York: Doubleday & Company, Inc.), 1972.

Rossiter Johnson, *Campfires and Battlefields* (New York: The Civil War Press), 1967.

Elsie K. Kirk, *Music at The White House* (Urbana and Chicago: A Barra Foundation Book), 1986.

H. Wayne Morgan, ed., *The Gilded Age: A Reappraisal* (Syracuse, New York: Syracuse University Press), 1970.

David Nasaw, *Andrew Carnegie* (New York: The Penguin Press), 2006.

Margaret Leech Pulitzer, *In The Days of McKinley* (New York: Harper and Brothers, Publishers), 1959.

Martin W. Sandler, *This Was America* (Boston: Little Brown & Company), 1980.

Jeffrey Simpson, *The Way Life Was* (Milan, Italy: Chanticleer Press, Inc.), 1974.

Edward Stanwood, A History of the Presidency from 1788 to 1897 (Boston: Houghton Mifflin Co.), 1912.

Robert C. Toll, *On With The Show* (New York: Oxford University Press), 1976.

Index

Note: BH and ZT stands for Benjamin Harrison and Zachary Taylor, respectively, throughout this index. Page numbers in italics represent pictures.